Man's Soaring Destiny

"The human species is on the threshold of a new experience as different from ours as ours is from that of the Pekin man." With these provocative words Julian Huxley opens the door on exciting new vistas of human expansion. Man, as the dominant type of life on earth, is the only organism capable of furthering the evolutionary process. This is his destiny ordained by nature.

The noted scientist illuminates some details in the rich tapestry of biological evolution. He shows that man, above and beyond his biological aspects, has mind and spirit . . . that he is capable of selective evolution . . . and that as a knowing creature he can use his tools of experience, mind, and spirit to shape his existence and determine his destiny.

". . . important reading for anyone concerned with the immediate as well as distant future."—
N. Y. Herald Tribune

Knowledge, Morality, and Destiny

Original title: New Bottles for New Wine

※※※※※※※※※※※※※※

Essays by

JULIAN HUXLEY

A MENTOR BOOK
Published by THE NEW AMERICAN LIBRARY

Published as a MENTOR BOOK
By Arrangement with Harper & Brothers

First Printing, September, 1960

MENTOR BOOKS are published by
The New American Library of World Literature, Inc.
501 Madison Avenue, New York 22, New York

PRINTED IN THE UNITED STATES OF AMERICA

CONTENTS

ILLUSTRATIONS
CHARTS AND DIAGRAMS

ACKNOWLEDGMENT

Many of the essays in this volume were originally composed as lectures, while others have appeared in journals. I have to thank the publishers of the journals and those who invited me to give the lectures for permission to reproduce them *in toto* or in amplified form. In particular, for A RE-DEFINITION OF PROGRESS Unesco and Messrs. Allan Wingate; for MAN'S PLACE AND ROLE IN NATURE *University of Columbia;* for EVOLUTION, CULTURAL AND BIOLOGICAL *Wenner-Gren Foundation for Anthropological Research, Inc.* and *University of Chicago Press;* for NEW BOTTLES FOR NEW WINE *Royal Anthropological Institute of Great Britain and Ireland;* for LIFE'S IMPROBABLE LIKENESSES, based on EVOLUTION'S COPYCATS, which appeared in the June 30, 1952, issue of *Life Magazine;* for NATURAL HISTORY IN ICELAND *Smithsonian Institution;* for POPULATION AND HUMAN FULFILMENT, published under the title WORLD POPULATION in the March, 1956, issue of *Scientific American; for* WHAT DO WE KNOW ABOUT LOVE?, which appeared in part as ALL ABOUT LOVE, in the July 12, 1955, issue of *Look,* Copyright 1955 by Cowles Magazines, Inc.; for THE BEARING OF SCIENTIFIC KNOWLEDGE ON BELIEF IN A FREE SOCIETY *University of Oregon;* for KNOWLEDGE, MORALITY, AND DESTINY *William Alanson White Psychiatric Foundation* and *Psychiatry;* for EVOLUTIONARY HUMANISM (Dyason Lecture 1953) *Australian Institute of International Affairs.* This last lecture has been incorporated in modified form in a revised edition of my "Religion Without Revelation", published earlier this year by Harper & Brothers.

I also have to thank Dr. Cott and Messrs. Methuen and Co. Ltd. for permission to reproduce from his "Adaptive Coloration in Animals" the drawing which appears on p. 134, and the illustrations of the hawkmoth, garden carpet moth, leaf-fish, and *Erémocharis* between pp. 144–145; PEP *(Political and Economic Planning)* and Messrs. Allen and Unwin Ltd. for the diagrams from "World Population and Resources" on pp. 153, 157, 159, 161, 163, 166, 167, 178 and 182; *Scientific American* for the diagram on p. 156; *The*

Observer for the diagrams on pp. 158 and 179; and Mr. K. Davis and Princeton University Press for the diagram from "The Population of India and Pakistan" which appears on p. 185.

PREFACE

IF asked to name the most remarkable developments of the present century, I suppose that most people would say the automobile and the aeroplane, or the cinema, the radio and TV, or the release of atomic energy, or perhaps penicillin and the antibiotics. My answer would be something quite different—man's unveiling of the face and figure of the reality of which he forms a part, the first picture of human destiny in its true outlines.

This new vision is based upon the enlargement of knowledge, not only or even mainly (as laymen and I fear also many scientists seem to think) in the natural sciences, but equally in the social sciences and the humanities.

During my lifetime, I have seen its gradual emergence, piece by piece. There was the discovery that atoms are not the ultimate units of matter, leading on to a coherent and comprehensive theory, first of matter, and then, through radiation studies, quantum theory and atomic physics, of matter and energy together; and the discoveries of physiology and medical science—hormones and vitamins, chemotherapy and antibiotics, the mechanism of nervous action and of muscular contraction, and many others—leading to a coherent and comprehensive picture of the working of the body in health and disease.

There was the rediscovery of Mendelism, leading on to a complete and comprehensive theory, first of heredity and then of organic evolution; and the discoveries of psychology, human and comparative—repression and the Unconscious, the measurement of intelligence and temperament, conditioned reflexes and Gestalt perception, the language of bees, the homing of birds and the behaviour of apes—leading towards a comprehensive picture of the evolution, the individual development and the working of mind.

There was the discovery of unsuspected ancient civilizations, like those of Crete and the Indus Valley, and the general pushing back of history until it met and fused with the flood of new knowledge pouring in from prehistory, archaeology, and palaeontology, so leading to a coherent view of human development as a whole; and also the rise of a more scientific and more universal history with its specialized subdivisions—social and economic history, art history, history of science, history of religions, and the rest—leading towards a comprehensive picture of civilized man's social and cultural evolution.

There have been the discoveries of exploration—on our earth, the attainment of the Poles, the ascent of Everest, the revelations of the bathysphere and the aqualung; and beyond it, the astronomers' astonishing exploration of space and its galaxies—leading to a more complete knowledge of our planet, and to a new and awe-inspiring picture of its place in the cosmos.

There have been all the applications of science, leading to a new and more comprehensive view of man's possible control of nature. But then there was the rediscovery of the depths and horrors of human behaviour, as revealed by Nazi extermination camps, Communist purges, Japanese treatment of captives, leading to a sobering realization that man's control over nature applies as yet only to external nature: the formidable conquest of his own nature remains to be achieved.

Finally, there has been the amassing of facts about the world's resources and their consumption, and about human numbers and their rate of increase, leading to another sobering realization—that resources are limited, and that population must be limited if man is not to turn into a cancer of the planet.

From these bits and pieces of new knowledge, new realizations and new understandings, man is capable of forming a new picture of himself, of his place in nature, his relations with the rest of the universe, his role in the universal cosmic process—in other words, his destiny; and on that, in turn, building new and more adequate beliefs.

During the post-war decade, I have found myself impelled to explore this formidable field, now from one angle, now from another. The present volume consists mainly of a selection from this series of tentative explorations. I am the first to acknowledge the gaps and inadequacies which they represent, but yet feel some assurance that my efforts have led me in the main in the right direction, and indicated some useful patterns of thought and belief.

TRANSHUMANISM

As a result of a thousand million years of evolution, the universe is becoming conscious of itself, able to understand something of its past history and its possible future. This cosmic self-awareness is being realized in one tiny fragment of the universe—in a few of us human beings. Perhaps it has been realized elsewhere too, through the evolution of conscious living creatures on the planets of other stars. But on this our planet, it has never happened before.

Evolution on this planet is a history of the realization of ever new possibilities by the stuff of which earth (and the rest of the universe) is made—life; strength, speed and awareness; the flight of birds and the social polities of bees and ants; the emergence of mind, long before man was ever dreamt of, with the production of colour, beauty, communication, maternal care, and the beginnings of intelligence and insight. And finally, during the last few ticks of the cosmic clock, something wholly new and revolutionary, human beings with their capacities for conceptual thought and language, for self-conscious awareness and purpose, for accumulating and pooling conscious experience. For do not let us forget that the human species is as radically different from any of the microscopic single-celled animals that lived a thousand million years ago as they were from a fragment of stone or metal.

The new understanding of the universe has come about through the new knowledge amassed in the last hundred years—by psychologists, biologists, and other scientists, by archaeologists, anthropologists, and historians. It has defined man's responsibility and destiny—to be an agent for the rest of the world in the job of realizing its inherent potentialities as fully as possible.

It is as if man had been suddenly appointed managing director of the biggest business of all, the business of evolution—appointed without being asked if he wanted it, and without proper warning and preparation. What is more, he can't refuse the job. Whether he wants to or not, whether he

13

is conscious of what he is doing or not, he *is* in point of fact determining the future direction of evolution on this earth. That is his inescapable destiny, and the sooner he realizes it and starts believing in it, the better for all concerned.

What the job really boils down to is this—the fullest realization of man's possibilities, whether by the individual, by the community, or by the species in its processional adventure along the corridors of time. Every man-jack of us begins as a mere speck of potentiality, a spherical and microscopic egg-cell. During the nine months before birth, this automatically unfolds into a truly miraculous range of organization: after birth, in addition to continuing automatic growth and development, the individual begins to realize his mental possibilities—by building up a personality, by developing special talents, by acquiring knowledge and skills of various kinds, by playing his part in keeping society going. This post-natal process is not an automatic or a predetermined one. It may proceed in very different ways according to circumstances and according to the individual's own efforts. The degree to which capacities are realized can be more or less complete. The end-result can be satisfactory or very much the reverse: in particular, the personality may grievously fail in attaining any real wholeness. One thing is certain, that the well-developed, well-integrated personality is the highest product of evolution, the fullest realization we know of in the universe.

The first thing that the human species has to do to prepare itself for the cosmic office to which it finds itself appointed is to explore human nature, to find out what are the possibilities open to it (including, of course, its limitations, whether inherent or imposed by the facts of external nature). We have pretty well finished the geographical exploration of the earth; we have pushed the scientific exploration of nature, both lifeless and living, to a point at which its main outlines have become clear; but the exploration of human nature and its possibilities has scarcely begun. A vast New World of uncharted possibilities awaits its Columbus.

The great men of the past have given us glimpses of what is possible in the way of personality, of intellectual understanding, of spiritual achievement, of artistic creation. But these are scarcely more than Pisgah glimpses. We need to explore and map the whole realm of human possibility, as the realm of physical geography has been explored and mapped. How to create new possibilities for ordinary living?

What can be done to bring out the latent capacities of the ordinary man and woman for understanding and enjoyment; to teach people the techniques of achieving spiritual experience (after all, one can acquire the technique of dancing or tennis, so why not of mystical ecstasy or spiritual peace?); to develop native talent and intelligence in the growing child, instead of frustrating or distorting them? Already we know that painting and thinking, music and mathematics, acting and science can come to mean something very real to quite ordinary average boys and girls—provided only that the right methods are adopted for bringing out the children's possibilities. We are beginning to realize that even the most fortunate people are living far below capacity, and that most human beings develop not more than a small fraction of their potential mental and spiritual efficiency. The human race, in fact, is surrounded by a large area of unrealized possibilities, a challenge to the spirit of exploration.

The scientific and technical explorations have given the Common Man all over the world a notion of physical possibilities. Thanks to science, the under-privileged are coming to believe that no one need be underfed or chronically diseased, or deprived of the benefits of its technical and practical applications.

The world's unrest is largely due to this new belief. People are determined not to put up with a subnormal standard of physical health and material living now that science has revealed the possibility of raising it. The unrest will produce some unpleasant consequences before it is dissipated; but it is in essence a beneficent unrest, a dynamic force which will not be stilled until it has laid the physiological foundations of human destiny.

Once we have explored the possibilities open to consciousness and personality, and the knowledge of them has become common property, a new source of unrest will have emerged. People will realize and believe that if proper measures are taken, no one need be starved of true satisfaction, or condemned to sub-standard fulfilment. This process too will begin by being unpleasant, and end by being beneficent. It will begin by destroying the ideas and the institutions that stand in the way of our realizing our possibilities (or even deny that the possibilities are there to be realized), and will go on by at least making a start with the actual construction of true human destiny.

Up till now human life has generally been, as Hobbes

described it, "nasty, brutish and short"; the great majority of human beings (if they have not already died young) have been afflicted with misery in one form or another—poverty, disease, ill-health, over-work, cruelty, or oppression. They have attempted to lighten their misery by means of their hopes and their ideals. The trouble has been that the hopes have generally been unjustified, the ideals have generally failed to correspond with reality.

The zestful but scientific exploration of possibilities and of the techniques for realizing them will make our hopes rational, and will set our ideals within the framework of reality, by showing how much of them are indeed realizable.

Already, we can justifiably hold the belief that these lands of possibility exist, and that the present limitations and miserable frustrations of our existence could be in large measure surmounted. We are already justified in the conviction that human life as we know it in history is a wretched makeshift, rooted in ignorance; and that it could be transcended by a state of existence based on the illumination of knowledge and comprehension, just as our modern control of physical nature based on science transcends the tentative fumblings of our ancestors, that were rooted in superstition and professional secrecy.

To do this, we must study the possibilities of creating a more favourable social environment, as we have already done in large measure with our physical environment. We shall start from new premisses. For instance, that beauty (something to enjoy and something to be proud of) is indispensable, and therefore that ugly or depressing towns are immoral; that quality of people, not mere quantity, is what we must aim at, and therefore that a concerted policy is required to prevent the present flood of population-increase from wrecking all our hopes for a better world; that true understanding and enjoyment are ends in themselves, as well as tools for or relaxations from a job, and that therefore we must explore and make fully available the techniques of education and self-education; that the most ultimate satisfaction comes from a depth and wholeness of the inner life, and therefore that we must explore and make fully available the techniques of spiritual development; above all, that there are two complementary parts of our cosmic duty—one to ourselves, to be fulfilled in the realization and enjoyment of our capacities, the other to others, to be fulfilled in service to the community and in promoting the welfare of the generations to come and the advancement of our species as a whole.

The human species can, if it wishes, transcend itself—not just sporadically, an individual here in one way, an individual there in another way, but in its entirety, as humanity. We need a name for this new belief. Perhaps *transhumanism* will serve: man remaining man, but transcending himself, by realizing new possibilities of and for his human nature.

"I believe in transhumanism": once there are enough people who can truly say that, the human species will be on the threshold of a new kind of existence, as different from ours as ours is from that of Pekin man. It will at last be consciously fulfilling its real destiny.

A RE-DEFINITION OF
PROGRESS

MYTHOLOGY fills a necessary place in the history of human ideas. It arises when man first demands some explanation of the strange surroundings in which he finds himself, some comprehensible guidance in the frightening chaos. The human mind has not at this stage been able to penetrate beyond the surface of things, to discover the deeper relations of events, or to illuminate the dark confusion with the light of science. Myth is thus a rationalization; it is an *ad hoc* support framed by our intellect to sustain our existence, and the formation of myths is bound to continue in any domain so long as our desire to know and to understand is confronted and overtopped by our ignorance.

In later stages, however, mythology is inevitably modified by new knowledge and experience, and in the long run becomes supplanted by science. Science may not be able to give ultimate explanations, but at least it can, as time passes and knowledge accumulates, provide rational understanding. The myth is thus eventually replaced by the scientific description, the comprehensible account of the facts of nature. The making of myths has thus not been confined to early stages in the development of man's ideas. Some myths, like that of Nordic racialism, or, as we shall shortly see, of progress, are quite recent. Although some myths are no more than primitive fairy-tales, others are so profound in their intuition that they can continue to serve a valuable function long after their literal truth has been discarded. Thus in the myth of the Fall of Man, Reinhold Niebuhr[1] rightly finds profundities and subtleties which are still capable of showing up the inadequacy of some of to-day's cruder so-called scientific approaches.

Yet even if myths can be stretched to include new scientific knowledge, as the myth of the Fall can be stretched to include the facts of Freudian psychology, even if they may retain a value long after their original crude rationalization has ceased to have a meaning, there yet comes a time when it is desirable to reject and demolish them, to start building a wholly new scaffolding for the human mind, on the frank basis of naturalistic description and scientific method.

This time of rejection is approaching for the mythology of man's destiny. There are many different sectors of mythology—myths of creation, those cosmic Just So Stories; myths of magic and power, peopling this world with spirits or some other Olympian world with the high gods of polytheism; myths of death and the hereafter; myths of nature, dealing with sun and stars, with thunder and eclipse, with the seasons and the fertility of crops; myths of sex and reproduction; myths of good and evil. But the myths of human destiny, though often intertwined with other subjects, have always taken a large place. By myths of human destiny, I mean all those fabulations which purport to give man, both as individual and as race or species, an explanatory picture of his life in relation to its setting, to rationalize the process of change we see everywhere both in and around us, and to indicate (sometimes optimistically, sometimes the reverse, but at least comprehensibly) the relation between human desire and purpose on the one hand and cosmic chaos and indifference on the other.

One such myth is that of metempsychosis in all its varied forms; it becomes most expressly a myth of destiny when linked with the doctrine of Karma. Another is that of the Golden Age, an ideal state from which man has fallen, whether through his own fault or not. Its most modern

---

[1] Niebuhr, R., *An Interpretation of Christian Ethics*, S.C.M. Press, London, 1936.

embodiment, I suppose, was Rousseau's idea of the noble savage, though a less radical version is found in the glorification of ancient Greece as the apogee of human achievement. All ideas of belonging to a Chosen People which one day shall accomplish great things for or in the world are myths of this general type. So, of course, are all the fragments of classical mythology dealing with that problem of Até or Doom which so concerned the Greeks. At almost every level of culture we could discover myths of this general nature.

One of the myths of human destiny is that of progress. Professor Bury in an interesting book[2] has shown how recent has been the growth of this idea. Apart from temporary flickers, it dates back no earlier than the Reformation. Its rise was undoubtedly connected with that of modern science, which, following on the great explorations, revealed not only new realms of possible knowledge, but new possibilities of control over culture.

The myth of progress has taken two main forms, which have sometimes remained separate, sometimes been intertwined. One is the myth of millenary progress, the other of its inevitability. Millenary progress is the myth of the Golden Age in reverse. It asserts that if only man gets rid of some old obstacle or creates some well-defined and realizable new social mechanism, humanity will leap forward to a utopian state of general well-being and happiness. The eighteenth-century apostles of revolution believed that what was needed was the abolition either of kings or of priests (or preferably of both). Some of the more zealous apostles of the nineteenth-century industrial revolution believed that what was needed was to make the applications of nineteenth-century science available to everybody, and to teach everybody the three R's: if these conditions could be fulfilled, then everything—to put it rather crudely—would be All Right. Inevitable progress, on the other hand, is an optimistic reversal of the grim Greek myth of Até, or of the pessimistic Christian doctrine of predestination. It asserts that, the nature of the world and of man being what it is, human progress is inevitable, and more particularly that it will inevitably be both smooth and rapid, now that man has become scientific.

In our Western world the myth of progress has now fallen on evil days. It was attacked in general terms by Bury in his previously-cited book, and by many writers since then

[2] Bury, J. B., *The Idea of Progress*, Macmillan, London, 1920.

on the more specific grounds that the idea of progress cannot be reconciled with the retrogressions of Fascism and Nazism and the horrors of the recent war. Among its most recent assailants is my brother Aldous.[3] He refers, for instance, to "the apocalyptic religion of Inevitable Progress [whose] creed is that the Kingdom of Heaven is outside you and in the future" and wants to "bully nature into subserving ill-considered temporal ends, at variance with the final end of men" (which he describes as "unitive knowledge of the Divine Ground of being"). Elsewhere he says that "the religion of Inevitable Progress . . . is, in the last analysis, the hope and faith (in the teeth of all human experience) that one can get something for nothing".

Thus according to the more sweeping of these critics, the idea of progress is not only a myth, but a bad myth. A good myth is one which, while frankly and inevitably unscientific, yet, with the aid of intuition and everyday experience and common sense, still manages to embody truth. But a bad myth is merely erroneous, and should be discarded as dangerous.

Meanwhile, however, the patient labours of the students of evolution, whether stellar evolution, biological evolution, or social evolution, have revealed that progress is not myth but science, not an erroneous wish-fulfilment, but a fact. On the other hand, progress as a scientific doctrine reveals itself as very different from progress as a mythical dogma.

The scientific doctrine of progress is destined to replace not only the myth of progress, but all other myths of human earthly destiny. It will inevitably become one of the cornerstones of man's theology, or whatever may be the future substitute for theology, and the most important external support for human ethics. There has not yet been time to work it out in detail; indeed, a number of facts relevant to its elaboration still await discovery. But its broad lines are now clear. It will be my purpose here to set forth some of its consequences and implications, with special reference to the intellectual and moral urgencies of the world at this moment of history. For it is all too clear that humanity's present situation, as seen in evolutionary perspective, is a crucial one, balanced upon one of the recurrent knife-edges of change.

I will confine myself to quoting a brief summary of our present position of evolutionary theory on the subject. Evolu-

[3] Huxley, Aldous, *The Perennial Philosophy*, Harper, New York, 1945, Chatto & Windus, London, 1946.

tion in the broad sense denotes all the historical processes of change and development at work in the universe: in fact, it *is* the universe, historically regarded. It is divisible into three very different sectors—the inorganic or lifeless, the organic or biological, and the psychosocial or human. The inorganic sector is by far the greatest in extent. On the other hand, the methods by which it changes are almost entirely those of mere physical interaction, and the highest rate of evolution so slow as to be almost beyond our comprehension, the "life" of a star being of the appalling order of magnitude of 10^{12} years—a British as against a mere American billion.

The biological sector is very much more limited in extent; however, with the emergence of the two basic properties of living matter—self-reproduction and variation (mutation)—a new and much more potent method of change became available to life, in the shape of natural selection. As a result the possible rate of evolution was enormously speeded up. Thus the entire evolution of life, from its pre-cellular origins to man, has taken little more than 2×10^9 years, and quite large changes, such as the evolution of the fully specialized horses from their small and generalized ancestors, or that of the first true birds from reptiles, have been achieved in periods which are nearer 10^7 than 10^8 years.

Finally there is the human sector. This is still further restricted in extent, being confined to the single species, *Homo sapiens*. But once more a new and more efficient method of change is available. It becomes available through man's distinctively human properties of speech and conceptual thought. Objectively speaking, the new method consists of cumulative tradition, forming the basis of that social heredity by means of which human societies and cultures maintain themselves and develop. But it also has a subjective aspect. Cumulative tradition, like all other distinctively human activities, is largely based on conscious processes, on knowledge and purpose, on conscious feeling and conscious choice. Thus the struggle for existence that underlies natural selection is increasingly replaced by a struggle between ideas and values in the shared consciousness of social beings, resulting in what we may call conscious or psychosocial selection.

Through these new agencies, the possible rate of evolution was again enormously speeded up. What is more, there has so far been a steady acceleration of the new rate. Whereas in the Lower Palaeolithic major cultural change required something of the order of 10^6 years, by the late Upper Palaeolithic the period was nearer 10^4 years, and in historic times came down to the century or 10^2 years. And during the last hundred years each decade has seen at least one major change: if we are to choose ten such, let us select photography, the theory of evolution, the electro-magnetic theory with its applications in the shape of electric light and power, the germ theory of disease, the cinema, radio-activity and the new theories of matter and energy, wireless and television, the internal-combustion engine, chemical synthetics, and atomic fission. To-day, indeed, even the most momentous changes, such as the discovery and first practical application of atomic fission, may take only half a decade, and there is as yet no sign of the rate of acceleration slowing down.

Evolution in the human sector consists mainly of changes in the form of society, in tools and machines, in ideas, in new ways of utilizing the old innate potentialities, instead of in the nature of those potentialities, as in the biological sector. Man's inherited mental powers cannot have changed appreciably since the time of the Aurignacian cave-dwellers; what have changed are the ways in which those powers are used, and the social and ideological frameworks which condition their use. This is not to say that what has happened to man since the Aurignacian period or since the time of ancient Greece is not evolution; it is a very astonishing bit of evolution. Nor does it mean that man's innate mental powers could not be improved: they certainly were improved (presumably by natural selection) in the earliest stages of his career, from Pekin man through the Neanderthalers to our own species, and they certainly could be improved further by deliberate eugenic measures. Meanwhile, however, it is in social organization, in machines, and in ideas that human evolution is mostly made manifest.

These three sectors have succeeded each other in time. Perhaps the next fact that strikes one concerning the process as a whole is that the physical basis and the organization of what evolves become more complex with time, not only in the passage from one sector to the next, but also within each sector. Most of the inorganic sector is composed of atoms or of the still simpler sub-atomic units, though here and there it attains the next higher level, of molecules. Further, in a few rare situations it must have reached the further stage of organic macro-molecules, which can comprise a much larger number and a much more complex arrangement of atoms. It was from among such giant organic molecules that the living or self-reproducing molecules of the biological sector were later evolved. These are more elaborate still, consisting of many hundreds or perhaps thousands of atoms. In turn, their vast but still sub-microscopic complexity provided the basis for an even greater visible elaboration. The complexity of the bodily organisation of a bird or a mammal is almost inconceivable to anyone who has not systematically studied it. And this visible complexity has increased with time during biological evolution. A bird or a mammal is more complex than a fish, a fish more complex than a worm, a worm than a polyp, a polyp than an amoeba, an amoeba than a virus. Finally, in the human sector, a new complexity is superimposed on the old, in the shape of man's tools and machines, idea-systems, and social organizations. And this, too, increases with time. The elaboration of a modern state, or of a machine-tool factory in it, is almost infinitely greater than that of a primitive tribe or the wooden and stone implements available to its inhabitants.

But it is not only complexity of organisation which increases with time. In the biological sector, evolution has led to greater control over the environment, to greater independence of its changes and chances, and to a higher degree of individuation. It has also led to an increase of mental powers—greater capacities for acquiring and organizing knowledge, for experiencing emotion, and for exerting purpose. This trend towards fuller knowledge, richer emotion, and more embracing purpose is continued in the human sector, though by different methods and at a much increased rate. But to it is superadded another trend—an increase in the capacity to appreciate values, to appreciate experiences that are of value in their own right and for their own sake, to build on knowledge, to work through purpose, and to inject ethical values into the process of social evolution itself. The ethical values may be limited and primitive, such as unquestioning loyalty to a tribe, or high and universal, like those which Jesus introduced into the affairs of the world; the point is that only in the human sector do they become a part of the mechanism of change and evolution.

These broad trends are not universal. In the biological sector, stability frequently replaces directional change. Even when broad trends exist, they need not be desirable from the long-term point of view. Thus most evolutionary trends, like those seen in the horse or elephant stock, are only specializations. After tens of millions of years of one-sided improvement for a particular way of life, they lead inevitably to an evolutionary dead end, after which no further major change is possible. However, a few trends do occur which promote an all-round improvement of organization, such as the evolution of early mammals from reptiles, or early man from mammals. These do not close the door on further major change, as was demonstrated by the large-scale evolution of mammals in the Tertiary, or of man's societies since the Ice Age; they are thus the only changes which are, from the longest-range point of view, desirable and progressive.

Thus, whatever may have been the origin of the universe and whatever its final fate, it has in fact shown a certain trend which may properly be called progress. This is discernible within the few hundred million years of its history about which we can draw reasonable conclusions, and can be extrapolated with a high degree of probability into the few thousand million years of the future about which we can make reasonable prophecies. This trend is measurable most clearly by the upper level attained by certain attributes of the existing world-stuff, rather than by their average level. These attributes vary according to the sector of existence which is being considered. In the inorganic sector the only criterion is complexity of organization. In the organic phase of evolution complexity continues to increase, but other criteria become more important—notably the capacity to control other parts of the universe, and to become more independent of changes in the environment, while in its later stages the dominant criterion shifts to increased capacity for knowledge, emotion and purpose, notably the capacity for profiting by experience. All these criteria are still involved in progress within the psychosocial phase, but new criteria are superadded—notably increased understanding and attainment of intrinsic values. As my grandfather said in the Prologomena to his Romanes Lecture in 1893, in human life the struggle for existence has been in large measure replaced by the struggle for enjoyment. To which we may add that, if we take the long view, from the palaeolithic period to the neotechnic culture of to-day, there has been a rise in the level or value of the enjoyments for which we strive, as well as an increase in the variety and quality of enjoyments which are possible.

Although we have no right to regard this trend as embodying a cosmic purpose or a Divine intention, we can properly say that it constitutes a desirable direction of evolution, as contrasted with those numerous other trends which are less

desirable or undesirable—trends leading to cultural degeneration or extinction, to one-sided specialization or to stagnation.

Some maintain that we should not even use the word desirable—that it is mere question-begging or anthropomorphic
self-satisfaction to say that any existing trend is better
than any other. That I deny. We can judge by results. Life
itself is, in a self-evident way, somehow *higher* than any
inorganic system or structure. Goethe's *Faust* or the Fifth
Symphony of Beethoven assuredly have higher value than
any creative achievement of savage man, let alone than any
animal activity; and the knowledge and comprehension arising from the mathematical, scientific and humanistic discoveries of the last three centuries are clearly of greater value
than those available to Aristotle, not to speak of those possible to primitive man or the highest of apes. A world with
antelopes and song-birds and butterflies in it is in some real
sense better—more beautiful, more wonderful, more interesting—than one with only worms and polyps and protozoa, and
that again is somehow better than a lifeless world. The
world after human civilizations had arisen in it was higher,
more significant, more worth-while, than when only barba-
rous.

It is true that the range of undesirable possibilities increases at the same time, that in the human sector at least any
rise implies the possibility of a deeper fall and greater good
involves the possibility of greater evil. But this in no way
impugns the positive trend I have outlined. The level of desirable qualities and attributes attained by the existing world
does rise; that does not cease to be a fact because of the
existence of any other facts, even of antagonistic ones.

I want now to deal with the question of the inevitability
of progress. In biological evolution progress is in one sense
inevitable, in another sense not. It is inevitable in the sense
that, given the struggle for existence and natural selection in
our world or any world similar to ours during the last thousand million years, it is apparently unavoidable that true
progress should occur in some of the lines of life. But it is
not universally inevitable: the great majority of biological
stocks either show no progress, the reverse of progress, or a
progress which is only partial and limited. It is conditioned
by accidents; if the identical stock which showed progressive
evolution on a continent could have been transplanted to a
small oceanic island with different competitors, it would
assuredly not have progressed. If the world had not had the

accident of a great climatic catastrophe befall it at the close of the Cretaceous, the ancestral mammals would not have supplanted the reptiles so completely nor embarked upon such rapid new advance. And it will always remain subject to accidents. If some virus or bacterium were to arise which exterminated the human species, that would almost certainly be the end of any hopes of major progress on earth. If the temperature of the earth were to fall sufficiently, progress would undoubtedly stop and would eventually be totally reversed.

In the human sector for some considerable evolutionary future, progress is probably inevitable, in the sense that the upper level of desirable qualities in point of fact is bound to rise. But it is not inevitable in the sense that it must be steady; on the contrary, there may be serious regressions interrupting the general rise of level, as we know from history and from all-too-personal experience. Nor is it inevitable in the sense that it must be universal. This or that culture, this or that trend, may ignominiously peter out or may crash in war or revolution. Nor would it be inevitable if dysgenic reproduction reduced the average level of innate intellectual and moral qualities beyond a certain point. But given the present state of the human race, its thirst for knowledge and betterment, and the extent of its accumulated tradition, I regard it as certain that some degree of progress will for some time inevitably continue to occur.

The objection is sometimes made that if progress is inevitable we need not worry or exert ourselves; it will happen anyhow, without our painful efforts. Or are we told that any theory of inevitable progress, however limited, is mere fatalism, and as such incapable of providing either guidance or comfort. These, however, are fictitious difficulties. They arise out of a false separation between our material and mental activities. If we take the monistic or unitary naturalistic view demanded by evolutionary logic, matter and mind cease to appear as separate entities; they are seen as two necessary attributes or aspects of the single universal world-stuff. In the inorganic sector the mental aspect is wholly latent, negligibly developed. But in the higher range of the biological sector certain configurations of the world-stuff have definite mental attributes. Regarded objectively, these configurations are the special arrangements of nervous tissue we call brains; physiologically they are organs for co-ordinating and directing action on the basis of sense-data and memory; but subjectively, certain of their activities are apprehended as mental or psychological—perception, thought, emotion, and will.

Freedom, said Spinoza, is the knowledge of necessity. However epigrammatic, this dictum does constitute a resolution, albeit in highly condensed form, of the problem of free will. The biologist would state the position rather differently. He would say that the human brain provides a mechanism, wholly novel in evolution, whereby alternatives can be confronted. The alternatives may be alternatives of truth, or of action, or of emotional satisfaction. That is unessential; what is essential is that they are truly alternatives, and that the fact of their confrontation makes it necessary to choose between them, to select one rather than another. Further, they are present together within the unity of consciousness; it is this simultaneous presence in consciousness which constitutes their confrontation, has its special accompaniments in consciousness, its necessary subjective aspects. When two opposing impulses are confronted, we have a sense of conflict and struggle; when the confrontation is between two closely balanced alternatives, a sense of indecision. Similarly the act of choice is accompanied by a sense of effort when a strong impulse has to be suppressed; by a sense of release when a lower impulse is transcended and flooded out by a higher; sometimes by a sense of rational decision; by a sense of powerful and deliberate will; or by will which is effortless because accompanied by a sense of certitude and inevitability.

Man is unique in being endowed with such a mechanism for confronting, weighing, and choosing between alternatives in the light of reason and past experience. To this situation, logical arguments about free will versus determinism are irrelevant. The fact is that we are able to select between alternate cause of action, and that this selection involves the activity known as will. It involves an act of will at the moment, and also the results of past acts of will. If we had set ourselves to amass a little more knowledge, if we had disciplined our moral activities better, or if we had kept our bodies healthier, the decision we have to take to-day might be different. As Schopenhauer wrote, "A man can do what he will, but not will as he will." However, he can train his will, so that it becomes a more efficient agency of choice and action.

Progress at the present juncture may be inevitable, in the sense of being in the nature of things. But it is also in the nature of things that progress will not come about without human choice, human effort, and human purpose. With the coming of man, evolution itself comes to have a subjective as well as an objective component. Man becomes a microcosm in which the objective trends of the macrocosm can be mirrored and from whose subjective depths purpose can flow out to influence the trends of the macrocosm and, within gradually expanding limits, subject them to its will.

Before coming to the possibilities of progress to-day, I must deal with some of the generalities of progress in the human sector, since this is the subject of numerous misconceptions. In the first place, the method of human evolution in general, including that by which progress can be effected, is different from that found in the biological sector. This I have already mentioned, but it cannot be too strongly reiterated. Natural selection, as operative in biological evolution, depending on the differential survival of types with different genetical endowment, has ceased to be of major importance. It still operates, but in a quite subsidiary way, and it is no longer the prime agency of change. The prime method of change is now change in cultural tradition. Much of the struggle and consequent selection is between traditions and ideas, or between nations, classes, or other groups embodying those traditions and ideas. The inter-individual struggle tends to become more a struggle for the means of enjoyment than for the means of survival or of reproduction. And finally, much of the struggle can be displaced from the objective to the subjective world, there to involve the success or failure of ideas or desires, instead of the life or death of organisms or gametes.

Man could avail himself of a method of genetic change, if he were deliberately to practise eugenics. This would, however, no longer be a form of natural selection but of artificial selection, such as he has already practised on domestic animals and plants, involving a conscious aim and a deliberate control of the mechanisms of heredity. It could therefore operate much more rapidly and much less wastefully than natural selection.

As to the course pursued by evolution, the results of the biologists' elaborate exploration of the biological sector do throw some light on the problem in the human sector. In the first place, changes in the environment are important contributory causes of evolution. Without the desiccation of the mid-tertiary there would not have been the rise of the Grass family to botanical dominance over large areas of the world's surface, or the consequent rise of the grazing herbivores such as horses and sheep, oxen and antelopes.

When we extend this idea of environment to cover the biological as well as the inorganic environment, environmental change becomes still more important as a factor in evolution. The most obvious example is the colonization of the land by green plants. Since all higher animals are directly or ultimately dependent on plants, the establishment of this green environment was an indispensable prerequisite to colonization of the land by animals. A still more basic fact is the general raising of the level of efficiency and competition in the entire biological environment and the filling of more and more niches by new adaptations. This it is which makes evolution both inevitable and unique. The non-biologist sometimes asks why, if apes once gave rise to man, existing apes do not again evolve into a human type. The answer is simple. Even if they had remained just as they were before the evolution of man (instead of, as is probable, becoming more specialized for an arboreal life), they could not evolve in face of the competition from the more advanced form to which their ancestral relatives once gave rise. There is no longer an empty niche waiting to be filled by the evolution of a human creature; any tentatives in this direction would bring the potential new men not into a vacant promised land but straight up against the ruthless competition of the actual men already in existence.

We must next mention specialization and its consequences. Specialization—in other words one-sided adaptation to a particular mode of life—eventually leads to an evolutionary dead end. After this point is reached no more major changes are possible, for reasons concerned with mutation and selection into which we need not here enter. The specialized line or group may then continue to flourish, apparently indefinitely, but with its variation restricted within comparatively narrow limits; as has happened with the birds, for instance, during the past twenty or more million years, or with the snakes. Alternatively, it may go under in competition with some new rival line or as a result of some climatic change, and either be totally extinguished, as were the ichthyosaurs and the dinosaurs at the end of the Cretaceous, or the sabre-toothed cats and the giant sloths during the Ice Age, or else reduced to insignificance, like the lung-fish in competition with more modern fish on the one side and amphibians on the other, or (alas!) the larger mammals of to-day as a result of the spread of civilized man.

There is another type of bar to evolutionary advance, resulting from the inexorable limitations of some form of physiological mechanism. Thus the employment by Arthropods of a hard dead external skeleton involves periodic moulting, and this has the further result of setting an upper limit to size. Even the largest arthropods, to be found among the marine Crustacea, never weigh more than a few score of pounds. Among insects, the adoption of the method of breathing by air-tubes or tracheae has set a much lower limit to their size—which in turn has limited the size of their brains and the evolution of any degree of plastic intelligence. As a result of this limitation, even those highest of all insects, the ants, have shown no progressive change for nearly fifty million years, and the entire group of insects would seem to be barred from further major progress.

It is natural to ask whether similar bars to progress, due to the limitations of some important social mechanism, also operate in the human sector of evolution. The answer would appear to be yes, though not very frequently. It may prove that the Chinese method of writing, by ideographic symbols, is an example of this, and that for Chinese civilization to enjoy its full potentialities of progress it will be necessary to change to an alphabetic method. The non-metric systems of measurement to which the British Commonwealth and the United States still cling, if not bars to progress, are at least brakes upon it.

In any event, since these limitations are not inherent in the genetic constitution, but only in some aspect of social tradition, they can be removed without the extinction or collapse of the entire cultural group. They can be removed; but in fairness let us add that the difficulties in the way of their removal, difficulties which are by no means all the result of selfish vested interest, may be very great, as with the case of switching over advanced industrial nations from a non-metric to a metric system.

The next question is whether the opposition, so crucial in the biological sector, between specialization and progress, between advance which is one-sided and limited and advance which is all-round and unlimited, is of importance also in human evolution. The answer is yes; but the opposition presents itself in a very different way. The evolution of Homo sapiens has so far been mainly an evolution of cultures and traditions, and cultures can interpenetrate and interact. In the past, when cultural isolation was much greater, a tradition may perhaps have become so specialized as to become incapable of vital interaction and fusion with other traditions; and in modern times, with the increased possibilities of state propaganda and state control, there have been examples, such as Nazism, of the building up of a tradition incompatible with any other type. But in general different cultures do interpenetrate and interact, and if there is extinction or a fall from dominance, it, for the most part, comes not as the result of force (here again Nazism is an exception) but as the result of the gradual abandonment of certain ideas in favour of others which are in the ascendant.

An obvious example of interpenetration is the influence of ancient Greek on Arabic thought, followed by that of Arabic thought on Western mathematics, medicine and science; on a smaller scale we have phenomena like the blending of Christian and West African (Yoruba) practices in such places as Cuba. As examples of a fall from dominance we may take the abandonment in civilized countries of the belief in magic and witchcraft in favour of more scientific or more spiritual conceptions, or the replacement of creationist by evolutionary ideas during the last hundred years.

What we really need to know, however, is whether specialization or one-sidedness in cultural tradition is in the long run as undesirable, or at any rate as preclusive of permanent progress, as it certainly is in biological evolution. It is difficult to give a clear-cut answer, for a culture or a tradition is not a sharply defined entity like a genetic constitution, but fluid and plastic; and also, as we have just seen, capable of interacting and uniting with other cultures and traditions in a way impossible to all biological entities save those few plant types capable of large-scale hybridization. What we can say, however, is that exaggeratedly one-sided emphasis in culture or tradition—in other words cultural specialization—is inimical, either at the time or later, to the fullest degree of progress. It needs to be corrected, and the necessary correction must sometimes be violent. The recurrent over-preoccupation of the Christian tradition with sin; the over-emphasis of the Middle Ages on symbol and analogy; the over-emphasis of Fascism on the importance of the State; the Nazi transference of national pride, in any event exaggerated, to the falsity of racialism; the over-emphasis on rank, prestige or ritual that afflicts so many barbaric cultures; over-emphasis on the differences in way of life between classes, especially when crystallized within a rigid caste system; over-emphasis on the authority of the ruler, as embodied in such traditions as the Divine Right of Kings—these are a few examples.

Divine Right and similar over-emphases needed revolutions for their destruction; Fascism and Nazism demanded a world war. Over-preoccupation with sin has led to violent attacks on all forms of enjoyment, which in their turn have provoked counter-reactions that swing too far in the opposite direction; over-emphasis on theological authority has put needless shackles on the advance of material knowledge.

During the past hundred years there has been in the Western world an over-emphasis on the material side of things—on quantity as against quality, on novelty for its own sake, on control over the forces of nature as against control over our own nature, on variety and multiplicity as against unity, on matter as against mind, on technology as against art (including the art of life), on means as against ends. This trend is taking us off the main line of possible progress, and must be corrected soon unless it is to bring about a reaction of over-compensation, so violent as to deviate man's advance towards the opposite side of its true line.

It will perhaps be objected that it is only by a succession of such actions and reactions that man advances, and that human progress must therefore pursue a perpetual zigzag, never on its true course (though generally in the same general direction), and punctuated by wasteful explosions of conflict, during which there may actually be a drift away from progress. Or alternatively that, whenever the oppositions of thesis and antithesis, which await reconciliation in a dialectical synthesis, are really important, the "reconciliation" is unlikely to be accomplished without violence. In either case, major advance would always require acute revolution, instead of gradual and peaceful evolution.

Here biology may shed a suggestive light. In biological evolution both acute and gradual change occur, and both may contribute to progress. The sudden extinction at the close of the Secondary Era (sudden in the geological sense) of some three-quarters of the main lines of reptilian evolution, together with the relegation to unimportance of all the remainder save the one branch of lizards and snakes—this, with the almost explosive evolution of the mammals which followed upon it, was an acute process, a revolutionary event. But the slow transformation, during perhaps fifty mil-

lion years of the Secondary Era, of one small and insignificant reptilian line into a primitive mammal, and the subsequent slow transformation during another fifty million of
the Tertiary of one mammalian line into ancestral man—
those were processes of extreme gradualism, to be followed
by the acute revolutionary processes of extinction or reduction and explosive spread, and it may well be that this co-
operation between the violent and the gradual is inevitable in
the biological sector.

If so, it is because biological lines or trends of evolution
are discrete, incapable of interpretation and fusion. In the
human sector, however, as we have seen, what evolve are not
gene-complexes but cultural traditions, and can therefore
interpenetrate. On the other hand, they do not always do so
completely, or at least sufficiently to form a single viable
tradition out of the fusion of two hostile or opposing ones.
When there is this failure of fusion, it seems that any conflict
can only be resolved acutely—by violence, war, or revolution. But when interpenetration is sufficient to allow fusion,
the peaceful processes of gradualism can operate to produce
progress.

Here is another advantage of the method of human evolution. The reconciliation of opposites can take place within
the plastic unity of tradition, without the wastefulness of
acute violence and extinction. This is the counterpart of the
corresponding advantage in the sphere of selection—the
replacement of the wasteful methods of natural selection,
with its inevitable differential mortality, by a selection of
techniques and ideas.

We can now consider our present situation. In evolution as
a whole, it is obvious that there are two major critical points
—the origin of self-reproducing matter or life, and the origin
of self-reproducing culture or man. But there are also minor
or secondary critical points, decisive not so much because of
their immediate effects as for the new possibilities which they
open up. The secondary critical point in inorganic evolution
was the formation of giant carbon-containing molecules,
rightly termed "organic" since without them living organisms would have been impossible. The secondary critical
point in biological evolution was the origin of learning—the
formation of mechanisms for profiting by experience. This
was of importance partly because without it the evolution of
man would have been impossible; but partly also because it is
at the base of all the most successful and developed products

of biological evolution, from bee and ant to mammal and bird. The secondary critical point in human evolution will be marked by the union of all separate traditions in a single common pool, the orchestration of human diversity from competitive discord to harmonious symphony. Of what future possibilities this may be the first foundation, who can say? At least it will for the first time give full scope to man's distinctive method of evolution and open the door to many human potentialities that are as yet scarcely dreamt of. Meanwhile anything that can be done to increase the interpretation of traditions and their fruitful union in a common pool will help, and is itself assuredly a prerequisite of full progress.

There remains an apparent antinomy which we must try to resolve, the antinomy between the idea of progress and that of individual perfection. That opposition has been forcibly put by Aldous Huxley,[4] who goes so far as to state that "the final end of man is the achievement of unitive knowledge of the Divine Ground of all being"; and that "a society is good to the extent that it renders contemplation possible to its members". He further identifies progress merely with "progress in technology and organization", and therefore as involving the view that "the end of human life is action".

The same opposition has been either expressed or actualized in a hundred different ways. "What shall it profit a man, if he shall gain the whole world and lose his own soul?" said Jesus. The emphasis on individual salvation, as against realizing the kingdom of God on earth, has been on the whole dominant throughout Christian history, and has been especially intransigent when the salvation is considered to be solely by grace. Dr. Joseph Needham has some pertinent remarks on this subject in his book of essays, *History Is on Our Side*. He points out how, in early civilizations, the prevailing relation with the environment has determined man's attitude to this two-faced problem. When, as in tropical India, the environment was too much for struggling humanity, the spiritual leaders of that humanity proclaimed the pessimistic view that only through the renunciation of that environment—the physical world—could the individual attain full or lasting satisfaction. But when, as in ancient China, the environment was amenable to human effort, religious

---

[4] Op. cit.

philosophy adopted a worldly attitude and proclaimed the intimate linkage of individual and society, of man and nature, in place of their opposition.

The same insistence on the paramountcy of individual development as is stressed by Aldous Huxley is also seen in the prevalent individualism of America, although the two points of view are bitterly opposed in other ways, American individualism stressing the need for self-development and self-expression, Aldous Huxley that for self-effacement or self-transcendence if the individual mind is to achieve the goal of losing itself in union with the non-individual "Divine ground", eternal and universal. In certain conditions, on the other hand, the emphasis has shifted away from the individual and is placed upon society. This is often so in tribal life, where the individual can scarcely be conceived of except as a fragment and instrument of tribal tradition; and in historic times it has prevailed in societies which are deliberately tightly knit and highly organized for war or peace—such as the pre-Colombian Inca empire, or, in our own times, the modern Japanese empire, Fascist Italy (though here Italian individualism was in large measure too much for Fascist theory), and Nazi Germany, whence the believer in individualism was eliminated by exile, by imprisonment or by death. In Communist Russia, too, there is less emphasis on the rights and potentialities of the individual as such; partly because as a result of the transposition of some of Hegel's views on the State into Marxist Philosophy, partly because of the conscious adoption of a theory of total, mass or classless society, and no doubt partly through the exigencies of a revolutionary situation.

The antinomy also has its evolutionary aspect. Our analysis shows that the mechanism of human evolution is a social one. But it also shows that the developed human individual is the highest known product of evolution, the fullest embodiment of progress in the universe; in any case society is certainly lower than the individual in not possessing a conscious mind, with all the flexibility and potentiality, both of thought and action, which that connotes. Here is an apparent dilemma, and one which, as we have just seen, has often been solved by emphasizing one of the opposing claims to the virtual exclusion of the other. At one extreme the overriding duty of the individual is regarded as being to himself and his own development, to salvation, to the full pride of selfhood, or to glorious self-transcendence; and society is merely the environment in which he must perforce carry out this duty. At the other extreme, the overriding duty of the individual is regarded as being to the community; and society is seen as the more important and valuable entity, of which the individual is merely an organ.

The opposition between the requirements and interests of the individual and those of society is and always will be profound. Indeed, all moral codes and systems of ethics are attempts to reconcile these opposites. The evolutionist intent on elaborating a workable theory of progress must attempt a similar reconciliation. In this, he can achieve a considerable degree of success, though assuredly not any smooth and perfect solution. We must remember that the individual evolves as well as society—only we generally call his evolution *development*. The life of the individual human being is a process, not a mere existence, and even the most transcendent and apparently timeless experiences are related to a dynamic development, and do not just happen statically.

The most important of all the prerequisites for future progress is the acceptance of the fact of progress, and the understanding of its nature; for we cannot expect to achieve what we do not believe in. We command nature by discovering and obeying her laws. The fact of progress has now been discovered; but it is not yet generally acknowledged, still less its laws adequately understood.

Once we accept the fact of progress, no longer need our beliefs be restricted to anything so partial or ephemeral as a particular nation, a particular religion, a particular culture. Nations or religions may be the necessary vehicles or the instruments of progress, but in so far as they are worthy of our devotion, they must be thought of as the embodiments of continuing processes in time. These processes in their turn, in so far as in a desirable direction, must now be thought of as merely parts of the overriding desirable trend that we call progress. This is truly a continuing process. It has lasted for thousands of millions of years, and shows no sign of drawing to an end. It has already raised the upper level achieved by the world-stuff from the aimless jazz of electrons and atoms through a whole series of astonishing stages. The first origin of life, with its attainment of self-perpetuating organization: the evolution of sense-organs, with the attainment of knowledge of the world around; the miracles of beauty, efficiency, and grace that are the higher birds and mammals: the evolution of brains which can store and profit by experience: the present culmination of life in the emergence of man—man the microcosm, the time-binder, with brain and mind capable of annihilating the sequence of events, and tying them together in the unity of consciousness; capable of confronting alternatives and making decisions; capable of acquiring knowledge and producing beauty almost immeasurably beyond anything previously realized by any single evolutionary line; capable of appreciating and creating values, and of utilizing them as standards and goals; capable of throwing his thought forward into the future and of realizing that advances equally enormous (but equally impossible to visualize beforehand) are possible in the millennia to come.

In a way most important of all, we have a universal scale against which to set the disasters and miseries of a nation, or of an entire age like our own. Against its broad measure these appear either as necessary destruction opening the way to new construction, or as temporary setbacks of no greater importance to the general trend of evolution than are the wavelets raised by a contrary breeze to the sweep of the incoming tide.

And as regards our own personal lives, although nothing can make up for blind and cruel blows of fate, we can see them in a truer perspective. Paradoxically enough, this enables us at one and the same time to realize our pettiness and insignificance, but also our unique value and importance. For we are at one and the same time mere organs of the evolutionary process, operating through society; and also, whether actually or only potentially, the transcendent outcome of evolution, through whom alone the full flower and fruit of progress can be actualized and embodied.

Through the doctrine of progress we can be both consoled and exhorted to effort; we can be guided and we can be warned; we can be given an enduring foundation, and also a goal. Our acceptance of the fact of progress and our understanding of the doctrine of progress constitute the major prerequisite of our further progress.

MAN'S PLACE AND ROLE IN
NATURE [1]

NATURE is not a mechanism, but a process. To define man's place in nature, we must discover what situation he occupies in the process; to determine his role, we need to discover something of the essential characters not only of nature but of man himself as a resultant within its process; and this exploration will lead to new views on the unity of knowledge. Our age is the first in which we can obtain a picture of man's place and role in nature which is both reasonably comprehensive and based on scientific knowledge. We can be sure that the picture is still very imperfect, that its comprehensiveness will be much enlarged, and that its scientific basis will be powerfully strengthened; but the fact remains that our century is the first in which any both comprehensive and scientific picture has become possible.

In the world picture resulting from the Darwinian upheaval of thought, man was no longer seen as standing over against nature. His place was in nature; he was as much a product of evolution as the animals and the plants. But in our grandfathers' time, even the biologists still took a restricted view of the evolutionary process. For one thing, they tended to look backwards, to think in terms of the origins of present structures rather than of continuing trends and their possible future. It was not for nothing that Darwin called his two greatest books *The Origin of Species* and *The Descent of Man:* the ideas of original creation and original sin and the fall were still in the background of Victorian thinking. For nineteenth-century biology, man's position was determined by comparative anatomy. The place assigned him was amongst the animals: Genus, *Homo;* Family, *Hominidae;* Suborder, *Anthropoidea;* Order, *Primates;* Subclass, *Placentalia;* Class, *Mammalia;* Phylum, *Vertebrata;* Kingdom, *Animalia.* True, he was rather peculiar in various

[1] Paper presented at Conference Five of the Bicentennial Celebration of Columbia University, 1954, and later published in *The Unity of Knowledge,* ed. Lewis Leary, Doubleday, New York, 1955.

ways; but that was not allowed to interfere with the principles of sound zoological classification.

However, human peculiarities persisted in manifesting
themselves in man's daily life. Men continued writing poetry,
going to war, making scientific discoveries, building palaces,
worshipping gods, founding colleges, training lawyers, and
many other activities undertaken by no other organism.
Though biological science was content to classify him as just
another animal, in his own eyes he was still the Lord of
Creation, apart from the rest of nature, and in some unspeci-
fied sense above nature. Furthermore, in spite of pessimists
and disheartened idealists, the unconscious assumption
widely prevailed that, however disreputably animal man's
origin might have been, the process of evolution had now
culminated in nineteenth-century civilization, with its scientific discoveries and its technical achievements. All that was
now needed to put humanity on the very pinnacle of progress was a little more science, a little more rational enlightenment, and a little more universal education.

We all know the disillusionment that has set in within the
brief space of half a hundred years. How the orderly mechanisms of nineteenth-century physics gave way to strange
and sometimes non-rational concepts that no one but mathe-
maticians could grasp; how the idea of relativity, and its
somewhat illegitimate extension to human affairs, destroyed
faith in the absolute, whether absolute truth or absolute
morality or absolute beauty; how our belief in the essential
rationality and goodness of man was undermined by psychology and sent crashing in ruins by the organized cruelty
of Belsen and the mass folly of two world wars; and how our
idealistic notions of progress as the inevitable result of
science and education were shattered by events. In brief,
man's first evolutionary picture of nature and his own place
in it proved false in its design and had to be scrapped.

Meanwhile, however, knowledge has marched on in many
fields: even disillusionment has brought a better understanding of our limitations, and the new knowledge is making
possible the redesigning of our world picture. The twentieth
century, besides introducing us to the new world of atomic
physics and quantum theory at one end of the scale and to
that of relativity theory and the expanding universe of spiral
nebulae at the other, has given us our knowledge of the
method and course of biological evolution; of the development and working of the human conscious and subconscious

mind, and of its interactions with the body; of the variety of human societies and cultures revealed by social anthropology and ethnology; and of the course of human history and pre-history—in other words cultural evolution—from the Upper Paleolithic to the present day.

As a result, our picture of man's place and role in nature has once more changed. Though obviously this picture too will change in the future, we may expect the change to be one of natural growth and development, not the substitution of a wholly new design; for the present pattern is, as I emphasized earlier, the first to enjoy a reasonably comprehensive basis of scientific knowledge.

What, then, is the picture that emerges? First, we discover that all nature is a single process. We may properly call it evolution, if we define evolution as a self-operating, self-transforming process which in its course generates both greater variety and higher levels of organization. Though single and continuous, it is divisible into three distinct subprocesses or phases, each with its own distinctive methods and results. They are the inorganic or cosmological, the organic or biological, and the human or psycho-social. The second is less extensive both in space and time than the first, out of which it arises, the third less than the second.

The cosmological phase covers all but a tiny fraction of the universe. It operates by methods of simple physical and chemical interaction and its tempo of change is exceedingly slow; its products show very limited variety and attain only a low level of organization. Nowhere in it can we discern any mental activity.

The biological phase we know of only on our own planet, though it is presumed to exist also on a small minority of other planetary specks. It operates by the self-reproduction and self-variation of organic matter, which give rise to the method of self-transformation we call natural selection—the differential reproduction of variants. With the aid of this method its tempo of change is faster, the variety of its results much greater, and the level of organization which some of them attain very much higher. Its operations affect not only organic beings but that portion of the inorganic sector which is their home. In its later stages, mental activities are obvious and important.

Finally, the psychosocial phase we again know of only on this planet, though it may possibly have arisen also in a small fraction of other abodes of life. It operates by the self-reproduction and self-variation of mind and its products, which give rise to the method of cultural evolution based on cumulative experience. As a result, the tempo of its change, the variety of its products, and the height of organization reached are again enormously increased, as are its effects upon the portions of the other two phases of the process within the range of its influence. In the psycho-social phase, mental activities are more important than material.

Man's place in this process needs to be determined both in space and in time. Spatially, astronomy has now defined his place with some accuracy. It is an extremely small place. He inhabits one planet of one among hundreds of millions of stars in one among hundreds of millions of spiral nebulae or galaxies dispersed in an ocean of space to be measured in hundreds of millions of light-years. Temporally, the determination is less precise, partly because our knowledge of the past length of the process is less accurate, partly because its future can only be estimated. We can, however, affirm that man has come into existence somewhere in the middle reaches of the process, neither close to its beginning nor to its end. If, as some prefer to believe, human civilization represents the climax of evolution, it is only a climax to date, and has unimagined possibilities of further change still before it.

The minimum age of our galaxy is estimated at four or five thousand million years, and the age of our planet at three to four thousand million. On that planet, matter became self-reproducing—in common parlance, life originated—somewhere over two thousand million years ago, man less than one million and civilization a bare five thousand years back. Since astronomers and theoretical physicists give life on this earth a future at least as long as its past, it is fair to say that man's temporal place in nature is somewhere roughly midway in the process.

So-called modern man and his civilizations are thus in no sense a final product of evolution, but only a temporary phase in the process. Furthermore, realization of our transitional and midway position demands that we cease thinking only of past origins and pay attention also to future possibilities.

A consideration of man's role in nature strengthens these conclusions drawn from a better definition of his place in it. In the last fifty years, thanks chiefly to the discoveries of the paleontologists, we have for the first time gained a reasonably accurate picture of the way in which biological evolution pursues its course in time. There has been, we find, a succession of organizational types, the later-appearing ones possessing a higher level of organization than the earlier. Structural organization rises from the pre-cellular to the cellular and the multi-cellular level; there follows the multi-tissued type, like the sea-anemone, and then the multi-organed type like the worm or the mollusc or the early anthropod. The multi-organed animal attains new mechanical and physiological levels, as in crustacea and fish, new and superior modes of organization of reproduction, as in insects and reptiles, and new levels of behaviour appear, as in birds and mammals and social insects. New methods of integration and homeostatic adjustment arise, such as the endocrine system and the temperature-regulating mechanism of higher vertebrates.

Each major improvement in organization brings into existence a new and higher type, which then proceeds to demonstrate its improved nature by its biological success, as evidenced by its rapid multiplication and extension. The single original type radiates out into a number of separate lines or sub-types, each exploiting, in some special habitat or way of life, the advantages of the general organizational improvement possessed by the type.

General evolutionary advance is marked by a succession of successful dominant types, each undergoing expansion and specialized radiation, and each in turn supplanted in its position of dominance by a later type which has evolved some new major improvement. The classical example, and the one most relevant to my present purpose, is that of land vertebrates. During the past three hundred million years, the amphibians were replaced as dominant type by the reptiles, the reptiles by the birds and the mammals, the birds and the mammals by man. The successful expansion and diversification of each new type were correlated with the reduction of the previous radiation, as dramatically illustrated by the extinction of many orders of reptiles towards the end of the Mesozoic.

Another important general characteristic of biological evolution is that the great majority of evolutionary trends are intrinsically limited: after a longer or shorter time they come to a dead end. In the most general and non-committal terms, directional change is normally succeeded by stabilization.

This obviously holds good for the relatively minor trends we call specializations, like the specialization of whales for a secondarily aquatic life or of horses for grazing and rapid running. But, as my grandfather T. H. Huxley was one of the first to point out, it holds good also for major organizational trends and improvements. The occupants of the biological scene are for the most part what he called "persistent types", which have remained unchanged in their essential characteristics from the moment when they have come up against their invisible limitations. The most spectacular are the so-called "living fossils" like the lungfishes, which have persisted as rare survivors of a once abundant group for over three hundred million years; or the lampshell Lingula, which is barely to be distinguished from its ancestors preserved in the Ordovician rocks of four hundred million years ago. But an entire successful group may persist. The Coelenterates, such as jellyfish, polyps, and corals, certainly first became abundant and successful well before the beginning of the fossil record in the Cambrian, that is to say much more than five hundred million years ago; and they are still abundant and successful to-day. This does not mean that there has been no evolutionary change within the group during this portentous length of time. New specialized sub-groups, for instance of corals, have arisen and old sub-groups have died out. But the coelenterate level of organization has never been transcended by such new sub-groups: the coelenterate type of construction and working has persisted, though variations have been played on its essential theme.

The same holds true even for the latest and most finished products of evolution. The ants, in many ways the highest invertebrate type, have shown neither advance nor essential change since the time, some fifty million years ago, when ancestral specimens were trapped in the resin that has hardened into Baltic amber. The bird type has not changed in its basic quality of warm-blooded flying machine for perhaps twenty-five million years, although much minor specialization has taken place, adapting different avian lines to different habitats, niches, and ways of life.

It is not only levels of organization and plans of construction which became stabilized; improvements in functional capacity and biological performance also reach a limit. The limit has long been reached in respect of terrestrial size, of elaboration of instinct, of speed in water, on land, or in the air. It appears biologically impossible to develop greater acuity of vision than that of hawks, and biologically unprofitable to increase the delicacy and accuracy of temperature regulation beyond that achieved tens of millions of years ago both by birds and mammals. Digestion, nervous conduction, mechanical support, muscular contraction, chemical co-ordination—all have long since reached the highest level of efficiency possible to animal life.

To be brief, it appears that some time in the Pliocene, between five and ten million years ago, the possibilities of major improvement in the material and physiological properties of self-reproducing matter had been exhausted. The purely biological phase of evolution on this planet had reached its upper limit, and natural selection was no longer capable of producing any further large advance.

This does not mean that all biological evolution has come to an end, as is often mistakenly alleged. New species are constantly being evolved, and we can be sure that new trends will continue to bring new types into being. But these trends will all operate on existing levels of organization, and no advance to a new and higher level will, it seems, be possible, nor any major improvement in biological efficiency.

You will observe that my statement contained two caveats. One was that the method of natural selection alone was incapable of producing further large advance; the other, that in Pliocene times the possibilities of material and physiological improvement had reached a limit. The two hang together. The possibilities of improvement in the mental or psychological capacities of life had *not* been exhausted: and when their improvement reached a critical value, a new method of evolutionary transformation became available.

The one line in which mental improvement reached this critical value was that of our hominid ancestors; and the new evolutionary method which became available to it was the method of the transmission and transformation of tradition. This method of communication by concept and symbol provided an additional mechanism of inheritance involving the cumulative transmission of acquired experience, and permitted a much speedier and in many ways more effective type of evolutionary transformation, which we may call cultural evolution. With the passing of this critical point, hominids became men, man became the new dominant type, and the human or psycho-social phase of evolution was initiated on our earth.

Biological evolution depends on natural selection, which was made possible when matter became capable of self-reproduction and self-variation. Psycho-social or cultural evolution depends on cumulative tradition, which was made possible when mind and its products became capable of self-reproduction and self-variation.

The emergence of man as latest dominant type imposed a further restriction on the evolutionary possibilities of the rest of life. Even should the conclusion prove unjustified that purely biological evolution has reached its limit and become stabilized, and some new animal type should arise which threatened man's dominant position, man would assuredly be able to discern and counter the threat in its early stages. Man is thus to-day the only organism capable of further major transformation or evolutionary advance.

Our knowledge thus now enables us to define man's role as well as his place in nature. His role is to be the instrument of the evolutionary process on this planet, the sole agent capable of effecting major advances and of realizing new possibilities for evolving life. This, however, is only a broad and general statement. To define his role more accurately we need to study in more detail the peculiarities of man as a unique psycho-social organism, and the trends and mechanisms of his new form of evolution.

Man's decisive uniqueness is his possession of a self-reproducing tradition. His many other biologically unique characteristics are either prerequisites for or secondary consequences of this, and need not be discussed in the present context. It was the primary uniqueness of self-reproducing tradition which enabled him to become the new dominant type in evolution. This property of man depends on his capacity for true speech, which in turn is correlated with his capacity for conceptual thinking. True speech involves the use of words as symbols to denote objects and ideas, as against all forms of animal language and communication, which merely utilize auditory or visual signs to express feelings or attitudes.

Thinkers discussing the distinctive characters of man have usually laid their main or sole emphasis on intellectual or rational thought, and on language as its vehicle. This is precisely because they were thinkers, not artists, or practical men, or religious mystics, and therefore tended to over-value their own methods of coping with reality and ordering experience. In addition, the verbal formulation of intellectual propositions promises greater exactitude and facilitates the accurate and large-scale transmission of experience.

But this intellectual and linguistic over-emphasis is dangerous. It readily degenerates into logic-chopping or mere verbalism. What is more serious, it takes no account of man's emotional and aesthetic capacities, exalts reason and logical analysis at the expense of intuition and imagination, and neglects the important role of arts and skills, rituals and religious experiences in social life and cultural evolution. The evolutionary philosopher (and also the true humanist, whether he be anthropologist, historian, psychologist, or social scientist) must take all the facts into account: he must attempt a comprehensive view of man's special characteristics, and of their effects on his evolution.

The distinctive feature of man is that he is a cultural animal. In the psycho-social phase, it is cultures that evolve. I am of course using *cultures* in the anthropologist's sense, of patterns of language and law, ritual and belief, art and skill, ideas and technology, which all have to be learned and all depend on symbols and their communication, instead of being innate and depending on sign-stimuli and their interaction with releasing mechanisms as in animals. In animal evolution there is a sharp distinction between soma and germ-plasm, between the organization for living and the organization for reproduction and transmission. In psycho-social evolution this distinction breaks down: cultural patterns are, in Washburn's words, both "shared and transmitted", so that culture is simultaneously both the soma and germ-plasm of the social organism.

All the components of culture are in the last analysis symbolic; they exist only in virtue of man's powers of mental conception, his faculties of abstraction and generalization, of creative imagination and systematization—in a word, of constructing organized patterns of conscious experience, thought and purpose. Cultures are based on pre-existing material conditions and issue in new material effects; but they are predominantly the creation of mental activity in the widest sense.

However, we need a term to denote mind in this broad sense, as including all kinds of conscious experience and activity, rational intellect and imagination, emotionally motivated beliefs and attitudes, mystical experiences and aesthetic expressions, deliberate technical skills and symbolic ritual actions. I shall use the term *noetic* for this purpose. Although it has been sometimes restricted to intellectual activity, it is derived from the Greek word for mind, and has been applied in this general sense by two pioneers, both having begun significantly as biologists. St. John Mivart used *noesis* to denote "the sum total of the mental action of a rational animal"; and Père Teilhard du Chardin, in his remarkable book *Le Phénomène Humain* (Paris, 1955), speaks of man and his activities as constituting the *noosphere*, as against the *biosphere* which denotes the total of the organic inhabitants of the earth.

I would accordingly suggest the term *noetic system* or *noosystem* to denote the complex of the shareable and transmissible activities and products of human mind, the pattern thought and science, law and morality, art and ritual, which forms the basis of human society. These noetic patterns will differ from culture to culture, and often within a single culture. The study of how they are transmitted and how they change and evolve in time should be the central quest of the sciences of man: we might call it *noogenetics*.

I introduce these terms merely to save time in later discussion. What is important is the functions which the systems carry out. Man's place in nature, we have seen, is at the present summit of the evolutionary process on this planet; and his role is to conduct that process to still further heights. The mechanisms by which he can perform that role are his noetic systems—self-reproducing cultural agencies, superorganic products of conscious human organisms. He is now the agent of evolution, whether he knows it or not; but he will perform his role better if he is a conscious agent.

His evolution is now almost wholly a cultural evolution, operated by the transformation of shared and transmissible noetic systems—in other words, symbol-based systems—and their communication, both in space and in directional time. Throughout its history, the human species has operated by means of a number of distinct and often hostile or even irreconcilable noosystems; and none of them so far have fully or accurately represented the realities of nature. Both these facts have impaired their functional value in psycho-social evolution, and have prevented man from adequately performing his evolutionary role.

Man differs from all other dominant types—indeed from all biological types whatsoever—in that he has not split up into separate sub-groups, has not radiated out into a number of biologically discrete lines of specialization and adaptation, but has remained biologically a single interbreeding group or species. Culturally, however, he *has* split up—into a number of social or cultural lines or "interthinking groups", each with its own noosystem as basis for its existence and its evolution.

It would clearly make desirable psycho-social evolution easier to undertake and to operate effectively if the entire species shared one noosystem, one single body of knowledge, ideas, and attitudes. From this angle, the unity of knowledge is part of the noetic unity which we must strive to attain if we are to fulfil our destiny. Knowledge in this sense includes the intellectual and practical fruits of science and learning— "the sciences" in their broad European connotation, both natural and human, both pure and applied, and not only academic knowledge but also "know-how".

The possible creation of a unity of knowledge by extending a common system of facts and ideas to the whole human species had a number of implications. Since the only potentially universal type of knowledge is scientific, in the broad sense of resting on verifiable observation or experiment, it follows that this unity of knowledge will only be attained by the abandonment of non-scientific methods of systematizing experience, such as mythology and superstition, magico-religious and purely intuitional formulations. Here is an enormous and vitally important task for intellectuals of the world—to foster the growth and spread of a scientifically based noosystem.

This will also help to remove the second major defect of all existing and past noosystems—their lack of correspondence with the facts of nature. The facts of nature of course embrace not only cosmic, physical, and biological nature but also the facts of human or psycho-social nature, including social organization and cultural evolution; what is more, they embrace not only the facts of static organization but also the dynamics of nature as a process.

In so far as we succeed in constructing a system which represents the facts of nature, we shall have created not merely another noosystem, but a noocosm—a noetic microcosm which both illuminates and in a certain sense embodies the macrocosmic process. Such a system would be a new organ of evolving life, an organ both of comprehension and of control, through which we could not only reach some comprehension of the cosmic process—nature in the fullest sense—but also implement its further progress.

I am not so naïve as to believe that only one noetic system can exist in any community. Actually, "one society, one noosystem" is the exception: in advanced societies, a number of distinct noetic systems normally coexist. To discuss this phenomenon in detail is beyond the scope of this essay. It must suffice to point out the following facts. First, the co-existing systems may be complementary, as in a stable society organized on a class basis. I may instance the attitudes and ideas of the peasants, the clergy, and the feudal lords in the Middle Ages, or those of the "labouring classes" and the Whig aristocracy in the eighteenth century. Though there may be some friction between such separate systems, they function essentially as parts of a larger though looser unity. Secondly, as a corollary of this, there are usually some key concepts and attitudes common to all classes or groups of a complex society; it is these which provide the total system with what unity it has. Thirdly, one of the partial systems is usually dominant, in the sense that it has more operative effect on the development of the society as an organized community. This is so, for instance, wherever power is concentrated in the hands of an oligarchy, whether the great Whig landowners of Britain in the eighteenth century or the Central Committee of the Communist party in the U.S.S.R. to-day.

Finally, there may be a struggle for dominance between partial systems, which then naturally appear in opposition, and may come into active conflict. In such cases we are witnessing an important feature of psycho-social evolution, a noogenetic phenomenon analogous to the rise of an improved type in biological evolution. Analogous, but by no means identical. In biological evolution the types are condemned to remain distinct, and the struggle must result either in their permanent competitive co-existence, or in the expansion and rise to dominance of one, accompanied by the decline and reduction or extinction of the other. Though the same sort of results may occur in psycho-social evolution, as witnessed by the continued co-existence of the theistic and the scientific system in Western Europe during the last three centuries, or by the rise of the Marxist system to dominance in post-revolutionary Russia, there are also additional possibilities. Elements of a less successful system may be incorporated in one which is newly dominant, as with the absorption by Christianity (and indeed by all higher religious systems in their early stages) of elements of magic and animism from more primitive systems; or, still more interesting, conflict may be transcended in a new unification, and opposing system may be more or less completely reconciled in a higher synthesis, as happened when the new central idea of religious toleration brought religious persecution and the wars of religion to an end in Christian Europe, and as is beginning to happen in the world community to-day with the first transcendence of conflicting nationalisms by a supra-nationalist system of ideas and practice.

This brings me to another aspect of noetic unity. Man's systems of shared experience and attitude acquire increased unity not only externally by extension through greater areas and greater numbers of people, but also internally by greater integration. This is accomplished by what may be called *noetic integrators*—symbolic or conceptual constructions which serve to interpret large fields of reality, to transform experience into attitude and unify factual knowledge in belief. The general role of noetic integrators has never, so far as I am aware, been adequately explored, though attention has been paid to integrating concepts in the intellectual fields of science and philosophy, and to the integrative role of symbols in ritual and art.

In science, an integrating concept is one which orders a mass of facts and ideas into an organized pattern: it may be styled an intellectual organizer, roughly analogous to the biological organizer discovered by Spemann which imposes a pattern of organization on the early embryo of vertebrates. Thus the pattern of scientific thought and knowledge imposed by the concept of the conservation of matter and energy is quite different from that determined by the medieval ideas of force and the four elements besides unifying a much larger quantity of facts.

Even in the purely intellectual and scientific spheres, many organizing concepts are successful because they integrate apparent disparates or even reconcile apparent opposites. Thus the concept of temperature reconciles the originally opposed concepts of hotness and coldness. On a vaster scale, modern physical theory not only integrates all the multifarious forms of physical existence in the single concept of matter and the diverse types of physical action in the single concept of energy, but reconciles the inertness of matter and the activity of energy in a still more embracing synthesis. Similarly modern evolutionary genetic theory not only demonstrates the unity of life—green plants, animals, bacteria, and the rest —all based on the common mechanism of the chromosomal gene-complex, but also reconciles constancy with change.

When we come to the fields of belief and morality, attitude and expression, in which values and emotions are involved as well as knowledge, this capacity of noetic integrators for combining or reconciling opposites becomes even more important. Many such integrators are symbolic constructs, and it is in the very nature of a successful symbol to be a complex unity, capable of bringing together many disjoined or even disparate elements in a single effective pattern.

I am using *symbol* in the broadest possible sense, to denote the whole range of noetic constructions to which man has assigned significance, from national flags to gods, from slogans to celebrations, from rituals to works of art.

Many early rituals, like ritual cannibalism or the rites of Adonis, combine the opposites of death and life, of sacrifice and fulfilment; and this persists in sublimated form in rites like that of the Mass. For Christians, the cross is charged with a multiplicity of emotional, ethical and religious values which it unites in its single symbol. In human personality, many separate faculties are united, many conflicting impulses at least partially reconciled: thus a personal god is a more effective integrator than an impersonal one. However, since a monotheistic god must logically come to include more aspects of reality than can be credibly or intelligibly symbolized as a single personality, trinitarianism is a more effective theological concept than unitarianism; it provides the godhead with three Persons symbolizing three aspects of the realities of human destiny, aspects so different that they could scarcely be found within the confines of a single personality, while yet insisting on the oneness of the trinity as symbol of the over-riding unity of the universe.

One final general point before I get down to my particular task: all noetic integrators have an intellectual core of some sort and degree; or, from another angle, all effective symbolic constructs have a knowledge aspect, all contain an idea or system of ideas, whether explicit and conscious, or unconscious and implicit. This applies to expressive constructs such as works of art and rituals as well as to scientific or ethical or theological integrators. This is another way of saying that, since all symbolic constructs and all noetic integrators have as their essential function the significant interpretation of reality as presented in available experience, they will perform that function better in so far as they embrace a larger field of experience and correspond more accurately with reality.

This is of the greatest importance for man's evolution. For on the one hand it stresses the desirability of continuing to extend our experience and enlarge our knowledge of reality; and on the other hand it warns against noetic fossilization, and emphasizes the danger of our symbolic constructs and noetic integrators becoming rigid and not keeping pace with the growth of our knowledge.

We are now in a position to consider the relation between man's place and role in nature and the unity of knowledge, or, as I would prefer to say, the unity of organized experience. If man's role is to be the instrument of further evolution of this planet, he needs the best possible noosystem to enable him to perform that role effectively. To start with, he requires to extend his knowledge of the unitary process of reality that we call nature, including of course the part of reality included in his own nature and his own psycho-social evolution; research must be vigorously prosecuted in every field of science and learning. Secondly, he must attempt to unify his knowledge by systematizing it and by discovering the interrelations between different fields of experience. For example, our age is the first in history in which we have acquired a comprehensive knowledge of historical fact, from the present back to the paleolithic, and therefore the first age in which it is possible to attempt a unified history, such as the *Scientific and Cultural History of Mankind* sponsored by Unesco. If this attempt is successful, it will mark an important advance in the unified articulation of factual knowledge. It has now become possible to produce similar unified articulations of factual knowledge in other major fields, such as physical geography, material resources, or biological evolution.

Such extensive systems or articulations of knowledge are valuable and necessary bases for noetic unification; but they need to be supplemented by the intensive mechanism of noetic integrators if we are to achieve integration in the domain of beliefs and attitudes, and therefore the over-all unification of dynamic noosystem.

How does all this apply to our immediate task? Let me recapitulate the essentials of the problem. Psycho-social evolution is cultural: it operates via the culture-complex, and is realized through the evolutionary transformation of cultures. Noosystems play a necessary and important part in cultural evolution; and noetic integrators provide a necessary and important part of the driving force and interpretative efficiency of noosystems. Our problem thus is to develop noetic integrators suitable for our present phase of cultural evolution. They must be consonant with the structure and the trends of man's present system of knowledge: they must also help to secure a pattern and direction of cultural evolution which will most effectively enable man to perform his evolutionary role in nature.

The most important facts and ideas which our new integrators must symbolize, focus, and order seem to me to be these. First, the fact of the unity of nature, of the entire reality of the cosmos—unitary monism as against any form of dualism, whether the dualism of natural and supernatural, of body and spirit, of actual and ideal, or of matter and mind.[2] Secondly, the fact that nature is a process, all reality a pattern of processes—evolution as against static mechanism, change as against fixity. Thirdly, the fact that evolution is directional, that it generates greater variety, higher organization, increase of mental activity, more definite and more conscious values—the idea of possible progress and advance as against stability or retrogression or mere alteration, of significant as against non-significant change or no change at all. We can reformulate this last point in terms of possibilities. Evolutionary advance consists in the realization of new possibilities by nature: thus we explore the areas and limits of possibilities, as against merely studying or accepting actualities. Finally, we have the fact that man's role is to be the instrument of further evolution on this planet—an evolutionary view of human destiny as against a theological or a magical, a fatalistic or a hedonistic one.

The precise form which the new integrators should take as effective noetic organs is not for any individual to prescribe: it can only emerge as the result of much co-operative discussion. Certain conclusions, however, seem inevitable. It is clear, I think, that the dualistic ordering of experience round the two incompatible integrators of natural and supernatural must go, and must be replaced by the idea of universal unity. Similarly the duality of material and spiritual elements in civilization must somehow be resolved in the unity of psycho-social culture, and that of mind and body in the concept of psychosomatic integration. Again the apparent

[2] Like so many philosophical terms, *monism* has been employed in a confusing number of ways. I use it simply to denote a unitary and comprehensive as against a dualist, pluralist, or restrictive approach.

opposites of individual and society became complementary within the concept of cultural evolution; and the conflicting desires for success in, and escape from, the limited present can be reconciled in the idea of progressive realization of possibilities.

Gods have been extremely potent noetic integrators in the last millennia of human history: but it is becoming clear that God, like all other concepts involving the animistic projection of man's mental and spiritual attributes into non-human nature, is ceasing to have interpretative value and needs replacing by some non-animistic construction, such as the concept of self-transforming and self-transcending reality. The ideas of comprehensible activity and orderly process will perhaps replace those of divine omniscience and omnipotence, and the concepts of operative sacredness and effective ideals supplant that of God's sanctity and goodness.

Assuredly the concept of man as instrument and agent of the evolutionary process will become the dominant integrator of all ideas about human destiny, and will set the pattern of our general attitude to life. It will replace the idea of man as the Lord of Creation, as the puppet of blind fate, or as the willing or unwilling subject of a Divine Master.

New integrators are also needed for more limited and more immediate fields of experience and action. For instance, the facts of national interdependence, the existence of grossly under-developed areas, the incipient schemes for supranational action in the spheres of politics, economics and so-called Technical Assistance, could all be integrated in the dynamic idea of joint participation in a common enterprise of world development.

The often rather futile discussion as to the status of the artist and the significance of art can be resolved by taking a functional view: the function of the artist is to bear witness to the variety and richness of reality, and to express it effectively and significantly in terms related to the life and aims of man.

Again, the role of writers, philosophers, columnists, and journalists would gain both clarity and dignity by being integrated under the head of interpretation: they are, or can be, the interpreters of reality, and the profession of interpreter of reality could in part take the place of that of prophet, which, in its original sense, has long fallen into desuetude.

For petitionary prayer we must substitute what may be described as dynamic meditation, a spiritual discipline which gives a set to the whole psyche and attunes it to wider and higher levels of reality. Our descendants will have to coin the right phrase to denote the noetic integrator for this purpose.

The ideal of social or professional success, based on a one-sided specialization of some single faculty or skill and evaluated in material or quantitative terms, needs to be supplemented and in large measure replaced by the ideal of wholeness. The integrator here is integration; the aim the development of an integrated personality, an inner harmony, with peace as its product. The concept of the Absolute would seem destined to disappear in all fields, whether of truth, beauty, goodness or any other value, to be replaced by those of satisfying wholeness, of self-transcendence, and of desirable direction.

Finally, I would prophesy that the central overriding integrator, round which man's entire noetic system is organized, will be that of fulfilment—satisfaction through fuller realization of possibilities. In the light of this concept, the sharp antinomies between individual and society, between nation and mankind, disappear, for each has its claim to its own fulfilment, and all are complementary within the total process of the evolutionary fulfilment of life. Past, present, and future are similarly united in its synthetic grasp, and the sharp opposition between the ideal and the real, between the abstract and the actual, is reconcilable in the concept of the increasing realization of possibilities.

This of course does not mean that conflicts will or should vanish: but they will appear as inevitable and often necessary steps in the reconciliatory dialectic process which can produce greater fulfilment. Nor does it mean that mankind will be furnished with a set of rules applicable to particular situations. It is of the essence of a good noetic integrator to be general and elastic: its function is to determine approach and determine attitude, not to provide detailed guidance.

Nor would general acceptance of fulfilment as central noetic concept ensure that human beings would always rule their actions and their lives in accordance with it. Men will continue to steal and kill, to act stupidly and deceitfully, as they have done in the past in spite of their general acceptance of the integrating concepts of theistic religions. But man's noetic systems do have an influence on his actions: they determine and provide the general policy and the general set of his cultural behaviour, through which he pursues his destiny.

It is further obvious that noetic systems differ in their efficiency and value, and I would maintain that in the world's present age, one organized round the integrating concept of fulfilment will achieve a greater degree of unity than any other, and will give man more help in the better accomplishment of his role in nature.

[1]EVOLUTION, CULTURAL AND BIOLOGICAL

WHEN I was invited by the Wenner-Gren Foundation to prepare "a guest editorial on a subject of my choice", concerning my views on anthropology, I was naturally flattered, but also experienced considerable trepidation. Even if an evolutionary biologist had any views on anthropology, how could they be of any value to professional anthropologists? However, I reflected, an evolutionary biologist, if he should not aspire to views *on* anthropology, might be expected to have some views *of* anthropology in relation to his own subject. This, then, is what I shall attempt—a view of anthropology *sub specie evolutionis,* in the belief that the general concepts and principles derived from biology will prove to have illuminating applications or implications for the more restricted and younger sister-science of anthropology.

Let me at the outset make a comprehensive disclaimer. I do not believe that any purely biological concepts and principles can be immediately applied or directly transferred to anthropology. In fact I know they cannot; the various past attempts at such direct transference and application have always resulted in confusion rather than clarification. The reason is simple: although the history of man is clearly part of a more general evolutionary process, its basis and mechanism are something *sui generis*. Man is a unique organism with unique properties, and there must be specifically anthropological concepts and principles whose application is restricted to man.

[1] Guest editorial written for the *Yearbook of Anthropology,* 1955.

In the last few decades it has become clear that the whole of phenomenal reality is a single process, which properly may be called evolution. Though the process of evolution is unitary, embracing the entire universe both in space and time, it is divisible into three very distinct sectors or phases, each with its own characteristic mechanism, tempo, and type of product—the inorganic or cosmological; the later and much restricted organic or biological sector arose as a later phase from the inorganic; and the still later and still further restricted human or psycho-social.

We have in the last half-century arrived at an adequate general understanding of the biological sector. This has been due to detailed study, first of what evolves—lineages of organisms of various types, including their structure, physiology and ontogeny, and their ecological relations; secondly, of the genetic basis of evolution—the mechanism of reproduction, hereditary transmission and transformation, including the gene-complex, variation, and natural selection; thirdly, of evolution as a process—the mechanisms and modes of its self-transforming course, as revealed in phases of change and stabilization, in radiation and extinction, in succession of dominant types, in emergence of higher material and mental organization; and finally by a synthesis of the relevant results in all three fields. Our knowledge of this interlocking trinity of subject-matter—the mechanisms for maintaining existence, the bases of reproduction and variation, and the modes of evolutionary transformation—had first to be gathered and then synthesized, to give us an understanding of life's total process.

The same must assuredly hold for the human or psycho-social phrase. Anthropology is the science of the psycho-social sector. It cannot expect to make full and comprehensive progress if it restricts its field. The study of social psychology and of the psychological mechanisms underlying various culture traits is important; so is a study of social structure and cultural working; and that of personality; and of social institutions and of systems and methods of education; and of culture-contact; and of kinship systems, totemic organizations, and religions; and of material artifacts; and of linguistic, technological, aesthetic, scientific, and other partial modes of evolution: but none is sufficient by itself.

As in the biological sector, so in the human: we need a knowledge of the mechanisms that maintain psycho-social existence, of their reproduction and variation, of the mechanisms and modes of their transformations in time, to give us a general understanding of the psycho-social process as a whole—in other words, of man.

But anthropology was inevitably a late starter in the scientific race, and it has to cope with a subject-matter both more complex and more confused than that of any other science. No wonder that understanding of the psycho-social sector of reality lags behind that of the biological and the inorganic.

Long before biology was born as a science, it seemed obvious that the individual organism provided the mechanism for maintaining existence in the biological sector. But though this holds for most higher animals, and though there is a marked trend toward sharper and fuller individuation in the course of biological evolution, later study showed that this naïve conclusion was not quite so obvious as it at first sight had appeared. In many forms it is difficult and in some impossible to determine the limits or even the nature of the individual organism. However, there does always exist some organization of living matter whose function it is to maintain itself in direct interaction with its environment. In the terminology of modern genetics, we may speak of this as the phenotypic system. It may be composed of single individual organisms, usually of two sexes, or of communities or societies of such separate individuals (as in gregarious mammals or social insects) or of colonies in which the individuals are physically united and lose much of their pristine individuality (as with the cells of a metazoan or the "individuals" of a siphonophore or a bath-sponge). But it is always a system for maintaining existence. The study of its structure and form constitutes anatomy and morphology; that of its methods of working constitutes physiology, behaviour, and psychology; that of its relations with the environment, including other organisms, constitutes ecology; and that of its development and growth constitutes embryology and ontogeny.

The biological mechanisms of reproduction and variation proved much harder to define. Their discovery awaited the invention of the microscope and the elaboration of scientific method, both experimental and statistical. It now appears that in almost all organisms, both plant and animal, the mechanism of self-reproduction is sharply distinct from that of self-maintenance. It may be called the genotypic system. In opposition to the phenotypic system, it is locked away and sheltered as far as possible from contact or direct interaction with the environment. It consists of the gene-complex—a system of self-reproducing bodies or genes, arranged in a definite order in larger bodies called chromosomes, and detached in the act of reproduction within a unit of general protoplasm (cytoplasm). The chemical behaviour of the cytoplasm is determined by the genes, but the gene-complex cannot survive and function without an envelope of cytoplasm: the two are interdependent, but with the gene-complex as dominant partner.

The mechanism of transmissible variation, again in almost all organisms, is twofold—*mutation* or change in intrinsic properties of parts of the gene-complex, and *recombination* of already existing mutants to produce new variants. You will observe that I expressly refer to *transmissible* variation. One of the notable facts established by modern genetics is the non-transmissibility of certain types of variation. Only those in the gene-complex of the reproductive cells are permanently transmissible: those affecting all other parts of the organism are not. Non-transmissible variance includes all so-called somatic variation—variations in the character of the individual body, whether occurring in the course of normal development (as in the differentiation of various tissues from the relatively undifferentiated ovum, spore, or other reproductive body, or in the alternation of generations in a moss or a fern); or induced by changes in the environment (as in the sun-tanning of white human beings, or the production of worker bees by a restricted diet); or the result of individual experience (as in the learning by solitary wasps of the location of their burrows, or by birds of the nauseous or dangerous properties of warningly coloured insects).

The two later categories of variation embrace all so-called "acquired characters", so that the proof of their non-transmissibility is a disproof of Lamarckism and all other similar theories of evolution. The first category, however, must be characterized as reproducible but genetically non-transmissible. The distinction between transmissible and non-transmissible variation coincides almost exactly with the earlier distinction made by Weismann between *germ-plasm* and *soma*. Though Weismann's original formulation needs to be slightly modified in the light of later knowledge, the opposition between germ-plasm and soma is still basic to all our genetic thinking. Some parts of the organism—in higher animals all the somatic tissues—are debarred from playing any role in reproduction, and variations in them cannot be transmitted; other parts—the gene-complexes of actual or potential reproductive cells—are the organs of heredity, and variations in them can be and are transmitted to later generations.[2]

Thus in the light of modern biology, variations fall into the two opposed categories of genetic and non-genetic. Furthermore, we can distinguish sharply between the mechanism of maintenance—the soma, including not only the living somatic cells but also their non-living products such as horn or chitin; and the mechanism of transmission—the germ-plasm, or more specifically the gene-complex or genetic system in the reproductive cells.

However, the sharpness of the distinction tends to break down in the simplest organisms, such as the bacteria, where the germ-plasm is much less cut off from contact with the environment; or the crystallizable viruses, which are in a sense nothing but germ-plasm, and whose "soma" is provided by the tissues of their host.

The greatest present handicap to the science of man would seem to lie in its lack of agreement in defining the objects of study in the three members of the interlocking trinity of its subject-matter.

The third member, the course of psycho-social transformation, I shall discuss later. As regards the mechanism for maintaining psycho-social existence, there is by no means agreement as to what should be analysed. This somewhat startling fact emerges clearly from works such as Bidney's *Theoretical Anthropology*. Some anthropologists say society, others culture, still others the individuals who make up the society or share the culture: and within each sect there is still a cleavage between the materialists and the mentalists (if I may coin a word)—between those who insist on a purely or mainly materialist interpretation of something, and those who want to explain human affairs solely or primarily in psychological terms. There is not even agreement on the definition of *culture,* that central anthropological concept: some anthropologists maintain that culture is an abstraction, others that it is the sum of human activities, or of the

---

[2] In this discussion I have neglected the plasmagenes, or self-reproducing cytoplasmic factors in heredity. Plasmagenes do exist, notably in plants, but they are few in number and small in importance compared with the nuclear genes, and furthermore are often subordinated to them in their effects. For our purpose they thus constitute a minor and subordinate fraction of the germ-plasm.

patterns of human behaviour within a given society, still others that it includes all "artifacts, socifacts, and mentifacts", to use Bidney's convenient terms for the different types of products of a culture or human society.[3]

A further confusion arises owing to two radical differences between psychosocial and biological evolution—first, the lack of any sharp distinction in the psycho-social sector between soma and germ-plasm; secondly, the presence of an increasing trend toward convergence superimposed upon that toward divergence. Culture, in the objectively definable sense which seems natural to a biologist, is at one and the same time both soma and germ-plasm, both a mechanism of maintenance and a mechanism of reproduction or transmission. This statement needs some minor qualifications: for instance, the system of material production is more concerned with maintenance, the educational system more with transmission. But the material objects produced and the skills that produce them also are directly transmissible (unlike the metabolic products and activities of the animal soma); and the knowledge and attitudes transmitted by education are also directly concerned with the maintenance of culture and the body politic (unlike the germ-plasm securely tucked away within the body organic).

This union of somatic and germinal functions in culture is another consequence of the new evolutionary mechanism available to life in the psycho-social phase—the mechanism of cultural tradition based on cumulative experience. This follows from the fact that cultural tradition depends on communication. Since communication occurs both extensively, in space, between contemporary members of a culture, and

[3] In some ways the situation in anthropology recalls that of biology some fifty years back. Then we had the protagonists of comparative morphology contending with those of physiological analysis; the violent (but as it turned out unreal) quarrel between the biometrician gradualists and selectionists and the mendelian mutationists and anti-selectionists, the dispute between the ultra-materialistic and the ultra-psychological students of animal behaviour; the curious preformationist theories of Bateson; the confusion between genetic determinant and character; the last stand of the Lamarckians and the vitalists against the advancing regiments of the Mendelians and the mechanists.

To-day this confusion has been largely abolished, partly by the final disproof of certain views, partly owing to the reconciliation of opposing theses in a higher synthesis, and partly by a linking-up of separatist movements in a combined attack on a unified front. We may reasonably hope that anthropology will undergo a similar development.

progressively, in time, between individuals of different generations, tradition and the culture arising from it inevitably combine maintenance and transmission functions—in other words, serve both as psycho-social soma and germplasm. Furthermore, transmission may occur by diffusion of various sorts between cultures, as well as within single streams of culture.

The new basis and mode of transmission and transformation available to psycho-social evolution have also important consequences for its course, notably in leading to convergence. Man differs radically from all preceding successful types in not having diverged into numerous biologically separate species and lineages. An incipient divergence, based doubtless on geographical isolation, permitted the differentiation of *Homo sapiens* into what in biology would be called subspecies—the races of mankind, each physiologically adapted to its geographical habitat. But since most human adaptation and improvement are cultural, genetic divergence did not proceed further, and was soon overtaken by the effects of genetic convergence, as man's expansive or migratory urges brought previously isolated populations into contact. Biologically, modern man has thus remained one species, a single interbreeding group.

However, the two complementary processes, of evolutionary divergence by increase of variety, and of evolutionary advance marked by improvement in general organization and leading to the emergence of new successful types, continued to take effect in the psycho-social sector, but in the domain of culture. As in the biological phase, major advance proceeds by large steps, each marked by the spread of the successful new type of organization. Among obvious examples are the discovery and spread of agriculture, of urban civilization, of alphabetic writing, of monotheism, and of science and scientific method.

The complementary process of divergent cultural evolution has always been a striking feature of man's history, and was markedly accentuated in its later stages, after the advance to the level of urban civilization. We need only think of the range and variety of cultures in the ancient world—Sumerian, Egyptian, Indus Valley, Hittite, Assyrian, Phoenician, and the rest. On the other hand, the same unique trend toward convergence after divergence, seen in the genetic make-up of man, operated also in his cultural evolution: the main difference is that a much greater degree of cultural than of biological divergence took place, and that the degree of unity produced by cultural convergence is still far below that reached on the genetic level. Whereas biological convergence must be achieved by physical interbreeding of divergent types, cultural convergence operates by various forms of culture-contact and diffusion.

With this preliminary clearing of the air we are now in a position to analyse cultural evolution in more detail. I must first justify the view that what evolves in the psycho-social phase is not primarily the genetic nature of man, or individuals, or society, or minds-in-society, but a new supraorganismic entity, demanding an appellation of its own. *Culture* is the appellation by which anthropologists denote this central subject of their science.

Culture, if I understand it aright, is a shared or shareable body of material, mental, and social constructions ("artifacts, mentifacts, and socifacts") created by human individuals living in a society, but with characteristics not simply explicable by or directly deducible from a knowledge of the psychological or physiological properties of human individuals, any more than the characteristics of life are simply explicable by or directly deducible from a knowledge of the chemical and physical properties of inorganic matter, or those of mind from a knowledge of the properties of neurons. Culture has a material basis, in the shape of resources of food, raw materials, and energy; but though the quantity and quality of material resources available will influence or condition the character and development of a culture, they do not determine it in detail, so that differences between cultures are no more explicable by or deducible from a knowledge of their material basis than from that of their psychological basis in the minds of individuals.

In describing and analysing a culture, we thus need to distinguish a number of distinct components. First, the material or resource basis: secondly, the basis of communication or language; thirdly, skills and techniques, including tools and machines, dress and adornment, buildings and vehicles, and works of art; then systems of social organization, including kinship and marriage systems, legal, political, economic and administrative systems, and status systems such as class and caste; then knowledge systems, including education, science, and higher learning; and finally attitude systems, ranging from manners to religions, and including personal and social ethics, tabus, and rituals.

But the mass enumeration of cultural components is obviously not enough. We must also undertake the analysis of culture as a self-operating and self-reproducing system. Here, the best method of approach would seem to be the functional one, analogous to the broadly physiological approach in biology. How does a culture work? What operations and functions must it perform, and how and with what organs does it do so? The chief alternative is the structural or morphological approach, analogous to the method of comparative anatomy in zoology. This is obviously useful as a first step, but can and should be incorporated in a broad functional analysis. It is dangerous when utilized to the exclusion of the functional approach, or as dominant to it.

The dangers of over-emphasis on the structural approach are evidenced by the history of zoology. As Radl wrote in his *History of Biological Theories* (1930), many zoologists in the late nineteenth century were so busy comparing one structure with another that they forgot to ask what the structures were or did. The first effect was the growth of a forest of largely hypothetical (and we may add also largely sterile) family trees; the second was a compensatory over-reaction in favour of physiology and experimental analysis. The next step was an attempt at reconciling purely structural anatomy with purely experimental physiology in the concept of the organism as a working or functional whole; and the final result has been the development of an all-round approach (as evidenced, for instance, in J. Z. Young's recent *The Life of Vertebrates*), in which comparative anatomy, though still basic, is treated functionally, physiology has become broadly comparative, and both have been combined in an ecological-evolutionary approach.

I feel sure that a similar synthesis or reconciliation will take place in anthropology, though the details of the process will be different—for instance, the comparative anatomy of structural patterns is much easier to study in zoology than in anthropology, while the reverse is often true for the analysis of function.

Let me now return to the problem of culture and its investigation. Culture in the broad objective view appears *sub specie evolutionis* as a self-maintaining system or organization of intercommunicating human beings and their products, or if we wish to be a little more precise, of the results of the intercommunication of the minds of human individuals in society.

Though a culture thus depends on individual human beings and their psychological activities, its characteristics, as I have already emphasized, cannot be deduced from theirs. The intrinsic (genetic) psycho-physical properties of the human population of a society, and the intrinsic peculiarities of single individuals within it, can and do to some extent condition the form and development of the culture, but do not determine it. In fact the boot is on the other foot, or at least the emphasis is the other way round: the effective (or in biological parlance the phenotypic) characterization and achievements of human beings in a society are to a very large extent the result of the pattern of culture in which the human individuals live and the cultural forces which play upon them.

The studies of Kroeber on genius have shown that geniuses appear—in other words, that exceptionally gifted individuals are able to realize their talents effectively—not at a constant or even approximately constant rate in time, nor with a uniform extension in different areas, but in bursts; and that these bursts are related to the stage of development of the culture into which the potential geniuses are born.

Ogburn and Thomas have demonstrated that the progress of scientific discovery shows a somewhat similar phenomenon: outstanding discoveries and inventions are often and perhaps usually made independently by more than one man at about the same date. Here again the determining factor is the stage and type of cultural development.

This fact of multiple independent discovery is of course only a special, though outstanding, feature of what many thinkers have noted—the intrinsic momentum of science. Once a science has reached the stage of having a coherent theoretical basis, it will inevitably proceed (provided it is not discouraged by authority) to make further discoveries and further extensions of its theory. It becomes, in fact, a quasi-autonomous cultural entity, an organization of facts, ideas, and practices which is bound to progress until it has exhausted its possibilities—in other words, has realized the implications of its theoretical basis.

Analogous phenomena are found in other cultural fields; for instance, the localized outbursts of masterpieces and the deterministic trends of style in the arts, as in ancient Greek sculpture, or in European painting since the Renaissance; the development of Christian theology during the first millennium A.D., and of scholastic philosophy during the second.

Indeed, this intrinsic momentum appears to be a general property of all cultural organs involving creative thought or activity. It results in trends of cultural evolution. These resemble in an interesting way the trends of improvement to be seen in biological evolution: both types of trend continue in the same general direction for a considerable period of time, until they reach a limit of some sort, when they become stabilized (and often enfeebled, reduced or extinguished).

The limit, when the biological or cultural system has "exhausted its capacities for development", "fully realized its possibilities", or however else we may describe it, may be determined either intrinsically, by the very nature of the evolving system or faculty, or extrinsically, through the interference of some other system, or by the operation of external forces. In biology we have examples of these different types of limits, in the limitation of visual acuity by minimum size of visual cells; of size and intelligence in insects by their tracheal system; and of accuracy of temperature-regulation in mammals by the efficacy of the forces of natural selection. I leave it to my anthropological colleagues to find comparable examples in cultural evolution.

I must add an important caveat. Some "culturologists" and some believers in economic or social determination maintain that individuals as such play no part in moulding human history, but are wholly moved by superorganic social and cultural forces. However, while it is clear that the "great man" theories, according to which single individuals are responsible for all or most of the decisive advances and regressions, turns and twists of history, cannot possibly be upheld, neither can the extreme opposite view.[4]

It is one of the uniquenesses of man that in him the broad trend toward individuation and the greater importance of the individual organism and the individual event, which characterizes evolution in general, has reached and passed a critical point. In the inorganic phase, differences between individual atoms and molecules are submerged in the statistical behaviour of aggregates. In biology, individual events such as mutations produce the differences between individual

---

[4] Even Plekhanov (*The Role of the Individual in History*, International Publishers, New York, 1946), while upholding cultural determinism in general ("For a great man, the general character of his epoch is 'empirically given necessity'"), admits the importance of the exceptional individual.

genes which provide the basis for evolutionary improvement; and in higher animals, notably birds and mammals, selection operates largely on the differences between the highly individuated single organisms within a species, though the operation is still on a statistical basis. But in man, individual differences are no longer wholly submerged in statistical processes, and the behaviour of single individuals may affect the course of psycho-social evolution. Thus, while the Mongols would assuredly have become an important organized power in the Middle Ages, the extent of that power would certainly have been less and its form different if it had not been for Genghis Khan; and similar considerations apply to the influence of Napoleon on the development of post-revolutionary France.

The importance of individuals is perhaps most clearly evident in the arts, for it is of the essence of a great work of art that it should be individually unique. In Italian painting, for instance, while inescapable cultural forces were influencing a high percentage of talented men to become artists, and were producing over-all trends of style, it is the masterpieces of individuals which have been of decisive value for man and his cultural evolution. Although in a different culture, such as that of modern America or Russia, Giotto and Titian, Michelangelo and Leonardo would quite likely not have become artists, and would certainly have painted quite different kinds of pictures, the fact remains that if these particular individuals had not existed, not only would the world be a poorer place, but the history of art would have been different.

Since scientific discovery is a cumulative process, and since it concerns objective fact, the distinctive role of individuals is not so marked in the sciences as it is in the arts, and simultaneous discovery is not infrequent. All the same, it is impossible to believe that the advance of science would have been so speedy, or indeed quite the same, without individuals like Newton or Einstein. Even where independent or simultaneous discovery has occurred, the actual contribution or effect of one individual may be much greater than that of the others. Thus Wallace hit on the theory of evolution by means of natural selection independently of Darwin; yet we can be certain that the advance of biology into its evolutionary stage would have been both slower and different if Darwin had not existed.

An example which illustrates both aspects of the relation between individual and culture is that of particulate inheritance. As is well known, Mendel discovered and published the basic facts of this and established its elementary laws. But the development of science as a cultural process was apparently not ripe for their acceptance, and his discovery remained ignored until it was re-made independently by three workers thirty-four years later. Only after this did Mendel become recognized as the founder of the science of genetics.

Here I must make a brief methodological divagation. The *method of approach* to any scientific problem is clearly of extreme importance, and will to a large extent determine the type of discovery made. Putting the matter the other way round, the method of approach is itself largely dictated by the type of answer you want to obtain: it is, in fact, a kind of question. Furthermore, the question will alter with time and the progress of discovery: when one method has yielded the main crop of answers that it could be expected to provide, it is time to ask another kind of question, by adopting a new method. A biologist cannot suggest methods for anthropology to practice. What he can do, however, is to summarize the various methods of approach adopted in biology, in the hope that anthropologists may be able to discover implications helpful for their own science.

The original approach inevitably was descriptive: biologists set out to describe as fully and accurately as possible the variety of organisms and the phenomena which they exhibit. This approach is designed to answer the basic question, What are the facts?

The descriptive approach was soon supplemented by the comparative. This was first focused round the question of grouping or classification. What pattern or system of characters does an assemblage of organisms have in common; and what distinct types are there at various levels of characterization? This led to the classification of organisms in a hierarchical system of groups—species grouped in genera, genera in families, families in orders, orders in classes, and so on.

Implicit in such a system was the idea of physical relationship. With the acceptance of the fact of evolution, this implicit postulate became explicit, and the question posed by the comparative method became correspondingly altered; behind common patterns, men were reaching for common origins. The result was a phylogenetic classification, a classification intended to express evolutionary descent and relationships rather than just a convenient pigeon-holing system. The animals placed in the order of Carnivora, for instance, were all presumed to be descended from a single common carnivore ancestor, and a common mammalian ancestor was postulated for them and all the other orders placed in the class Mammalia.

However, while common ancestry accounted for the shared resemblances of a group, the problem of the differences exhibited by its members remained. For this, a new method of approach was needed, a method which we may call that of differential analysis. It asked the question, What is the cause of the differences between the members of a related group? The method has been most successfully (because most easily) employed in analysing the visible differences between minor varieties of a single interbreeding population and demonstrating that those which were heritable depended on differences in hereditary unit-factors, later called genes. The modern science of genetics is built on this, the mendelian method, of analysing after crossing.

When the different forms are populations inhabiting geographically different areas, such as two geographical races or subspecies of one species, extrinsic factors also must be taken into account. In such cases it is found that their differences, though due genetically to differences in their intrinsic genic make-up, also have a historical component, which is correlated with the geographical or ecological difference in their habitats, and with the degree and duration of biological isolation between them. The differences are thus the result of an evolutionary process of divergence requiring time.

Finally, when the different forms cannot be interbred to yield a fertile cross, as occurs between different species or higher taxonomic categories, the genic factors involved in producing the difference cannot be experimentally discovered, and can be only partially deduced through analogy and other comparative procedures. In such cases, where experimental crossing is impossible and the number of causative factor-differences is large, special methods of multi-variate analysis may be needed to give satisfactory results.[5]

However, there are limits to the usefulness of such differential analytic methods. Mendelian analysis, for instance,

[5] See, e.g., C. P. Stroud, 1953, *Systematic Zoology* (Washington), 2, p. 76.

tells us that a *difference*, say in flower-colour between two
varieties of plant, is due to a *difference* between two genetic
factors or genes.[6] But it tells us nothing, or at least nothing
worth knowing, about what the genes *are*, or of how they
work. To obtain answers to such questions we must utilize
other methods of approach—constitutive as well as differential, integrative as well as analytic. By constitutive I mean
an approach involving questions as to the constitution or
nature of what is being investigated; and by integrative I
mean one which attempts to comprehend the interrelation-
ships and total pattern of a system of analytically detectable
components.

In regard to genes, constitutive inquiry has already shown
that they are portions of chromosomes, that they consist of a
certain kind of nucleic acid in association with proteins, and
possess a molecular structure permitting binary multiplication by self-copying. And the integrative approach has led
to the concept of the gene-complex, a system of interrelated
units with mutually adjusted interactions. For the problems
of complex yet unitary patterns, *Gestalt* and other similar
approaches are required, and non-quantitative mathematical
formulations of patterned systems are being attempted.

The constitutive approach soon demands vectorial dia-
chronic enlargement, by the addition of a directed time-
dimension. We then ask questions about processes—how
does a given initial state of things become converted in time
into a different state? In genetics, for instance, we try to
unite gene and character by considering them as the end-
points of a single chemical and physiological process or chain
of processes—and in micro-organisms are already meeting
with considerable success.

Similarly, once we have introduced a historical component
into our study of differences between taxonomic groups
(subspecies, species, and higher categories) and have arrived
at the conclusion that evolutionary divergence has been at
work, we are inevitably impelled to ask what trends are
involved, what is their shape and their direction, how do
they operate, and how do they produce their observed results?
This approach, in the hands of men like Simpson and Ford,
Mayr and Dobzhansky, is already giving us interesting answers in terms of the effects of natural selection in different
circumstances—adaptive improvement, minor non-adaptive

6 Strictly speaking, two *alleles*, or forms of one kind of gene.

diversification, trends of specialization, parallel evolution, limits to improvement, stabilization, and so forth, so that we are beginning to work out a science of evolutionary process.

The evolutionary biologist, fortunate in the more mature stage of development which his science has reached, may perhaps be permitted to suggest some lines of study to the anthropologist. In the first place, an evolutionary approach seems to me essential. We shall never fully understand human culture unless we look at it as a portion of the evolutionary process—both a product of past evolution and a basis for possible future evolution.

The evolutionary approach in anthropology has been bedevilled by false starts and false premises—notably the erroneous idea that biological evolution could be represented by a single straight line of inevitable progress, and the Comtian conversion of this into an evolutionary strait jacket for culture.

When anthropologists realize the fact that evolution always involves divergence as well as advance, stabilization as well as improvement, and when they have reached a fuller understanding of the mechanisms of cultural maintenance, transmission, and transformation, we may reasonably forecast a broadly similar course for anthropology, including the prospect of an eventual triumphant synthesis.

If anthropology is a science, then for anthropologists culture must be defined, not philosophically or metaphysically, nor as an abstraction, nor in purely subjective terms, but as something which can be investigated by the methods of scientific inquiry, a phenomenal process occurring in space and time. The process has mental (subjective) as well as material (objective) components, but both of these can be studied naturalistically. As a naturalistic and operative entity, the culture of a given society cannot be understood merely as the sum of the behaviour and products of the individuals comprised in the society. It is composed of super-individual patterned systems of activity, potential as well as actual, all to a certain degree integrated in an over-all pattern of the whole.

In any scientific attempt to study and understand cultures, it is the patterned systems that are important and significant, rather than the individual activities in which they issue. Thus, in human communication, Cassirer cites de Saussure's distinction between *la langue*—the super-individual system of grammar and syntax—and *la parole*—the actual words or way of speaking used by particular individuals. We find the same distinction in every cultural activity—in law, between the legal system of rules and precedents and its specific application in particular cases; in art, between a style and the individual works of art produced; in social structure, between a system of local government, say, and the actual work of local bodies; in science, between a comprehensive theory and the mass of phenomena which it ties together; in kinship relations, between the theoretical system and the way it works out—or does not work out—in everyday life; in morality, between the systems of tabus or ethical injunctions and individual moral actions.

Further, we observe that a cultural pattern-system may be either latent or patent, either needing to be deduced from the individual phenomena or already consciously formulated by the culture. As is to be expected *a priori*, conscious formulation is a later development. Thus all languages are highly complex systems, but it is only late in human development that the system is consciously formulated in rules of grammar and syntax; the theories of aesthetics do not emerge until after millennia of the practice of art. Even where some conscious intellectual formulation exists *ab initio*, its extent and its precision will in general increase with time. Thus, in religion there is the development from fluid and non-rational myth to precise and highly rationalized theology; while science grows from a mere recognition of empirical regularities into an elaborate system of theories and laws capable of increasingly precise mathematical formulation.

This increasing patency of cultural pattern-systems in psycho-social evolution is analogous to the increasing differentiation of functional organic systems in biological evolution. An Amoeba has no visibly differentiated systems of support, locomotion, circulation, digestion, conduction, sense-perception, or reproduction; among Metazoa, a separate circulatory system did not appear until the Annelid level of organization was reached, a temperature-regulating system not before the later Mesozoic: sense-organs such as eyes and ears show a steadily increasing degree of differentiation and precision: behaviour-systems become more differentiated (with greater variety of instincts), and at the same time more flexible and precisely adjustable (with the development of learning capacity). But since biological evolution depends essentially on the self-reproduction of matter, and cultural evolution on that of mind, it is inevitable that the differentiation of organic functional systems will be manifested in increased material specialization, that of cultural systems in increased mental specialization—that is to say, increasingly full, precise, and conscious formulation.

With these preliminary considerations out of the way, let me try to define and analyse the cultural process a little further. A culture consists of the self-reproducing or reproducible products of the mental activities of a group of human individuals living in a society. These can be broadly divided into artifacts—material objects created for carrying out material functions; socifacts—institutions and organizations for providing the framework of a social or political unit and for maintaining social relations between its members; and mentifacts—mental constructions which provide the psychological framework of a culture and carry out intellectual, aesthetic, spiritual, ethical or other psychological functions.

The categories inevitably overlap, since all cultural activities have a mental component, all artifacts have been shaped by mind, all mentifacts have a material basis or vehicle, and all cultures are embodied in societies. Thus a piece of pottery may be both a useful artifact and a beautiful mentifact; socifacts like codes of law and morals incorporate much of spiritual and ethical mentifacts; and we all know how the intellectual mentifacts we call scientific theories and laws become transposed into technological artifacts. Nevertheless, the distinction is a useful one.

A more satisfactory analysis is made possible by changing the basis of classification of cultural elements from origin to function. In such a teleo-functional view, we perceive that every culture has certain components. In the first place, it exists in a particular material environment, and has a certain material basis. The environment does not *determine* the culture, but does *condition* and may *limit* it—for instance, through extremes of climate, or the prevalence of debilitating disease.

Secondly, the material basis, though by no means the sole determinant of culture, has a still greater influence: it is not possible for a society dependent on hunting or food-gathering to develop the kind of culture found in agricultural peasant societies, or for a pre-scientific society to develop the kind of culture found in technological civilizations based on machine-power.

Then all cultures are embodied in societies, and all societies must have a structure. Cultures therefore must include institutions and other social components. The most obvious of these are kinship systems, law, armed forces, and administration, together with political and economic institutions on the one hand, codes of manner and social customs on the other. Functionally, they may be classified into those which subserve the survival and well-being of the social unit as such, and those which regulate the personal relations of its members. Alternatively, they can be grouped under the heads of authority and custom. In addition, there is social quantity: the number of people included in a given social group, and still more the density of population, have a marked effect on the culture.

We also have the material components of culture (as opposed to its material basis). These include utensils, tools, buildings, vehicles, machines, manufactures, and industrial products. Functionally they can be classified according to the human needs and desires which they subserve—nourishment, health, shelter, clothing, enjoyment, adornment, communication, and so forth. The type of material production has repercussions on social organization: thus, industrialization has involved the supersession of guilds of artisans by trade unions, and the rise of the joint stock company and the giant firm or ring. It also has had repercussions on thought and ideas.

But before proceeding further I must mention the function of communication. This is fundamental: all culture depends on communication between individuals and between generations. The basic cultural organ of communication is language, so that linguistics must always be a basic branch of anthropology. The effectiveness of transmission of communication is later enhanced by various inventions—writing, the alphabet, printing, telegraphy, radio.

Other methods of communication are provided by symbols, and still others by the various arts, notably poetry and drama (including the cinema), painting and sculpture, and in special ways by architecture and music. But with these we reach the last category of cultural components—those with primarily mental or psychological functions, as against primarily material or primarily social functions. For while language is the medium of communication, the arts provide mentifacts—organized constructions of significance to be communicated from one human mind to others. Symbols like the cross or a national flag have an intermediate function. They have a denotative function like words, and can serve in the same sort of way as do recognition-markings and other releaser patterns in animals; but they can also function as vehicles of complex and multiple significance.

Mentifacts thus serve as the psychological framework of culture, the mental organs of man in society. They express awareness or experience in various organized ways—aesthetic and symbolic as well as intellectual—and communicate and transmit these organizations of experience to others. As Père Teilhard de Chardin and others have spoken of the *noosphere* constituted by human culture, as opposed to the *biosphere* of organic life, I have ventured to suggest that their function might be called *noetic*, and collectively they would then constitute the noosystem.

Besides symbols and works of art, the noetic components of a culture include rituals and formal celebrations, beliefs and superstitions, mythology and theology, tradition and history, philosophy and science. They include the totality of accumulated and available factual knowledge as well as the organized formulations of knowledge provided by mathematics and logic, scientific theories, and philosophical ideas; and finally the assumptions and attitudes that characterize a culture, including the vitally important epistemological premises on which its thinking is conducted.

Such an analysis is essentially static. But the biologist is driven to view culture historically, as cultural evolution, and to see cultural evolution as a part of the evolutionary process as a whole, albeit a special part, with its own peculiar methods and results. Once we adopt this approach, we cannot escape the conclusion that the most important characteristic of a culture is what I have called its noosystem—the sum of its mentifacts, and the way they are organized.

Artifacts often give a readier characterization and indeed may provide the easiest or, in the case of extinct cultures, the only measures of classification: institutions and other socifacts express more simply the physiology of a culture—the ways of its social working. But its evolutionary position and possibilities are ultimately determined by the quantity and quality of its awareness and the modes in which it is organized.

It is true that a culture may appear as in large measure determined by its economic and material basis; or, as by Rousseau or in a rather different way by Marx, institutions may be regarded as barriers to progress set up by vested interests, which need only be destroyed for an ideal society of men to come automatically into being. Yet these again are but partial or short-term views. The existing material basis and economic organization of a culture depend on the utilization or application of past knowledge. Again, institutions and their forms—like a church or a monarchy, a council of elders, or a civil service—depend on human ideas and beliefs about human nature and about men's relations with each other and with the universe: and though they may become fossilized or corrupt and impede or resist progress, yet even if they were swept away, new institutional embodiments of human ideas and beliefs would have to be constructed to serve as the culture's social framework.

Once more, biological parallels are available. The material environment does in large measure determine the characters of its organic inhabitants—think of the contrast between the faunas of the deep sea and the surface waters, between the floras of the sub-arctic, the desert, and the humid tropics. Furthermore, what an animal type inherits from the past, in the way of genetically determined anatomy and physiology and behaviour, conditions and limits its capacities in the present and its potentialities for the future. But the environmental determination is not complete, as is shown by the coexistence of high and low types in the same environments, or the evolutionary emergence of quite new types in an essentially unchanged habitat; and the limitations imposed by the framework of genetic structure cannot be transcended by abolishing that framework, but only by adaptively altering it. Further, comparative anatomy gives only a static picture, and comparative physiology only an immediate one. Fuller comprehension awaited their synthesis in the concept of evolutionary process.

We can to-day obtain a picture of biological evolution as a whole. It is a process of deployment of self-reproducing and self-varying matter, directed by the forces of natural selection. It involves two main types of change—diversification and advance. Diversification connotes an increase of specialized variety. Advance connotes a rise in the upper level of organization, both of material physiology and of awareness: it involves the realization of fuller control or fuller exploitation of the resources of the environment, fuller self-regulation or independence of its arbitrary or hostile forces, and an increasingly comprehensive and increasingly accurate picture of its events and operations. From the point of view of life as a whole, diversification also represents an advance, for it means a fuller and more efficient exploitation of resources in favour of a larger and richer biomass. And diversification and advance taken together involve the emergence of new or fuller realizations of the self-reproducing material of life.

Biological relativity holds throughout the process of organic evolution, in that all organisms show adaptation: if this were not so they would have become extinct. Yet this temporary relatedness of immediate adaptation is in point of fact transcended by a more inclusive and dynamic relatedness: we must also consider the relation of the organic type to the general process of biological evolution—a directional relatedness which takes account not only of its position in the process, but also of its direction of change, in relation to an increased realization of those possibilities of life concerned with a fuller awareness and a more effective exploitation of the environment.

In the psycho-social section, the same broad scheme of evolutionary relatedness still holds, but the process operates with different methods and with different principles of action. Once the cumulative transmission of experience was available, and accordingly mind as well as matter became capable of self-reproduction and self-variation, it was inevitable that evolution would take place overwhelmingly in the cultural rather than in the biological sphere, and with an enormous acceleration of tempo; and equally inevitable that the noetic or mentifact system would be the most important part of evolving cultures.

With the aid of reason and imagination, cultures build up a volume of more or less extensive and more or less organized factual knowledge, together with resultant ideas and ways of thinking, and a system of more or less coherent and more or less conscious beliefs and attitudes, together with resultant values and purposes. It is these which constitute the decisive long-term factors in cultural evolution.

In the long run, knowledge is the more important, because it conditions and modifies the beliefs and attitudes. Knowledge is potential action and potential control, both in the external material world and in the inner world of thought, valuation, and belief.

Cultures, too, all show adaptation: if they were not adaptively related to the business of maintaining themselves in their environments they would have become extinct. The result is cultural relativism—the fact that no cultural absolutes can be shown to exist, whether in the cognitive, the aesthetic, or the moral sphere. Insistence on the relativism of human values, especially perhaps moral values, has been very fashionable in certain circles. Just as the biological relativism of organic adaptation led some biologists to dispute the validity of distinguishing higher and lower types of organism, and so to deny the possibility of anything which properly could be called advance or progress in biological evolution, so the discovery of the cultural relativism of moral and other values has led a number of social scientists to dispute the idea that one culture can be higher than another, and so to deny the very possibility of advance in cultural evolution —in other words, of human progress.

However, as in biology, the adaptive relations subsumed under the head of cultural relativism are essentially temporary or immediate, and are transcended by a more inclusive and dynamic evolutionary relatedness. In human evolution, however, the properties of the culture (including the speed and direction of its change) must be considered in relation not only to the effective utilization of its environmental resources, but also to the satisfying enjoyment, by its individual members, of their capacities for experience and achievement, for knowing and feeling, willing and acting. The scale of culture thus has a dual measure: it is related not only to efficiency of exploitation but also to fulfilment of potentiality.

In a broad view, the overriding importance of knowledge and its organization for progressive cultural evolution is obvious. It was the capacity for cumulative transmission of experience which enabled animals to become men, and permitted our Pliocene ancestors to pass the critical point between biological and psycho-social evolution and to open the path toward human evolutionary dominance. All the major steps toward greater efficiency of material exploitation or of social organization, and toward alleviating or improving the human lot, have depended on increase or improvements in knowledge of some sort or other. The improved knowledge may be in the form of skill, as revealed by the slow improvement of tool-making techniques in the Lower and Middle Paleolithic. Or it may be constituted by an empirical discovery, like that of agriculture, which initiated an entirely new and higher level of cultural organization; or by an invention concerned with the transmission of experience, like writing, printing, or radio. Or it may be in the form of an improved organization of knowledge and experience, as in ancient Greek philosophy, or in the comprehensive world-picture organized by Christian theology. Or it may be pure scientific discovery with immediate applications, like the discovery of bacteria and its application to the treatment of infectious disease; or pure scientific discovery without immediate practical application, but with an effect on man's world-picture and his view of destiny, like the discovery of the fact and mechanism of evolution. Or, finally, it may be in the form of a new and improved organization of assumptions and methods of approach, as in the adoption of scientific method in field after field of inquiry during the past three centuries, with simultaneous abandonment of magical assumptions or explanations in supernatural terms.

Of these advances, the most important for cultural evolution are those which open up possibilities of quite new modes of material existence; which provide radical improvements in the mechanism of cultural transmission; which alter man's general approach to the intellectual and practical problems of life; and above all those which lead to a new picture or model of human destiny. The effectiveness of such organizations of knowledge can be estimated by the degree to which they lead to the emergence of new types of cultural organization, comparable to new dominant types in biological evolution, which spread and increase at the expense of previous types. Examples are afforded by the spread of neolithic culture (based on agriculture), of civilization or urban culture (based on writing and division of labour), of Christian and Islamic culture (based on new pictures of human destiny), and, in recent centuries, of industrial and technological culture (based on scientific method in the natural sciences).

Those which involve a new picture of human destiny are the most comprehensive, and may include elements of all the others. They are, in fact, the true noetic microcosms, and their importance can be estimated in terms of their relatedness to the over-all process of reality. The more fully and the more accurately they internalize the evolutionary process, the more effective will they be, in the long run, as systems of potential action.

From this angle, the most important single step in cultural advance is that which we are now in process of taking—the application of scientific method to the problem of man's evolutionary possibilities. To start with, it markedly changes the directedness of culture, and may even reverse the sign of that directedness. Most noetic systems consciously or unconsciously look backward, are based on traditional authority or on a nostalgic belief in a prior Golden Age or state of perfection, and the cultures built on them are accordingly in large measure resistant to change, and especially to the idea of change. A few noetic systems have looked forward instead of backward, but usually to some millenary and final fulfilment. In so far as Imperial Rome had a conscious goal besides that of increased power, it was to impose the Pax Romana and the efficient Roman system on the rest of the world. Soviet Communism deliberately proclaims the classless socialist State as its inevitable millennial goal. But in so far as the goal is a final one, it limits and distorts the process of cultural change by imposing on it both the myth of an ideal but static end-state, and the dogma of authoritative truth. In Marxist Communism we can see clearly how the myth of an ideal final state has taken the place of the salvation myths of earlier religions, and how the authoritarianism of Marxist doctrine can impede scientific and cultural freedom just as much as the Church ever did in the past.

The scientific method of acquiring truth and knowledge is free from these objections, since it explicitly recognizes that man's knowledge can never be complete or his truths absolute. But it does enable man to discover more knowledge and to arrive at a fuller approximation to truth, and so at once introduces a positive vectorial component into any culture which practices it. However, so long as it is applied in a limited field (for instance only in the natural sciences), or is still liable to be overridden by dogmatic authority (as in Soviet biology in recent decades), it has no more than partial importance. Only when a forwardly directed, dynamic ideal of cultural advance is combined with scientific method, or —what comes to the same thing—when scientific method is consciously adopted and prosecuted in all fields of human endeavour, only then can the noetic system begin to be a true microcosm, only then will cultural relativism become transcended by a more comprehensive relatedness, and cultural change begin to adapt itself adequately to the over-all evolutionary process of greater realization of inherent possibilities.

The capacity for the cumulative transmission of experience marked a critical point in the evolutionary process—the passage from a biological to a cultural mode of evolution. The attainment of a correctly related noetic system will mean the passage of a critical point within the process of cultural evolution—from the proto-cultural to the full cultural phase, from mainly unconscious evolution to change consciously directed. And just as the passage of the former critical point permitted the emergence of man as a new dominant type, the psycho-social type, within evolution as a whole, so the passage of the latter will permit the emergence of a new and dominant pattern of organization within the psycho-social process, and will enable the human type to fulfil itself by relating its modes of change to its inherent possibilities. It will permit the full humanization of man.

But I must not soar too far up into the clouds: the noosphere has its earthly base, which it quits at its peril. I will conclude with a re-statement (illuminated, I hope, by the foregoing analysis) of the evolutionist's view of human culture.

Biological and cultural evolution resemble each other in both showing a combination of two major trends, one to differentiation or divergence, the other to improvement or advance. In addition, cultural evolution shows a trend which is almost absent in animal evolution—toward convergence and consequently toward an eventual unity superimposed upon diversity. Both of these trends are subject to limitations, and in point of fact frequently reach final limits. In biological evolution, the amount of divergence possible to a group such as the teleost fish or the birds is limited by the variety of habitats or ecobiological niches which are available to their type of structural or physiological organization. It is, for instance, impossible for teleost fish to produce a type adapted to terrestrial desert existence, and equally impossible for birds to increase their variety by colonizing the deep sea.

Occasionally, however, a biological lineage finds its way out of its limitations and up to a new level of organization. Such major steps in advance are recognizable *ex post facto*, by the emergence of the lineage as a new dominant type, which demonstrates its dominance by its rapid development into a new fanning-out of combined divergence and improvement. This did not occur among either birds or teleost fish: they both appear to be incapable of breaking through their organizational limitations. It did occur, however, among body fish as a whole, when one lungfish-like lineage evolved to the amphibian level of organization capable of terrestrial life; even more strikingly, it occurred among the Reptiles, when one lineage of one of the numerous major divergent types of the reptilian radiation gave rise to the new dominant type we call the Mammalia. The other reptile lineages, though diverging to produce types as strikingly different as snakes and dinosaurs, tortoises and crocodiles, flying pterodactyls and whale-like ichthyosaurs, all remained on the reptilian level of organization, and have either become extinct or have persisted on that level up to the present.

Biological classification aims at reflecting the facts of biological evolution. It is often assumed by zoologists that it does so by distinguishing groups according to their ancestry. Each taxonomic group, according to this view, is distinguishable because it is descended from one ancestral lineage. Thus, all species of weasels and stoats are pigeonholed together in the genus *Mustela* because they are all descended from a single weasel-like ancestor; all families of carnivores are pigeon-holed in the order Carnivora because even such divergent creatures as seals, tigers, bears, and weasels are all descended from a single proto-carnivore lineage; all orders of mammals in the class Mammalia because their universal possession of hair, milk, and warm blood is only comprehensible if they are all descended from a single proto-mammalian lineage with these properties.

Recently, however, it is becoming apparent that these taxonomic assumptions are fully valid only for a classification concerned with evolutionary divergence. Others are needed for a classification which also takes account of evolutionary advance. Thus G. G. Simpson in his *Meaning of Evolution* states that the latest and dominant group of bony fish "called Teleostei in formal classification", is "apparently a structural (and functional) grade" independently evolved by several lines; and this parallel evolution of improvements appears to be a common feature in smaller-scale deployments, like that of the horse family (Equidae).

Actually, the idea of a common grade of improvement in place or in addition to that of a common ancestry is implicit in much taxonomic practice. Thus from the strict common-ancestry point of view, birds and mammals are parts of the great reptilian radiation, and should be classed as orders on a par with other reptilian orders like Crocodiles or Dinosaurs. However, they both developed such outstanding improvements in general organization that they became new dominant groups more varied and more abundant than any reptilian order—the birds primarily in the air and the mammals primarily on the land. For this reason, they are called classes, with new orders as their major subdivisions. Both are actually monophyletic groups; but whereas this fact of common ancestry is the basis of our classification of other products of the reptilian radiation, in their case the decisive factor is advance to a new level of organization. *Aves* and *Mammalia* are grade labels as well as ancestry labels.

Sometimes, indeed, our taxonomy designates only grades. This would be so for teleost fish if Simpson's views are confirmed. It was once so for the subkingdom Metazoa, originally intended to cover all multicellular animals. Later, however, when it became clear that sponges had evolved independently to the multicellular level, the zealots for ancestry classification placed them in a new subkingdom, the Parazoa, leaving Metazoa as a combined grade and ancestry label for the rest of the multicellular animals.

I personally would like to see a new, evolutionary classification, which would combine the advance and ancestry principles. We would then have *groups*[5] of common ancestry—classes, orders, and other familiar designations, and *grades* of advance (advance sometimes independently achieved, sometimes in common), for which new designations would be needed. Thus, Birds and Mammals would continue to rank as two classes, but would be included in a single grade, which might be called *Homotherma,* since temperature-regulation is their diagnostic improvement. Other obvious grade labels for Vertebrates would include terms already in use, such as *Gnathostomata* for forms with jaws, *Tetrapoda* for those with walking limbs, and *Amniota* for those with a protective "private pond" for the embryo. I would hope that *Metazoa* would be restored to its original use as a grade label and that Man would be placed in a new major grade, which might be called *Psychozoa.*

Of course, it is not the labels that are important, but the principles and assumptions on which the necessary labelling is done. I venture to suggest that the adoption of a broadly similar outlook would permit real progress in anthropology. Its assumptions of principle are roughly as follows. Evolution still operates in man, but overwhelmingly as a cultural, not a biological process. Cultural (psycho-social) evolution shows the same main features as biological evolution. From one angle, it shows short-term improvement ("adaptation") and long-term improvement ("advance") together with some

[5] *Clades,* from the Greek for branches, is perhaps preferable, as more precise.

apparently non-adaptive accidental and consequential results; from another, it shows divergence (resulting in greater variety), advance (resulting in progressive improvement) and limitation (resulting in stabilization or regression); and from still another, more comprehensive angle, it reveals a succession of dominant types, resulting in progress, as manifested by a rise in the upper level of achievement and an increased realization of possibilities. But finally, cultural evolution differs importantly from biological in respect of selection and mechanisms of change, of transmission of the old and incorporation of the new, of the presence of diffusion and a consequent tendency to convergence as against divergence, of the immensely increased importance of mind and mentifacts, notably the accumulation and better organization of knowledge, and in many other ways.

With such an outlook, the sterile controversies about cultural evolution (sterile because based on misconceptions) would be resolved; anthropologists would be able to see their subject in the conceptual framework of combined divergence, stabilization, extinction, and advance; they would reach a truer and more satisfying picture of cultural evolution than those provided by historians and sociologists like Spengler, Sorokin, or Toynbee; and they would open the door to a scientific theory of human progress, free from wish-fulfilment and over-optimism on the one hand, and from captious relativism and over-pessimism on the other. By envisaging the problem of acculturation in the world of to-day as an inevitable accompaniment of the emergence of a new dominant cultural type, they could bring a new illumination to bear upon it; and by reminding politicians and administrators of the value of variety-in-unity—variety of cultural expression within a unitary framework of knowledge, ideas, and purpose, they could help to minimize the evil effects of the process and maximize its desirable results. Finally, by insisting on the overriding importance of knowledge and its organization in the form of ideas, assumptions, and beliefs, they would ensure that anthropology would make a vital contribution to the march of history. By clarifying the role men's ideas of destiny have played during past cultural evolution, they would make it easier for man to achieve his true destiny in the future.

NEW BOTTLES FOR NEW WINE: IDEOLOGY AND SCIENTIFIC KNOWLEDGE[1]

T H. HUXLEY played a leading part in the development of anthropology. Indeed, the great Virchow, speaking in England in 1898, said that his work in this field would alone be enough to secure his scientific immortality.

His interest in ethnology (as the subject was then generally called) grew out of his interest in the general question of evolution. Already before 1859, he had satisfied himself of the falsity of Owen's statement that the brain of man contained structures not found in the apes or any lower animal, and had concluded that the physical differences between man and higher apes were smaller in extent than those between the higher apes and the lower monkeys. But with the publication of the *Origin of Species* evolution became a matter of acute and embittered controversy, and the relationship of man and apes its burning focus.

The discovery of the Neanderthal skull, and requests from Lyell for anatomical help over his book on *The Antiquity of Man,* led Huxley to take an interest in physical anthropology, and *Man's Place in Nature,* published early in 1863, included evidence from this field, as well as from that of comparative anatomy.

This, his first book, was an important landmark in the history of science: it gave an irrefutable demonstration that man, physically speaking, must be considered as merely one among animal species, a primate mammal specialized in peculiar ways. This was a necessary first step towards a truly scientific anthropology, in which all attributes of human life, social as well as physical, psychological as well as material, are treated as natural phenomena to be studied by the methods of science. It made one of the first breaches in the barrier set up by theology and philosophy between man and the rest of the universe.

[1] The Huxley Memorial Lecture for 1950, delivered before the Royal Anthropological Institute of Great Britain and Ireland.

Huxley continued his keen interest in physical anthropology till the early '70s. In addition to various detailed papers, he interested himself in a grandiose scheme for establishing a collection of photographs of representatives of all the peoples and tribes in the British Empire, and wrote an important pioneer paper on the geographical distribution of human races or, as he wisely called them, "the chief modifications of mankind".

If T. H. Huxley did not pay special attention to social anthropology, this was partly due to its less advanced development and partly to his natural bias as a comparative anatomist towards physical anthropology. But he was much interested in it, as shown by his address to the Anthropological Section of the British Association in 1878. In this, he refers to Herbert Spencer's work on sociology; to that of Max Müller and Tylor on the natural history of religions, which he calls "one of the most interesting chapters of anthropology"; and to Lane Fox's ethnographical museum, which he describes as "one of the most extraordinary exemplifications that I know of the ingenuity and, at the same time, the stupidity of the human race".

However, his greatest contribution to anthropology was the fact that he brought his remarkable mind to bear upon it as a single subject, in relation to other subjects of scientific study. He saw it, not as a set of separate specialized problems, but as part of science as a whole, and was able to help materially in integrating it into the great scientific movement of the mid-nineteenth century.

One of T. H. Huxley's outstanding qualities was his encyclopaedism, humanist as well as scientific. He was not merely interested in a vast range of subjects—comparative anatomy and German literature, evolution and ethics, painting and physiology, embryology and anthropology, education and biblical criticism—not only able to illuminate and forward each and all of them separately but also to help to relate them in broader constructions of thought and to distil them in more potent syntheses.

Anthropologists know very well that no human culture or society can flourish without the support of some general framework of thought, even if the thought be largely tacit and its synthesis incomplete. Accordingly I make no apology for taking as my subject our present need for unifying interpretation and constructive synthesis. That need is even greater to-day than in my grandfather's time. This is due partly to the increase of specialization, partly to the increase in mere bulk of knowledge, and partly to the disruption of the background unity still possessed by nineteenth-century thought.

Specialization has led to the accumulation of vast quantities of new knowledge; but also to the paradoxical result that much of that knowledge has cut itself off from any central common pool and from cross-fertilizing contacts with other currents of thought. Some branches of science and learning have shown tendencies towards isolationism and autarkic self-sufficiency strangely similar to those shown by various nation-states in their economic and cultural affairs. This has had its counterpart in education, notably in the compartmentalization of subjects of study at our universities. Wherever and however manifested, these tendencies act so as to sterilize great volumes of knowledge and to impede the growth of a common tradition and a common basis for human action.

Next is the increase in the mere amount of factual knowledge available. This has been quite prodigious. We have some idea of the quantitative changes in other fields. Thus, the growth in area of Greater London since 1914 is about the same as its growth between Roman times and that date: demographers tell us, staggeringly enough, that the net increase in the world's population since T. H. Huxley began his professional career is roughly the same as the total it had achieved in the whole span of human existence on earth up to that time. However, no one, so far as I am aware, has attempted to make a similar estimate for the increase in the number of facts in the world during the same period. If they were to do so, I anticipate that the result would be even more staggering. Mountains of facts have been piled up on the plains of human ignorance—facts economic and social, facts historical and physical, astronomical and archaeological, geological and art-historical, agricultural, chemical, biological, geographical, psychological. The result is a glut of raw material. Great piles of fact are lying around unutilized, or utilized only in an occasional or partial manner.

Of course, there has been a great increase also in interpretative theories and principles in all the separate branches of science and learning. But this has not always kept pace with the increase of facts; and, furthermore, there has been scarcely any attempt at a synthesis of the specialized theories of separate disciplines, in a general interpretation or even in a common synoptic view. Our old bottles are bursting or have already burst: we need new containers for the potent new vintages now brewing.

In some ways, the third factor in the present situation, the loss of a common background of thought, is the gravest. In my grandfather's day there was still some unity of approach. Authoritarianism had been decisively defeated in the intellectual battle. Its defeat left the field in the possession of a broadly liberal philosophy, resting on an assumption that the scientific method was universally applicable and science intrinsically beneficent, on an essentially optimistic conception of human nature, on a belief in the necessary validity of individual freedom as it appeared to nineteenth-century liberalism, and on a half-unconscious faith in civilization and its more or less inevitable progress.

To-day, that unity has disappeared. We have learnt by experience the distortions of which civilized human beings are capable, the depths to which our boasted human nature can sink. We have witnessed a huge setback to whatever progress there may exist. Science has in some quarters come to be looked on as an enemy. The scientific method itself leads sometimes to uncertainty and apparent irrationality. Psychoanalysis has often been misinterpreted to imply the depreciation of reason. Wholly new theories of man in society have emerged, like Fascism, Nazism, and Marxist Communism, which seem irreconcilable with each other and with any kind of Western liberalism. The very assumption that unity is possible is itself in danger of disappearing.

I would go so far as to say that the lack of a common frame of reference, the absence of any unifying set of concepts and principles, is now, if not the world's major disease, at least its most serious symptom. It is particularly obvious and particularly serious in the Western world. We of the West are confronted by a very real dilemma. We see the fragmentation of Western thought into a series of conflicting and largely irreconcilable tendencies—Science, Roman Catholicism, the Welfare State or the Fair Deal, Big Business, the cult of the Common Man, and the rest—in place of its synthesis into a harmonious picture and its condensation into a common point of view; and we contrast this with the obvious and powerful appeal of the coherent point of view provided by Communism in the East. But then we recall that Marxist Communism is an authoritarian orthodoxy, whose enforcement has already led to many undesirable results—

social, political and intellectual—and whose continuance is likely to be as disastrous to itself as that of any other enforced authoritarianism in the past.

And so we find ourselves in the apparent dilemma of having to choose between an ineffectual chaos of thought on the one hand and the suppression of freedom of thought on the other.

But the position, grave though it be, is certainly not hopeless. For one thing, civilization has survived equally grave crises in the past, human reason has resolved contradictions of equal magnitude. For another, the dilemma between chaos and authoritarianism is apparent only. It *is* possible to have voluntary agreement, agreement by persuasion, without any other enforcement except that of reality: the highest freedom is to understand and voluntarily to accept the compulsion of the facts. And the present situation is a new one, in which new facts and new knowledge are available over new fields to an unprecedented extent, and could be distilled to provide us with the truth that alone can set us free.

There is no panacea for such a situation. But I do suggest that, if we look at the position objectively, as a problem in applied anthropology, and scientifically in the light of all the relevant knowledge and methods available, we can get some way towards an answer.

Note that I specify "in the light of all the relevant knowledge available". For whatever the enemies of science may say, they cannot gloss over the fact that it has produced a steadily growing body of established knowledge, which we neglect at our peril. It is no longer possible to secure belief in *a priori* or mythological assumptions about the nature or origin of man, any more than it is possible to do so about the nature and origin of disease. Man is an organism, although a very peculiar one, and his history is a continuation of biological evolution, although by new methods. We can investigate and describe the properties and potentialities of evolving man as we do other natural phenomena, and can empirically study the course of evolution, both biological and human, as an integral process.

The conclusion is forced on us that the most important, if not the most urgent, task of our times is the development of a new set of integrative, directive, and transmissive mechanisms for human societies and for their continuity down the generations. These must include systems in which the community at large can share, of shared interpretation, shared belief and faith, and shared activity. Such general terms have different meanings to different people, but it will I hope appear as I proceed in what sense I am using them. Meanwhile, I will only say that among the minor but pressing needs of to-day is the semantic need for a satisfactory and agreed terminology, both for scientific purposes and for general use, in the field of—I was going to say sociology, and then history, and then social psychology, and then political science, but once more the terms are inadequate—in the whole field of human relations, including social anthropology.

First of all, the phrase *integrative* (or *unitive*) *mechanisms* can often be used to cover mechanisms of transmission also. This is not true on the biological level, where integrative mechanisms, such as the nervous and endocrine systems, are quite distinct from the transmissive mechanisms of the gene-complex in the chromosomes. But on the human level, parts of the integrative mechanism unite men in time as well as in space, binding the generations together and providing the continuity for all collective existence that is not focused impossibly on the present alone.

Any such mechanism must have its over-all framework of ideas, its ritual, and its morality of action, its emotional driving force. I would use the word *religion* for such a system, since it is the only word in common use which includes these three connotations, but unfortunately its usage has become so restricted to one particular type of unitive system that it is useless as a general term. Alternatively, there is the word *ideology*. Quite apart from its ugly associations with systems of ideas that we know to be forced and believe to be false, it has the defect of implying only cognitive elements in the system, whereas an integrative system, as an organ of society, must always involve emotion, action, expression, and will, as well as (or in conjunction with) rational thought. In point of fact, however, the systems to which the term ideology is usually applied—Fascism, National Socialism, and Communism—have all contained other than cognitive elements, and I shall employ it, though sometimes *belief-system* and sometimes *interpretative system* will be more useful. But though terminology is important, discussion of it here would be both tedious and useless. I must hope that my terms will define themselves *ambulando* as I proceed.

Let me point out at the outset that belief and faith, though by their nature they include a non-rational element, need not be either irrational or anti-rational, unscientific or anti-scientific. They can perfectly well be coherent with reason and with scientifically established fact, and any belief-system which is going to be of value in the world of to-day must be thus coherent with reason and science, because rationality and scientific knowledge are an important part of that world. And this implies further that it must not be dogmatic: to be coherent with science it must surrender the completeness of its certitudes, and with that its own unchangeability. Big words with capital letters, like the Absolute and the Eternal, must be banished from its vocabulary.

This is only a heavy-handed way of saying, what ought to be self-evident but is usually disregarded or even denied, that an ideology or belief-system is conditioned by current reality; that it should be congruent with the facts of nature and with established knowledge: and that it should be flexible and capable of adaptive change and development.

At the present stage of social evolution, current reality includes scientific ideas just as much as it includes political structure or technological capacity. The ideology and belief-system of peoples who could suppose that death was never due to natural causes, who did not know the cause of thunder, and were ignorant why the sun "rises" and "sets", were (and indeed in some cases still are!) very different from our own.

Sometimes scientific discovery has had an obvious and central effect on ideology. The facts of astronomy, for instance, have not merely made it impossible to believe certain aspects of theology, but have brought a feeling of human insignificance which has had various effects on general outlook —of late, after the earlier misplaced reverence for Natural Law and the assumption that it was the edict of a divine law-giver, either pessimism, or a sense of being alien to the universe as a whole, or, in reaction against that, an intellectual and spiritual isolationism, or the existentialist's over-insistence on the individual human self.

I believe that, by the time its implications have been properly grasped, the discovery of evolution is destined to have a more revolutionary effect upon ideology than any other scientific discovery yet achieved. The effect will also be a less depressing and more constructive one than that of astronomical discovery. For evolution bridges the gaps between man and animal, between mental and material, and between the organic and the inorganic. Evolution shatters the pretence of human isolationism and sets man squarely in his relation—and a very important relation—with the cosmos. It is the most powerfully integrative of concepts, forcibly and inevitably uniting nebulae and human emotions, life and its environment, religion and material nature, all into a single whole. The facts of evolution, once clearly perceived, indicate the position we men should take up and the function we are called on to perform in the universe. "Stand there," they say, "and do thus and thus." If we neglect to do as they order, we not only do so at our peril but are guilty of a dereliction of our cosmic duty.

I have no space here to enter on any detailed exposition of the facts of evolution. What seems relevant to my present purpose can be condensed into a few sentences, but sentences pregnant with implications.

First of all, then, reality—in the sense of the cosmos of which we form a part in so far as we have knowledge of it—reality is a process, and that process is evolution. Biological evolution, the development of different forms of animal and plant life on this planet, is one small but important aspect of this universal process. The process of evolution as we know it to-day exists on three distinct levels—the inorganic or cosmic, the biological or organic, and the human or psychosocial.

Cosmic evolution means the process of change in the stars and nebulae, in the inorganic constituents of the cosmos, in so far as they are not caught up in the effects of the other phases of evolution. These constitute the enormous bulk of the whole; but their changes are slow almost beyond imagination, and the complexity of organization arrived at is almost infinitely below that produced by organic evolution in any familiar animal.

Here and there in this dragging and apparently meaningless drama of lifeless matter, spots appear in which more complicated organizations of matter become possible, sometimes indeed organizations capable of self-copying and therefore alive. The astronomers tell us that we may expect that at least a few hundreds of these theatres of life have arisen in our own galaxy: but we have knowledge only about one—our own earth.

Living matter does not always copy itself exactly. From the basic fact of self-copying and the secondary fact of inaccurate copying or mutation, natural selection automatically follows; and natural selection is a far more rapid agency of change than anything available on the inorganic level. As a result of its operation during two thousand million years or so, it has in fact produced the organizations we call higher animals, which would, if they were not so familiar, stagger us by the almost impossible complexity and delicacy of their construction. A dog would be a miracle if it were not just our familiar Prince or Toby.

More extraordinary still, it has produced mental as well as physical organization. From the study of bacteria or amoebae, jellyfish or green plants, we would have no right to conclude that they possessed mental attributes: but with an ape or a cat or a bird we cannot avoid this conclusion. Their minds are certainly very different from ours, but minds they certainly possess.

Finally, it is possible to detect a trend in biological evolution which deserves to be called progress. Evolutionary progress can be defined as improvement of vital organization permitting increase in control over the environment and in independence of changes in the environment, together with the capacity to continue evolution further in the same general progressive direction. It also involves an increase in internal harmony and individuation—the degree to which living matter is organized into well-marked and well-integrated individuals—an increase in range of knowledge (or, more accurately, of the environmental effects which life can detect), and finally an increase in mind, an intensification of the mental properties of organisms. Biological progress would have occurred, as an objective fact, even if man had never existed.

Eventually the stream of evolutionary progress passed a second critical point, and a new level of evolution was attained. In one out of the million or so animal species, mind developed to a stage at which it gave its possessor the power for true speech and conceptual thought. The result was man. With this, a new method of evolutionary change was introduced—cumulative change in the behaviour and achievements of a social group by mentally transmitted tradition, instead of change in the potentialities of individuals by physically transmitted systems of nucleoproteins. And this again immensely speeded up the rate of the evolutionary process.

There is complete continuity between the three phases or levels, but yet a critical point between each one and the next, after which the process alters in character.

Evolution on the human level, although it has been operating for the barest fraction of geological time, has already produced very extraordinary new results, impossible even to conceive of on the biological level—for example, Dante's *Divina Commedia*, guided missiles, Picasso's *Guernica*, Einstein's theory of relativity, ritual cannibalism, the Parthenon, the Roman Catholic Church, the films of the Marx brothers, modern textile mills, Belsen, and the mystical experiences of Buddhist saints. Most extraordinary in principle, it has generated values. No one can prove that values play a part in the process of biological evolution, but no one can deny that they do so in human affairs. In lower organisms, the only ultimate criterion is survival: but in man some experiences and actions, some objects and ideas, are valued for their own sake.

The ideologically most important fact about evolution is that the human species is now the spearhead of the evolutionary process on earth, the only portion of the stuff of which our planet is made which is capable of further progress. Men are the sole trustees, agents, representatives, embodiments, or instruments—each word has its merits and demerits—of the only process of progressive evolution with which we have any direct concern.

Man, in fact, is a microcosm—but in a somewhat different sense from that of earlier centuries. He is, as it were, a distillation of the universe at large, the macrocosm. The picture that he constructs of the universe, including of course himself, however distorted and full of gaps it may be, is the only representation that exists on this earth of the macrocosm as a unit. And the novelties that he produces in history, however crude and misdirected some of them have been, involve the only large-scale advance of the evolutionary process still operating on our planet. There is thus a new categorical imperative that has taken form and voice from the facts of post-Darwinian science and humane studies—that man's destiny, his duty and privilege in one, is to continue in his own person the advance of the cosmic process of evolution.

There is mystery in this: who can prophesy the possibilities of man's future achievement when we are only now beginning to understand his present properties and those of his natural environment? There is morality: if the highest good is not quantitative but qualitative, then population-increase at some point becomes a threat, and any opposition of principle to birth-control becomes immoral; if cumulative knowledge is the necessary foundation for success in coping with the problems of life and its improvement, then dogma is a threat, and any claim to exclusive possession of the truth or to suppression of free enquiry is immoral; if our destiny is to continue this mystery-play of cosmic change down the millennia, then improvident exploitation of resources is immoral; and so on.

There are faith and hope—reasoned faith and tempered hope, but none the less valuable for that. There is love, for without love of one kind or another—love of beauty, love of holiness, love of life and its possibilities, love of other people, love of knowledge—we never achieve anything constructive. Above all, there is participation—the sense that we are participants with the whole cosmos in its and our unbelievable adventure, so much stranger than anything that we could imagine out of our own heads.

Some of you may have been thinking that, instead of delivering a scientific address, I have been indulging in a flight of fancy. It is a flight, but not of mere fancy. It is my small personal attempt to share in the flight of the mind into new realms of our cosmic environment. We have evolved wings for such flights, in the shape of the disciplined scientific imagination. Support for those wings is provided by knowledge created by human science and learning: so far as this supporting atmosphere extends, so far can our wings take us in our explorations.

However, it is time that I returned nearer home, to ask what role ideologies and integrative belief-systems have actually played in different types of human society, and, at one further remove, what role science and new knowledge have played in producing and altering the ideologies and integrative systems themselves. Only so can we begin even to consider the problem of harnessing our new knowledge of evolution, of domesticating it, as it were, and making it perform a social function.

First of all, then, the biologist naturally sees the course of human evolution as the differentiation and development of portions of the world-stuff organized as groups—not in the form of the interbreeding units or *species* of pre-human evolution but of psycho-social groups—"inter-thinking units", in the arresting phrase of G. G. Simpson, the American palaeontologist, or "human collectives" as the Marxists often term them. Just as the main method of biological evolution is the adjustment, by means of natural selection, of a mechanism of biological heredity capable of reproducing itself and any viable changes that may take place in it, so the main method of human evolution is the adjustment, by means of psycho-social selection, of a mechanism of cultural heredity, involving the cumulative transmission of tradition.

The mechanism of biological heredity can be analysed in purely material terms: so can most of the mechanisms of natural selection, though in higher animals non-material (psychological) properties may enter in, as in the evolution of colours and patterns with an adaptive function. But the mechanism of social and cultural heredity cannot be so analysed. What is transmitted always has a mental and psychological component, actual or potential. Even where what is socially transmitted appears at first sight to be purely material, there is a psychological component. With money, for instance, there has to be understanding of the use of tokens for exchange, there has to be agreement as to the use of a particular currency: otherwise we could not transmit it.

Sometimes the psychological function subserved by the transmission of an object or event is quite different from that which it originally had. The value to us of a record of, say, a boy going to school in Sumeria 4000 years ago is in large measure that of giving us a sense of the continuity of human history and the permanent similarities of human nature— *humani nil a me alienum puto,* such a document reminds us. A ritual object, such as a bull-roarer, may have no aesthetic value, and may have entirely lost the operative magical significance to which it owed its original function: yet it may have the psychological function of helping us in the comprehension of our human past.

Often, however, what is transmitted is intended to continue exerting the same psychological function—a flag, for instance, a theological system, a social ritual, an idea. I say *intended;* for the ritual may become fossilized, the idea may become irrelevant in new conditions, the theological system may become distorted.

But the mental components are always there. What is more, they cannot be separated from the material components. A man is not a mind plus a body, but a unitary conscious organism, a mind-body. So the organic coherence and continuity of a society or collective are assured by the existence of something which is transmitted: and that something always involves both mind and matter. Sometimes, as with an idea, the mental aspect is the dominant one; but even there it cannot be transmitted except by means of material sound-waves or visible marks on paper. In other cases, what is transmitted is determined by mind, or shaped by it, or at least conditioned by it. It is only through psychological participation of one sort or another that individual human lives are tied together through space and time. Mind builds the boat in which the social unit floats through time, and it is only by utilizing the psychological components of transmission that the social unit can acquire any organic unity.

Nor can it be said that either component of social reality is subordinate or secondary to the other. The idealist and the theologian maintain that spirit has the primacy. This led in the past to various errors and unfortunate results. To-day, however, in this age of physical science and dialectical materialism, it is the opposite view which is dangerous. The net effect of Marxism, for instance, whatever the subtleties of its philosophers, is to produce the notion that all which really counts is material conditions and social machinery, and that emotions and ideologies, sciences and arts, however necessary to society, are automatic or epiphenomenal secondary products.

The modern triumphs of physical science have led to too much importance being attached to science in general as against other human activities. Furthermore, science has tended to become equated with physics and chemistry, experiment and quantitative measurement, so that quality and value, not being amenable to this type of treatment, have come to be neglected; our thinking has been split into the so-called scientific or quantitative, and the non-scientific or qualitative. Psychology itself has tried to achieve scientific respectability by quantifying itself, with the result that much of mind eludes its attention.

While it is obvious that many ideas are only rationalizations, that many beliefs are secondary to material and social conditions and have been generated by them, yet sometimes it is impossible to give either aspect the primacy; and in still other cases the existence of beliefs, however generated, has a decisive influence on material and social events.

An obvious example is the belief of the Aztecs that human sacrifice was necessary to placate the sun-god and to ensure that the sun continued to rise each day. This led to the ceremonial slaughter of hundreds of thousands of human beings, thus making constant warfare necessary in order to provide the victims; and so, by alienating the neighbouring peoples, became one of the prime causes of the Aztecs' defeat by the Spaniards.

Or again, the Egyptians' belief that continued existence in the after-life was only possible through the regular provision of food and other offerings resulted in the establishment and endowment of a mortuary priesthood, and so eventually led to a very large area of the country's land and resources coming into the hands of the priests and escaping from the more efficient methods of exploitation adopted by the kings. Payment for masses for the souls of the dead had a not dissimilar effect in medieval Christendom, and every schoolboy knows what were the material results of men's ideas about indulgences.

Another example of the economic result of a belief is seen in India, where the entire agricultural economy has been affected in a deplorable manner by belief in the sanctity of cows.

Belief in the spiritual efficacy of pilgrimages to sacred spots and holy places has produced very extensive material effects. Canterbury and Compostella spring to mind, Mecca and Jerusalem, Benares and Qalat Seman round the pillar of the Stylite; and anyone who visited Italy in Holy Year can testify to the resultant overcrowding.

The only possible conclusions from the facts of evolution are that mental and psychological events are also material events, but experienced from the inside instead of studied from the outside; that the mental properties of life—knowing, feeling, willing—on the whole make for biological success, since they have been intensified during evolution; and that in higher animals and especially in man, methods have been developed for extending the range and operative value of mind beyond the confines of the individual, through the establishment of causal chains from mind to mind, from mental event to mental event, by means of various material expressions or symbols. Gestures, call-notes and cries, and facial expressions are the primitive means of mental intercommunication: but in human society, thanks to new properties of our minds, symbols, both arbitrary and otherwise, and finally language and works of art, can serve as vehicle between mind and mind, so that forms of mind as well as

forms of matter become capable of reproducing and transmitting themselves.

We could theoretically conceive the existence of brains as
automatic, as efficient, and as devoid of mental experience as a modern calculating machine. However, for reasons
beyond our comprehension, the biological utility of brains of
a high order of complexity seems to depend on their possessing mental as well as material properties—the capacity for
perception, for instance, as well as for the physical transmission and registration of sensory symbols, for emotion as
well as for the setting of our organic machinery in preparation for this or that type of action. If this were not so, we
can be certain that mental functions would not have been
evolved, for natural selection is the sole or prime agency of
biological evolution, and it is incapable of producing anything except on the basis of its biological utility.

Once a new piece of biological machinery has been
evolved, however, it often proves to have various secondary
implications or potentialities which have nothing to do with
its primary biological utility—correlates or consequences as
opposed to original (and originating) properties. This is
particularly true of mind. Once the faculty of conceptual
thought and therefore of abstraction had been evolved, logic
and mathematics and science were there *in potentia,* however
much effort was needed for each step towards their actualization; and once what I may call the synoptic faculty had been
developed, the unitive faculty by which present sensations,
perceptions, emotions, memories, images, deductions, mental
constructions, and much else can all be brought together in
a single mental experience or act of consciousness, almost
infinite creative possibilities lay open—in comprehension, art,
imagination, and morality.

With this, new and illuminating pictures of the world-
process become apparent to us. Note that I say pictures: not
interpretations, still less explanations—but pictures, which
reveal in a flash something which had not previously been
apparent. Biological evolution is seen as a manifestation of
the almost infinitely improbable and varied potentialities of
self-reproducing world-stuff. Man's evolution, including
human history, is seen as a manifestation of the potentialities
of mind once it too had become self-reproducing through
cumulative tradition. We have no right to say, with some philosophers and many theologians, that human history is either
produced or directed by some external mind or absolute

spirit: but we cannot avoid saying that it *is*, in one very significant aspect, mind or spirit. This does not imply an idealist position, but a genuinely monistic one, a unitary naturalism. Mind and matter are, in human affairs as in human bodies, always united as two aspects or faces of a single reality.

In the sphere of human mind, as in that of animal body, much of the variety is improbable and fantastic in the extreme; and again, among the variety the significant fact stands out that with the passage of time new levels of achievement are attained, new and higher potentialities actualized. But there is only one side of the picture. The realization of mind's possibilities takes place only against immense resistance. There is the inertia and perversity of lifeless matter to be taken into account, since only in and through matter can mind realize itself. There is the unconscious but effective hostility of other living species, notably pests and agents of disease. There is the biological foundation of mind, the self-reproducing matter of our bodies, with its own momentum of demands for food, and of over-production of population until quantity acts as a brake on quality. There is the inertia of social institutions which have developed in relation to one phase of human development but become set and crystallized so as to resist the next onward impulsion. And there is the frustration and the waste engendered by conflict—conflict not only between individuals and groups, but within mind itself, both within individual minds, and also within the common pool of mind and its products belonging to the evolving society.

But it is time to return to my main theme—the need for a new belief-system or ideology. Many people will say that any deliberate attempt to create a belief-system is unnatural and doomed to failure; such things cannot be turned out artificially but must have a natural growth. I do not think that this is necessarily true. After all, the present epoch differs from all previous periods in possessing a far more extensive and detailed knowledge about the universe in general and about human societies in particular—though this knowledge must be synthesized and processed before it can serve as basis for a new belief-system. For this, new techniques of teamwork and group research and new forms of co-operation between specialisms will be required, as well as new types of educational curriculum and new techniques of teaching. In so far as an effective new belief-system must have a religious aspect, it will doubtless need to wait for the appearance of a prophet who can cast it into compelling form and shake the world with it.

Any new ideology will change and grow—indeed, if it is to be based on science, it must retain that combination of flexibility with assurance that is one of the hall-marks of the scientific method. But that does not in any way prevent the main outlines of its structure from being deliberately synthesized, as any piece of apparatus can be synthesized provided that we have enough scientific and technological knowledge.

In setting about such a task, we need the help of science in three main ways. First, we need to explore the psychological foundations of ideologies and belief-systems: what psychological needs they meet, what compulsions they suffer, by what inner machinery they are moulded and their development is guided—in other words, their genetics, their embryology, and their developmental physiology.

Then we need a survey of the structure and functions of belief-systems in as many different societies as possible—their comparative physiology, their comparative anatomy: what they do and what they consist of. Next we must supplement this comparative study with a historical and relational one, seeking to discover the way in which ideologies and belief-systems change with changes in economic, social, and political structure, and in knowledge, skills, and creative expression—their phylogeny and evolutionary history. Further, we need a survey of those elements in our present world and our knowledge about it, with which any new belief-system should be consonant—the social, intellectual, and factual environment to which it must be adapted. And finally we (or our descendants) will have to have a try at the business of synthesis itself, the actual construction of a belief-system, or at any rate a working model of a belief-system.

The first thing that strikes an outsider confronted with an anthropological question of this sort is the astonishing variety of the social mechanisms which have in point of fact some such unitive or integrative function, even when we omit all those in which the ideological component is weak or negligible—accepted techniques and customs of life which have no particular emotional or intellectual charge associated with them, but are just passed on from one generation and accepted by the next. The variety of belief-systems is indeed bewildering, especially their functional roles. Thus a theistic belief may mean belief in divine immanence, possession or transcendence, in polytheism or monotheism, in local and concretely personified divinities or in a remote and universal Absolute. The fact of death is ascribed by one people to professional witchcraft, by another to routines of sorcery by non-professionals, by yet others to a god or gods, to natural causes, to ancestral spirits, to Fate, to devils or demons, or to human sin. Again, the universal problem of "wrong" thoughts and actions, and of relief from their burden, is met in different societies by all kinds of assumptions and beliefs, many of them mutually contradictory, concerning sin, guilt, shame, and conscience, and concerning salvation, asceticism, non-attachment, sacrifice, an after-life, mystical self-transcendence, and purgation.

How can all these be truly functional or adaptive? And if adaptive, how can any be truer than any other? Essentially the same problem confronts the biologist, faced with the equally astonishing variety of animal types. How can such different types of organizations as those of a tortoise and a wasp both be adaptive and useful to their possessors? And still more difficult, how can we say that a wasp is "higher" than a worm, or a man "higher" than either, or even than an amoeba, when all manage to exist and survive?

In another essay in this volume I have dealt with the biological problem of evolutionary progress, and its indubitable existence in spite of universal adaptation. As regards belief-systems, I would make the following points. Adaptation, whether in anthropology or biology, is not anything absolute; it merely connotes a relation to a particular environment, and one which permits survival. The environment to which belief-systems are related is not just "nature" (which of course includes man's own nature), but man's knowledge about nature. When that knowledge is primitive and crude, his ideas and beliefs cannot be closely related to the true facts, and all kinds of rationalizations and fantasies can and do play a part, as well as various primitive assumptions (such as magic), which later knowledge forces him to reject.

Thus, the essential relation to be investigated is that between belief-systems and the advance of knowledge. A tendency to the increase in quantity and coherence of established knowledge is the most obvious and perhaps the most important among the general trends of human evolution.

Meanwhile, some system of beliefs is necessary. Every human individual and every human society is faced with three overshadowing questions: What am I, or what is man?

What is the world in which I find myself, or what is the environment which man inhabits? And what is my relation to that world, or what is man's destiny? Men cannot direct the course of their life until they have taken up an attitude to life; they can only do that by giving some sort of answer to these three great questions; and their belief-systems embody that answer.

Beliefs, in their origin and for much of their history, are inextricably entangled with ritual, since, as has been stressed by many workers and has been generalized in illuminating fashion by Susanne Langer in her book *Philosophy in a New Key*, ideas, beliefs, myths, rituals, and forms of art are all expressions of man's basic symbol-making faculty. Rituals are always in some measure acted beliefs, beliefs always in some measure subjectivized rituals.

The most obvious integrative practices or ideas are those whose function it is to emphasize the distinctiveness which is almost always rationalized into a feeling of superiority to other groups: thus the Greeks assumed their cultural superiority to all other peoples, and emphasized this by the use of the word *barbarian* for non-Greeks. Many tabus, whatever their origin, come to include this as a later function. Pride in one's own local or special gods is another such mechanism. The culmination is the transference of sacredness to the group itself. This is what the ancient Hebrews did in proclaiming themselves the Chosen People, what the Nazis did with their false racialism, and what the U.S.S.R. are now doing in their insistence on what they claim as the unique achievements of Socialist Man.

In the development of a new ideology for the One World of the future, the world's oneness will constitute a real difficulty, for such ideas tend to emphasize distinctiveness as against others and readily spill over into hostility. The solution would appear to lie in emphasizing the uniqueness of man, his distinctiveness in having the future of evolution entrusted to his charge.

Another unitive function is that of celebration. The dance after a successful hunt; the firing of cannon to celebrate a successful battle; the celebration of solemn anniversaries, as of Armistice Day, of the Fourth of July in the U.S.A., of the Fourteenth of July in France, though they celebrate some particular event, exert a general integrative function. Or the celebration may be of some natural recurrence. The obvious examples here concern the turning-points of the agricultural year—spring, fertility, the summer solstice, harvest, the passing of winter's grip, and so on. These, of course, were originally magico-religious in nature: but they certainly exerted most powerful unitive functions as well—we need only think of the Adonis cult of Byblos and Afqa, bringing thousands of scattered people together to celebrate their common destiny as utilizers of the great discovery of agriculture (besides uniting them in a common consciousness of the mysteries of their own existence); the rites of Osiris in Egypt; May Day celebrations in all their transformations, down to their modern function of celebrating the solidarity of Labour; Christmastide festivities (with their switch of emphasis towards New Year celebration in countries like Scotland).

Then there are the celebrations of stages in man's journey from the womb to the grave—name-giving, *rites de passage* and initiations, graduation, confirmation, marriage, and the rituals of death. While many of these appear at first sight to have only individual or restricted relevance, they all actually perform important integrative functions. Initiation ceremonies at puberty not only unite an age-group, but impress on the initiates their new membership of the group of young adults of the same sex, their unity of participation in its privileges and duties. Funeral rites unite the participants in a sense of common fate as well as of the continuity of the generations.

Once men come to be concerned with the realization of new possibilities of experience and of personal development, rather than the simple passage from one natural stage of life to the next, new types of ritual or celebration are required. These may be concerned with promotions in hierarchies of rank, or with degrees of learning or steps of progressive initiation into sacred mysteries. The society of the future will need to devise new ways for coping with the variety of such situations.

Ancestor-worship gives integration through continuity, as well as helping to emphasize the distinctiveness of the group. The glorification of national history subserves a similar function in societies which have a history, while myths of origin and legends of founding heroes played a similar role in earlier societies.

There are rituals which cement the social relationships of individuals or groups—the exchange of gifts, of ceremonial feasts, of ceremonial visits. The hypertrophied role which such exchanges play in Polynesian life is well known. Sometimes a precise integration is arrived at, as in the Kavirondo Bantu of East Africa, where Wagner points out that ceremonial visits are made to "precisely those persons to whom a man can turn for economic support, for help in a quarrel or dispute, for a share in garden land, or on whose goodwill he depends to conduct his marriage successfully". The visiting cards and other formalities of social intercourse in recent Western European "Society" played a somewhat similar role.

Men may be united through trouble or disaster. Thus the ceremonies of the northern Maya, in throwing sacrifices (including human victims dedicated by the community, as well as individual offerings) into the cliff-bound waters of the *cenote* at Chichén Itzá certainly gave them a sense of unity in face of drought or famine or war.

The list becomes too long for more than bare enumeration. Participation in a ritual meal, that widespread practice which is sublimated in Holy Communion; recurrent acts of common worship, prayer or praise; sacred mysteries as at Eleusis; ritual dramas, seen at their highest pitch in fifth-century Athens; pilgrimages; the tribal gatherings of Australian aborigines; festivals of sport like the Hellenic Games, where potentially hostile political groups were united in a common rivalry—these and much else exert some kind of socially integrative function.

Even where religion is esoteric or restricted, and where, as in ancient Egypt, its main celebrations take place inside enormous temples from which ordinary people are excluded, it still can exert an integrative function. The people conceive the temple as a sort of power-house for the generation or manipulation of forces necessary for the safety of the community, and the king and priests as the requisite specialists.

This introduces us to the notion of vicarious participation, which in one form or another plays an important part in many ideologies, culminating in the central Christian idea of vicarious sacrifice and suffering. This idea, of the vicarious performance of tasks or bearing of burdens by different sections of the community, is basic to any developed social organization, as well as providing an outlet for some of the deeper elements in human nature, and any new ideology will need to pay careful attention to it.

Nor must we forget the function of belief-systems in relation to guilt and sin. This chiefly concerns individuals and their separate "salvation" or personal development: but it has its integrative aspects too. Such rituals and beliefs can unite men in a common consciousness of evil and error. All humanity is saddled with a burden of guilt, conscious or unconscious (Freud has, of course, shown the way to an explanation of how this comes to be so); all humanity has capacities for evil and for error as well as for good and truth, and everyone is guilty of sins and mistakes. Accordingly, men can be united by the common urgency of freeing themselves from these burdens. Only so will they be able to devote themselves to the more positive and more essential task of fuller living, which any comprehensive ideology must inculcate.

Crude ideas on this subject can have most unfortunate effects on integrative ideologies. If men neglect the basic fact of the evil in human nature (including the intellectual evils of stupidity and error, and the spiritual evil of self-righteousness) and then proceed to ascribe the obvious evils of existence entirely to social conditions, the resultant ideology is likely to be a utopian millenarism, in which the present reality is sacrificed to an imaginary future. This was true of some versions of the Victorian belief in progress, and characterises communist and all revolutionary ideologies.

Such "pie-in-the-sky" ideologies bring us to the escape and compensatory functions of belief-systems. To all people at some time, and to many people much of the time, the world is an unpleasant or even horrible place, and life a trial or even a misery. All normal people at some time are oppressed by a sense of their own inferiority or, at least, inadequacy. Little wonder that many ideologies, religious and otherwise, are concerned with providing escapes from the unpleasant reality, compensation for the paralysing feeling of insufficiency. The escape may be *via* an imaginary millennium, or may have a more restricted goal (such as the last generation's idea of a War to end War), or may be into a Promised Land, or into bliss in a Next World. Sometimes escape is sought from the burden of self, its inadequacy and its limitations— whether through the orgiastic rituals of some ancient religions, through asceticism, through meditation, through a sense of union with the divine, or through an agreeable sense of certitude in one's own rightness or salvation.

When an ideology of escape becomes escapism, it is clearly bad. It was this compensatory and escapist aspect of Christianity that Marx had in mind when he made the unjustified generalization that religion is the opium of the people. We must, however, note that escape is not necessarily a wrong or cowardly aim. All existence is always to some degree in some prison or other, and it is good and right to escape into greater freedom. Self-transcendence, the desire for social progress, practical idealism, hope itself, are all forms of escape, and can be good and right if they do not escape from external reality altogether into celestial pies and wishful imaginings, or from the internal reality of human imperfection into self-righteousness (itself a grave form of sin) and impossible certitude (itself a form of wishful thinking).

Ideologies and belief-systems may also have as one of their functions the preservation of the power and interests of the ruling class or group. But to assert, as does dialectical materialism, that this is the sole function of all belief-systems (or even the main function of most), is itself a piece of ideological dogma, and demonstrably far from the whole truth.

Religions are, of course, among the most potent integrative mechanisms known—the very word signifies that they bind men in the bonds of common purposes. To discuss their integrative functions would take a book. Here I can only touch on a few relevant points. First, religions can divide as well as unite, so that a study of what gives them divisive properties is very important for learning what to avoid in building up an ideology which could be integrative for humanity as a whole. One of the most potent divisive factors is the claim to complete or absolute truth, whether of revelation, dogma, righteousness, or anything else. Systems based on any such absolute inevitably come up against new facts and new discoveries which are in opposition to their pretensions. The only method then open is to assert that the new ideas are also absolute, in the opposed sense of being absolutely wrong; and this at once creates division, and shuts the door on synthesis and development. A claim to absolute truth may be dressed up to appear as a claim to universality: but in point of fact it is always particular and not general, and can never become truly universal. *Le mieux c'est l'ennemi du bien*, and a pretended absolute is the enemy of true universality and of a real increase in truth.

Religions can also be divisive in denying the unity of human nature, and attempting to project evil and guilt out of the individual and on to somebody or something else—usually a class or a foreign nation. Instead of treating the conflict in the soul as a natural phenomenon, which may be only transitory, since it is capable of being reconciled in the integration of personal development, the conflict is stabilized, made more permanent, and projected as an inter-group division into the outer world, where it then is capable of hindering human integration.

There is still a more subtle way in which religions can be divisive. They can divide reality itself. This they do whenever they insist on the existence of the supernatural. In its earliest stages, when religion perhaps scarcely deserved the name, since it consisted largely of magic, it was naturalistic, though its naturalism was false or erroneous, for it was based on the belief that magic was part of the nature of things. Sacredness, whether good or evil, *Mana,* numinous qualities, magical potency, good and bad witchcraft—they were supposed to inhere in natural objects or people or rituals or forms of words, and were not regarded as emanating from another realm.

Personification is probably rather less primitive than magic; in any case, its share in determining the character of human belief-systems seems to have increased during early prehistory. Thus, religious and magic forces came increasingly to be personified as spirits or gods, and this increasing tendency to personification was accompanied by an increasingly sharp division of religion into two disparate realms, of natural and supernatural. But the division was often far from complete. The gods of classical Greece, however supernatural in some respects, had partly material natures and lived largely in the natural world. Divinity then was not, as so often now, regarded as an attribute only of supernatural beings. It was quite natural to the ancient Romans to deify their emperors and call them *Divus;* for their divinity merely meant that some of the sacredness inherent in the natural order of things was, as it were, distilled and concentrated in their persons, as holders of their sacred office. In this the Romans were continuing the tradition of the priest-king, which culminated in the Egyptian empire, and of which Shakespeare's "divinity that doth hedge a king" is the latter-day dilution. The idea that divinity could accrue to a man as son or descendant of a god was also current in the ancient world, as witness all the legends of demi-gods. On tombstones from Asia Minor in the century around the beginning of the Christian era, men of various religions are often described as "Son of God, Saviour." And, of course, Christian theology combines this concept of divinity by sonship with that of divinity by incarnation: the divine, banished to the supernatural realm by a process of personification pushed to a too logical conclusion, returns to dwell in a natural human body. All concepts of divine immanence, possession, and incarnation are attempts to bridge this unnatural division between natural and supernatural.

The modern naturalistic approach acknowledges the existence of the quality of sacredness or holiness among other realities, accepts the fact that men can reach transcendent heights of personality or experience, and reminds us that ideals and abstractions are facts of nature, just as much products of the cosmic process as trees or stones or human beings; and in so doing makes it possible to repair the split in reality and to create a truly unitary and unitive ideology.

The relation between such things as ritual and ideology may be obscure and implicit, as among many primitive peoples, or obvious and explicit, as in Christianity with its developed theology, but the ideological framework always has an important power of determining the rest. In fact, once man has learnt to think deliberately, the core of any socially integrative mechanism is bound to be ideological, centering round man's idea of the cosmos and of his own destiny. It is this which will give such mechanisms their set and their effectiveness, and will qualify the associated rituals, doctrinal formulations and the rest.

Man's view of his destiny inevitably changes with the progressive illumination revealed by new knowledge. The latest revelation—scarce dreamt of and never substantiated in earlier ages—is that of evolutionary science. In its light, as I have set forth earlier, man is enabled and, indeed, forced to view his destiny as the trustee, spearhead, or effective agent of any further evolutionary progress on this planet. That is the destiny which he cannot escape. He can attempt to shirk it or shut his eyes to it, but he will still be performing it, though maybe inefficiently or even badly. If he accepts this new illumination, and the view of his destiny which it implies, the basis of a new ideology is thereby at once determined. So, too, is a certain general attitude to reality. This must be a naturalistic attitude, since evolution manifests the unity of man, including all his spiritual properties and achievements, with the rest of the universe. Human intellectual and spiritual constructions, together with machines and societies, birds and plants, minerals and suns and nebulae, are all parts of the one cosmic process: no part is any less natural than any other.

The essence of human destiny is thus to introduce evolving life, in the person of man, to fuller realization and new possibilities. For this we need to chart the potentialities of nature, especially human nature. Among those new possibilities, hardly or not at all available to pre-human life, are those of comprehension, beauty, love, wonder, significance, creation, morality, holiness, and conscious enjoyment; and all these can either exist as subjective experience, or as expressed concretely in matter or through action. Furthermore, through that capacity for fusion or interpenetration which is an outstanding characteristic of mind, they can be blended and built up in all kinds of ways. Effective morality requires comprehension; creation may be the creation of beauty, or significance, or both, and should involve elements of love as well as of comprehension.

By general consensus these possibilities differ in value. Their differences are of two sorts. They may differ simply in regard to their rightness or wrongness. The knowledge on which comprehension rests may be false or incorrect; the products of material creation—bridges, machines, exchange systems—may not work, or may work badly; the products of aesthetic creation—poems, paintings, symphonies—may be bad, in not adequately expressing or transmitting emotion or understanding: a code of morality may be false or bad, in that it produces evil rather than good results.

But they can also differ in level—in being higher or lower, in embodying more, or completer, or higher values. Comprehension may differ in extension, depth or fulness; works of art may differ in quality and greatness; morals in nobility and efficacy. Finally, there are what I have called the highest experiences, like those of the great mystics or great discoverers, those that may come at the sound of a musical masterpiece as opposed to just a good melody, or at the sight of a great picture as opposed to a good piece of painting, those involved in genuine dedication or sacrifice and in love at its highest or fullest, as opposed to affection and ordinary decent behavior; these, all agree, are not merely quantitatively different, but qualitatively higher, in their very nature: yet there are all degrees, and the lower ranges may still be good in themselves.

It is thus part of human destiny to be the necessary agent of the cosmos in understanding more of itself, in bearing witness to its wonder, beauty, and interest, in creating new aids to and mechanisms for existence, in experiencing itself, and so introducing the cosmos to more new and more valuable experiences.

Be it noted that these possibilities always arise from a participation of individual minds with other elements of the cosmos, or at least from their joint involvement. The mere perception of a leaf, for instance, involves the existence of the leaf, of some exceedingly complicated anatomical structures and physiological processes, and the innate capacities of our minds for perceiving colour, size and form, not to mention the unconscious adjustment of perception to past experience.

Neither beauty nor scientific law exists *per se*, on their own, in objects: their generation requires the participation of human minds and their interaction with objects. Even works of creative imagination can only be realized with the aid of, or on the basis of, past experiences of external reality. (I should be inclined to say the same in principle about the ineffable experiences of the mystics, reached by abstracting the mind from the outer world; but here the situation has not yet been properly explored or analysed.) The external element in this joint involvement may be predominantly human affairs and other human beings, including their minds; but this in no wise invalidates the general point.

Thus, for man to fulfil his destiny, he must think of himself as in partnership with the cosmos. Just as he cannot exist adequately if he exhausts or overspends the material resources of the earth, so he cannot realize many possibilities of beauty or wonder if he too much destroys or tames the beauty, strangeness, and variety of nature—as by putting dams and pylons and bungalows all over Snowdonia or the sea-coast, or killing off big game, or draining every drainable pond or lake. Evolution thus insists on the oneness of man with nature, not merely in respect of biological descent and chemical composition, but because nature is the indispensable basis of his material existence, and also the indispensable partner in his mental and spiritual achievements.

Such an ideology has something important to tell us about the fundamental units of humanity, the individual and the community. The direct and actual realization of those possibilities which it is man's destiny to actualize is always effected in and by individuals. A state or a society cannot experience significance or holiness. If a society becomes significant, it is in the minds of its citizens; if it achieves holiness, as in all deifications of the state or its rulers, the holiness is thrust upon it by individual minds. An evolutionary ideology is thus a valuable reminder of that real primacy of the individual which all totalitarian ideologies attempt to deny or destroy. The community, together with its organs, including the state, provides the framework for individual lives, and is the vehicle of the continuity and change required for further evolution: of itself it cannot realize any new possibilities for life, but only some of the means for the attainment of that end.

The individual has primacy in another way. Not only are human individuals, in the shape of developed personalities, biologically and intrinsically higher than the community or the state, but they include the highest products of the cosmic process of which we have any knowledge. But, while human individuals have their biological individuality fully determined for them by the automatic processes of differentiation and growth, they have to develop their mental individuality, or personality, after birth: and this development can reach very different levels of completeness and richness, effectiveness and achievement. Thus, one of the main possibilities which it is man's destiny to realize is the production of more fully developed individual personalities.

Our evolutionary ideology needs to bring to men's notice the possibilities open to human beings and the techniques by which they may be realized—possibilities of aesthetic and intellectual experience, of more acute perception and awareness, of health, of physical and mental control, of memory, of quick and effective education, of integration, of spiritual as well as of physical training, of hypnosis and the unconscious mind, and little-explored regions like mystical experience and so-called paranormal phenomena. If so, the common man of the future will be ashamed if he does not attain a far higher level of experience and personality than today's miserable average, and states and societies will be judged by the opportunities they provide for such attainment.

But the human community is as indispensable as the human individual. Indeed, it is impossible to think of a human individual apart from some human group; the two both play as indispensable and complementary roles in the situation in which the cosmic process now finds itself as do heredity and environment in the development of an organism.

Accordingly, both the present and the future of the community must enter into our ideology. In the present, there is ordinary civic duty from the individual, and in return his satisfaction in feeling useful. The community provides the mechanism for all that is distinctively human; while its structure can, to a considerable degree, guide human impulses into civilized channels and away from the horrible outlets of primitive cruelty and violence. The community ensures the continuity of the traditions and ideas in and by which individuals live. In addition, the community is the necessary vehicle and mechanism for desirable long-term change as well as for continuity.

Further, any modern ideology must concern itself with the community of man in its entirety, the potential One World of all the races, nations, classes, and individuals, past, present, and to come, that go to make up the human species; and accordingly must think of the narrower (if now better organized) community of the nation in relation to this larger and more lasting whole.

The idea of the community and its future thus enters into our ideology to satisfy man's desire to work for something bigger than himself and more enduring than his own group or community, and his need to compensate for the imperfections and miseries of the present.

Crude individualism leads to crude hedonism as well as to selfishness and ruthlessness; and over-emphasis on individual development to a disguised hedonism, to sterile asceticism, or to selfishly individual salvationism. Crude communism, if I may use the word in a rather unusual sense, as a system that maintains the primacy of the community, leads straight to totalitarianism, the Führer principle, and state-worship, while over-emphasis on the future evolution of the community will enthrone millenary illusions as supreme. In such circumstances, men forget that, as has been well said, "eternity is now", and that their destiny and their duty can only be truly fulfilled by present realization and achievements, as well as by concern and sacrifice for a distant future, however roseate.

To the individual personality and his development I must now return. A great deal has been written about man's psychological and spiritual needs, often on the assumption that needs can be equated with cravings or wishes, and that any and every such need ought somehow to be satisfied. This is as false as it would be to assert that man's desires for eating are to be equated with his needs for food, and that his greed should somehow be satisfied as much as his hunger. We must consider the matter from a quite different angle: how does the personality work, how does it develop, and how could its working and the mode of its development be improved?

Let me take a couple of instances. We owe to Freud and his followers the discovery that all normal infants are saddled with a burden of guilt, conscious or unconscious, as a result of having to repress the impulses of aggression in the primal infantile conflict of hate and love for the parents. We have a "need" for getting rid of this burden, for resolving the conflict, for moral or spiritual certitude. One way of doing so is by projecting our guilt outwards on to others, and so making them appear as a legitimate enemy, against whom our impulses of hate and aggression can then find a permitted outlet. But the existence of this need and of the sense of its satisfaction does not guarantee its rightness. On the contrary, history demonstrates over and over again that it has often served not only to justify war but to make wars bloodier and more cruel.

The sense of guilt can only be rightly overcome by recognizing the fact of one's own guilt-complex, and by facing the internal conflict and reconciling its two parties in the higher synthesis of an integrated personality. Absolute certitude of complete moral rightness can never be obtained, for all men are inevitably subject to moral error; and the sense of having obtained such certitude is always a false illusion, and bound to produce bad results.

The so-called need for intellectual certitude springs largely from the real need for action in a world too complex for our ignorance to understand. It is often met by the provision of dogma, whose absolute truth is buttressed by authority or guaranteed by revelation. This is temporarily satisfying, but in the long run has always broken down in the face of the accumulation of new facts and new knowledge. Absolute intellectual certitude, indeed, is as impossible as absolute moral certitude. In this sphere man has invented a better method for dealing with the problem—the method of science. This, by denying the possibility of absolute or complete knowledge and insisting on the value of doubt, has, in the short space of three centuries, permitted man to build up a greater volume of established and properly organized knowledge than was possible in all previous history.

In this there is a lesson for all other aspects of existence. The scientific method of the working hypothesis, as the only gateway to the erection of comprehensive theories, laws, and principles, to the establishment of firmer knowledge, and to the securing of more successful practice and better control of nature, can and should be utilized in other spheres —in morals, in politics, in social affairs, in religion.

In other words, any new ideology must not be dogmatic, and must refrain from any claim to absoluteness or completeness; it must utilize scientific method, so as to be expansive, flexible, and unitive instead of rigid and eventually restrictive or divisive. Tolerance, respect for cultural and individual variety, acceptance of difference—these are some of the counterparts of the scientific method in other fields. However, they themselves should not be employed rigidly or in any absolute sense, but in the same sort of way that the principle of the working hypothesis is applied in the natural sciences.

The question of course remains, how such a mere intellectual analysis can become a social force, how a set of ideas can develop into an ideology, how the evolutionary concept of man's destiny can come to effect that destiny.

What celebrations will be devised of human achievement and human possibilities, what pilgrimages and gatherings, what ceremonies of participation, what solemnizations of the steps in individual lives and personal relations? What rituals and techniques of "salvation", of self-development and self-transcendence will be worked out, what new incentives and new modes of education, what methods for purgation and for achieving freedom from the burdens of guilt and fear without inflicting harm on oneself or on others, what new formulations of knowledge and consequent belief? What modes will the future find of distilling its ideas of its destiny into compelling expression, in drama or architecture, painting or story, or perhaps in wholly new forms of art?

To such questions I cannot presume to attempt answers, but will merely point out that they pose themselves, and must sometime and somewhere be answered. What I am sure of is that some such naturalistic and evolutionary synthesis as I have indicated is inevitable, and that the resultant view of human destiny is essentially true, to whatever extent further analysis may modify or develop it. And if it is essentially true, it will prevail. It will prevail through the efforts of those whom its truth compels to belief, and their belief to action. As always happens with new truths and beliefs, those believers will at the outset be but a tiny minority: but such a minority is capable of leavening the whole lump.

NEW LIGHT ON HEREDITY

LARGE-SCALE scientific advance depends primarily on finding the naturalistic explanation of some natural process or set of facts. Usually what is important is the material basis of the process; once that has been discovered, the explanation becomes evident. Thus Galileo and Newton gave a naturalistic explanation of the movements of the heavenly bodies; while the whole of modern chemistry dates from the discovery of the atomic basis of matter. Of course, scientific advance depends also on the discovery of new facts. Think of discoveries like Galvani's, of muscular contraction under electric stimulus; or Röntgen's, of a new kind of radiation so enigmatic as to have to be called X-rays; of Fleming's, that the growth of mould might prevent the growth of bacteria. But such discoveries of fact, however novel and exciting, are important mainly because they set people puzzling after new explanations of old processes, or on to the trail of a new and unexpected process to be explained.

Genetics is no exception. Fifty years ago it was not a science at all—just a series of speculations, weighed down by superstition and leavened by a few tentatives of scientific study. Yet to-day it is rapidly becoming recognized as the most central and most fundamental of all the life-sciences. And if we ask how this spectacular progress has been achieved, the answer is simple: through the discovery of the material basis of heredity.

In 1859, when Darwin published *The Origin of Species*, practically nothing was known, scientifically speaking, about either heredity or reproduction. Pasteur had not yet proved that all life came from pre-existing life; the chromosomes had not even been detected; and it was only just being realized that sexual reproduction involved the union of two cells, the tiny male sperm and the bulky female ovum. Only in the

1880s was it established that the essential part of this process is the joining up in one nucleus of two sets of chromosomes from the nuclei of the male and female cells, *chromosomes* being visible threads constant in number for any one species. In fact, the chromosomes obviously *must* have the main say in heredity, for they are the only things that are contributed equally by both parents to the new life; and yet we know that offspring take after their fathers as much as they do after their mothers. Equally significant is the fact that the normal complement of the cells of the body is two entire packs or sets of chromosomes, but that before sexual reproduction the two packs separate from each other, so that each sexual cell, whether egg or sperm, receives only one. The normal double number—two packs—is of course restored by the union of egg and sperm at fertilization.

But the actual mode of inheritance of particular visible characters remained obscure and all sorts of speculations were rife. Perhaps the chief source of confusion was that no one had really clearly distinguished between what an animal or plant looks like—its visible and measurable characters— and what it can transmit to future generations—its genetic constitution. The German zoologist, Weismann, had made a good beginning by pointing out that quite different-looking individuals could be alike in their hereditary capacities. Some of the variation that we find in any assemblage of animals or plants is due to differences in the conditions of life (like the fleshiness of plants brought up in salty conditions or the conversion of the permanently aquatic axolotl into a land salamander by a meal of thyroid) or to use or disuse (like the larger arm-muscles of a blacksmith). These we call *modifications;* and we now know, as Weismann asserted on theoretical grounds, that they are not inheritable. But if you bring up all your experimental group in identical conditions, individuals will still differ somewhat among themselves, and this part of the variation is due to internal differences and *is* inheritable.

The failure to distinguish between these fundamentally different sources of variation had allowed all sorts of erroneous views to flourish, notably the Lamarckian superstition that so-called acquired characteristics could be inherited. However, Weismann's work did little or nothing to undermine another basically erroneous view: that heredity involved the blending of parental characters—and also the blending of whatever it was in the hereditary constitution that determined those characters. Darwin himself had assumed this to be true, though the results of the assumption puzzled him sorely. And towards the end of the century this view still vitiated the conclusions of the school of biometricians, like Galton and Karl Pearson, who attempted to understand heredity by purely mathematical methods. It was reserved for Mendel to make the further decisive discovery, complementary to that of Weismann, that similar-looking individuals could yet be quite different in their hereditary capacities. For instance, Mendel's classical cross between tall and dwarf peas gave a ratio of three talls to one dwarf in the second generation. But when the talls were bred from, it was found that only one out of every three, on the average, would breed true; the other two, when intercrossed, once more threw 25 per cent. of dwarfs. Now this, of course, depends on the fact, familiar enough to-day, of *dominance*, another of Mendel's discoveries. The gene for tallness is called dominant, but its partner, which produces dwarfness when in double dose—in other words when it is received from both parents —is *recessive*, which means that it does not show, does not produce any visible effect, when it is present with the dominant gene for tallness.

However, Mendel's most fundamental discovery, on which indeed the whole of modern genetics rests, was that the basis of heredity consists of material units in the reproductive cells; that these units are self-perpetuating and self-copying and do not blend or get diluted when crossed; and that they can be recombined to give new and true-breeding combinations. Thus, when Mendel crossed his tall and dwarf strains of garden peas, although the dwarf *character* disappeared in the first generation, which was all tall, something that determined that character had not been affected, for perfectly normal dwarfs reappeared to make up a quarter of the next generation. The same thing happened to the greens in a cross between strains possessing yellow and green seeds. Mendel rightly concluded that there must be permanent material units, or factors, responsible for the determination of tallness versus dwarfness, and of yellow seeds versus green seeds; that these existed in pairs in the body of the individual, but with only one or other of each pair present in the reproductive cells. The unit-factors now go by the more convenient name of *genes*, and each gene can exist in different forms or *alleles*, like yellow-determining versus green-determining in peas. Mendel then made a cross involving two pairs of alleles—between one strain which was tall with green seeds by another which was dwarf with yellow seeds. Again the recessive characters, green and dwarf, disappeared in the first generation, all of which were tall and had yellow seeds; but in the second, not only did he recover the two original types, but obtained two novelties as well: tall yellow and green dwarf—recombinations, we call them. And some of these bred true.

Mendel's strange sad story is well known—of how he published his results as far back as 1865; how none of the leading biologists of the time paid any attention to him or them; and how, sixteen years after he died, a disappointed man, they were unearthed independently by three biologists in 1900 and rightly hailed as epoch-making. The next ten years of research, under Bateson's leadership in England, established the fact that Mendelian heredity existed in every kind of animal and plant, and made many detailed discoveries about its workings. The decade ending in 1920 saw the leadership pass to America. Here, Morgan and his group of young men, using the ideal research material provided by the fruit-fly Drosophila, and supported by the results of the many workers who had been studying the chromosomes themselves under the microscope, proved once and for all that the chromosomes are the main organ of heredity. They contain the material basis of heredity, in the shape of the hundreds or even thousands of separate genes, arranged end to end in a definite order. And Mendel's laws, besides many other facts and rules of heredity, are due simply to the visible manœuvres of the chromosomes—the way they behave in ordinary cell-division before the formation of sexual cells, and at fertilization.

The other great advance of this period was the discovery of how inherited variations originate. The Morgan school found that new mendelizing characters—characters which are inherited according to Mendel's law—arise by *mutation:* a sudden but permanent change in a gene producing an effect of definite extent. For example, one gene concerned in producing the usual red colour of the fruit-fly's eyes, mutated spontaneously on a number of separate occasions to a different state in which it produced, or determined, white eyes. This same gene also, on other occasions, mutated to several other mutant alleles which produced different shades of pink in the eye. In the next ten years the rate of spontaneous mutation was measured and other kinds of mutations were discovered, for instance, mutation due to the addition or subtraction of whole chromosomes, or sections of chromosomes, and eventually it became clear that wherever a mendelizing character-difference existed, it must have originated by mutation.

Then Müller discovered, in 1927, how to produce mutations artifically, by means of X-rays, and at a rate several hundred times as great as that found in nature. We now know that other radiations too can provoke mutational changes in genes, and so can certain chemicals and probably other agencies. Almost invariably, the nature of the mutation, including the effect it has on its possessor, bears no particular relation to the agency that caused it: it looks as if most mutation is due to a physical or chemical shock, which causes a slight alteration or rearrangement of the structure of a gene.

Let me now point out that Mendelism immediately explained various everyday facts which otherwise remained a puzzle on any other theory. How, for instance, can one account for the wide differences—many of them obviously of genetic origin—which are often to be seen between the brothers and sisters of a single human family? The mendelian answer is simple: by recombination—recombination which shuffles and redistributes the parents' genes in all kinds of new arrangements.

It also clears up the skipping of a generation by some characters, the apparent non-inheritance of genius, and in general the cases where children do not inherit some strongly marked characteristic which their parents possess. Such cases are puzzling only because, before Mendel had taught us how to view the material basis of heredity, people confused inheritance in the popular sense—the reappearance in children of characters found in their parents—with genetics in the scientific sense—the transmission and distribution of material units of heredity along the stream of the generations. The gene for a character that skips a generation is transmitted all right, but it is recessive, so that the character itself cannot reappear until the second generation at earliest. Genius, in the proper sense of extraordinary gifts, must almost always be due to a recombination of genes which is, statistically speaking, extremely improbable. This automatically gets taken to pieces before the genius reproduces, so that although its constituent genes are transmitted, their reappearance in the same special combination is even more astronomically unlikely than its original emergence. And this is, of course, merely a special case of the general mendelian principle that what is transmitted in heredity is not the particular gene-outfits of the parents, but new rearrangements of the genes that make up those outfits.

During the same period, every animal or plant that was properly investigated was found to contain a store of mutated genes in its chromosomes. These constitute a reserve supply of variability which can be drawn on to adapt the species to changed circumstances if need be. Meanwhile, Darwin's great principle of natural selection came finally into its own. There is nothing mysterious about natural selection. It is a shorthand phrase to describe the results of the automatic and obvious process of differential survival; the fact that, on the average, more individuals containing variations that are favourable in the conditions of their life will survive than of those with less favourable variations. If you plant equal numbers of cold-resistant and cold-susceptible plants in a cold climate, the next generation will contain more of the former and fewer of the latter: that is a very simple example of natural selection at work. Then mathematics was enlisted and proved that a mutation which gave its possessors even only a slight advantage in each generation—say 1 per cent., which means that a hundred of the mutated form would survive on the average, against ninety-nine of the old type —would replace the old gene and become the normal type in a very short space of time, biologically speaking. And in principle it became clear that mutation plus natural selection could account for the facts of evolution.

The next step was the discovery that the rate of inheritable variation itself is under a certain degree of genetic control. Mutation provides the basic raw materials of evolution; mendelian recombination then distributes these raw materials of change in every possible arrangement, many of them new and valuable. From the point of view of the species, it clearly matters that the rates of production and redistribution of these units of change should neither be too low to risk getting caught short if change is demanded, nor too high to interfere with the stability of the species and its adjustment to current conditions. It was found that genes exist which regulate the rate of mutation of other genes, with the inevitable consequence that during evolution, mutation-rate has been broadly adjusted, by natural selection, to evolutionary needs. Then, it is obvious that different types of breeding system will allow different degrees of mendelian recombination. Thus, when there is obligatory inbreeding, as in plants or animals with self-fertilization or with sexual reproduction wholly suppressed, there can be no recombination at all; while with obligatory wide outcrossing, as for instance in maize, there will be a great deal. Some species and groups, by cutting down the degree of outcrossing, have gone in for the short-range advantages of stability and of completeness of adaptation. But many of these are likely to die out if any marked alteration in conditions, such as a sharp change in climate, demands new adaptations. Most animals and plants have struck some degree of balance between stability and plasticity by adopting outcrossing systems which yet involve a certain degree of inbreeding.

So far all the discoveries I have mentioned have had to do with obvious mendelian genes—genes concerned with readily distinguishable character-differences and distributed according to Mendel's laws. However, two puzzles remained. One was the existence of heritable character-differences which are not sharply marked off, but run into each other—so-called continuous characters like human stature, for instance. Quite recently, however, by rather complicated experiments with the exceptionally favourable material provided by Drosophila, it has been shown that the factors responsible for such characters are mendelian in the sense that they are lodged in the chromosomes, but that they act in co-operating groups, each member of a group exerting a small quantitative effort, plus or minus, on some continuous or quantitative character, like size, or proportions, or fertility. Because there are always many similar units at work in a group, they have been styled *polygenes*. The single factors in any group of polygenes cannot be isolated by ordinary mendelian methods. However, the knowledge that they are lodged in the chromosomes, and so must be subject to mendelian principles in their transmission, makes it possible to use the mathematical methods invented by the biometricians half a century ago, to make much more accurate estimates of their distribution and behaviour in heredity. And this discovery turns out to be of some practical importance.

The second puzzle, of methods of inheritance that cannot possibly be fitted into the mendelian scheme, has also quite recently been solved in principle. They are due to the existence of genes outside the nucleus, in the general protoplasm of the cell, and therefore called *plasmagenes*. Since plasmagenes are loose in the cell, not joined up to form super-units of accurate composition like the genes in the chromosomes, the number of them in any one cell can vary and their distribution to later generations does not follow the regularities of the mendelian laws. Perhaps the most striking examples of plasmagenes are those associated with the bodies which contain the green chlorophyll of plants—the plastids. They are self-copying and occasionally mutate, and so are clearly genic in nature, though they are subject to a certain amount of control by the main body of genes in the chromosomes. Although plasmagenes play only a small and subsidiary role in heredity as a whole, the discovery of their existence enables us to fit various otherwise puzzling facts into the modern extended gene-theory of genetics.

A very spectacular recent step in the progress of genetics has been the discovery of the chemical nature of genes. Through the use of X-ray analysis, spectography under the microscope, and microchemical methods, we now know that genes consist of certain kinds of protein in association with certain kinds of nucleic acids; for brevity's sake, we call them nucleoproteins. The nucleic acid is a necessary part of the mechanism by which the copying gets done. Darlington calls it the midwife molecule for the birth of new genes. It seems to act as a sort of chemical template, closely applied to the elongated protein molecule, and somehow helping it to assemble new atoms into the same shape and pattern as itself. Particles of purified extracts of nucleic acid can even penetrate into the interior of some kinds of bacteria and there can permanently replace certain of their genes—a genetic transformation effected by chemical means. Furthermore, nucleic acids of one sort or another constitute the essential basis of viruses. Some plant viruses can be obtained as pure crystalline nucleoproteins; the protein component seems to be merely protective, while infection and further reproduction depend on the nucleic acid component alone. Our knowledge of the material basis of heredity has penetrated below the biological to the more basic chemical level. Clearly an almost unlimited new field has been opened up to scientific exploration. Indeed, the advance of genetics has led us towards the central secret of life itself, for after all the essential property of life, which distinguishes it from not-life, is the possession of an organization capable of reproducing or copying itself.

Fifty years ago we knew nothing worth knowing about

the material basis of heredity. To-day it is revealed as a vast system of self-copying units of nucleoprotein, most of them elaborately integrated in the highly organized structures called chromosomes.

LIFE'S IMPROBABLE LIKENESSES

THERE is a Japanese legend which tells of the sequel to the struggle for supremacy, during the twelfth century A.D., of two leading feudal families, the Heike and the Genji. The struggle ended in 1155 with the overwhelming victory of the Genji in the naval battle of Dan-no-ura, off the southwest tip of the country. The defeated Heike, true to the Samurai tradition, committed mass suicide by throwing themselves into the sea. Immediately afterwards, all the crabs of the region appeared stamped with the face of a resentful Japanese warrior, thus reincarnating the dead Heike nobles. The face-bearing crabs are called Heike-gani or Heike crabs; the Japanese will not eat them to this day, and an exceptionally homely or ugly man is likely to be told "You look like a Heike-Gani."

That is the legend. The facts are that the Heike *were* defeated at Dan-no-ura; that the crab *Dorippe japonica*, which is widespread in Japanese waters, *is* called *Heike-gani* and *does* bear on its carapace the exact likeness of a medieval Japanese warrior; and that, though edible, it is *not* eaten by the Japanese. Professor Yamayita, of the Institute of Folklore in Tokyo, tells me that in past centuries it was sometimes called *Oni-gani*, *oni* meaning a frightening kind of demon who may also be the spirit of a dead man.

Professor H. J. Muller, the eminent American biologist, showed me a specimen which he brought back from a recent visit to Japan. He agrees with me that *Dorippe* provides the only known case of the mimicry of man by another species of animal. It may, however, be mentioned that the white mark on the back of the common European garden spider is quite definitely a cross, and the resemblance may quite possibly have been of advantage in causing people to think twice about killing this kind of spider; anyhow, as Dr

Bristow, our great authority on spiders, tells me, it was in many places considered unlucky to do so, and this would have polished up any original rough cruciform pattern into a more detailed and striking resemblance. We would not expect to find this selective superstition or such a close resemblance in Moslem countries; but, unfortunately, the range of the species is exclusively Christian!

The resemblance of *Dorippe* to an angry traditional Japanese warrior is far too specific and far too detailed to be merely accidental: it is a specific adaptation, which can only have been brought about by means of natural selection operating over centuries of time, the crabs with a more perfect resemblance having been less eaten.

This statement is usually greeted with incredulity by the layman, but there are large numbers of equally improbable likenesses in biology which undoubtedly owe their evolutionary origin to selection—the astonishing resemblance of leaf-insects to leaves, of stick-insects to sticks, of flower-spiders and flower-mantises to flowers, or various harmless moths and beetles and other insects to wasps and hornets, and so forth. In all such cases, it can now be taken as established that the precision of the likeness is due to the action of natural selection—in other words that over many generations those individuals which happened to look a little more like their models survived and reproduced themselves on the average a little more often than those which looked less like the models. It can be demonstrated that even a very small biological advantage will in the course of generations add up to produce a large and striking result.

The objections raised against the idea that such strange resemblances are of biological advantage to their possessors and are therefore due to the action of natural selection run something like this: How can the animal know what it ought to look like? and even if it did know, how could it manage to achieve the likeness? Or contrariwise, as Tweedledee would have said, the likeness is just an accident, and has no significance for its possessor. Or alternatively, the likeness *is* miraculously exact, but how could it have been produced except by some omnipotent divinity who has thought up these striking methods of demonstrating his powers?

The answer to the first objection is very simple—the animal doesn't know anything about it; and even if it did, no efforts on its part could help to bring about the likeness.

Evolutionary transformation does not occur as a result of an animal's wishes or efforts. One major result of the modern science of genetics is a negative one—that the effects of disuse or of changes in the environment (like heat or cold or moisture, still less the sight of leaves or sticks) just aren't inherited. Its main positive upshot is as follows: that evolutionary change occurs through the natural selection of heritable variations or mutations; that mutations are due to chemical changes in the material units of heredity, the genes; that most mutations are harmful or useless, but the rare favourable ones are automatically preserved and incorporated in the race, just because they are favourable—their possessors survive and reproduce themselves a little more often.

The difficulty about the start of any such process is a more real one. The variations that actually get used by natural selection seem almost invariably to be small mutations, with quite slight effects on the animal's or plant's visible characters. That being so, now could we conceive that the first steps in the direction of a human face, for instance, could have been any use to our crabs? For clearly people are not going to be put off eating a creature by superstitious fears unless there is some fairly striking reason.

The answer of modern evolutionary theory is that in such cases natural selection has merely operated to polish up a prior condition which *was* purely accidental: and luckily for evolutionary theory, we can often point to the existence of accidental predispositions of this sort. In crabs, for instance, the back of the carapace is usually not smooth, but embossed in relief with bumps and depressions (which are related to the underlying structure of the body); and not infrequently the pattern thus produced bears a rough (and doubtless quite accidental) resemblance to some object or other, and in several cases to a human face.

On English shores there is a little crab of the genus Corystes, the pattern of whose shell is sufficiently like a human face for the species to have been given the specific name *cassivelaunus*, after the chieftain who led the ancient Britons against Julius Caesar. But the likeness is never more than a rough one, and in any case, Corystes is a very small crab which is not used as food by human beings. The result is that the resemblance has not only stayed rough, but is very variable, some crabs showing scarcely any likeness to a face. However, it is easy to conceive of an accidental resemblance, no better than the best among Corystes, which would be capable of arousing superstitious fear and wonder—how could a human face get imprinted on a crab's back unless some god or devil had put it there with some mysterious intent? And then the rest would follow automatically. The crabs which were more like a face, especially more like a face typical of the local culture, would tend to be spared, while their less miraculous brothers and sisters would continue to be eaten, until in the course of the generations (remember that perhaps a thousand would be available for our species, for an effective resemblance must have been in existence long before the battle of Dan-no-ura) the crude and accidental original had been polished up into the truly astonishing likeness of an ancient Samurai which the crabs now bear.

In passing, there is a possible way of testing the validity of this conclusion. If *Dorippe japonica* has a wide geographical range, we may expect that the crabs that live on the shores of other human cultures either gain no protection from the pattern of their carapace, in which case the resemblance to a human face will be much less exact; or they do gain protection, when we may prophesy that the resemblance will be an exact one, but will be to some rather different human type, and certainly not to a specifically Japanese warrior.

To return for a moment to Corystes, this little crab, though its resemblance to a human face is not adaptive, has another peculiarity which admirably illustrates both the way in which an extremely beautiful adaptation can be built up from non-adaptive beginnings, and also the specific nature of adaptation. In place of the short thread-like feelers of ordinary crabs, spaced somewhat apart on the head, the antennae of Corystes are longer than its whole body, are pressed together, and project directly forward —or rather upwards, for the animal lives throughout the day buried in the sand in an upright position, with nothing showing but the very tip of the antennae. This mode of life is an adaptation to escape the attention of skates and other predatory fish; at night Corystes comes out and crawls over the surface of the sand to forage. And the antennae are an adaptation to the mode of life: with the aid of interlocking stiff hairs along their edges, they form a tube through which the animal can breathe, drawing in a current of clean water through the sand to be passed over the gills. The adaptation is highly specific to burrowing in sand: in mud it would be no good, but would clog up. Mud-living crustaceans live in burrows, and draw in currents of water down the burrows by constantly vibrating the swimmerets on their abdomen.

The antennae of ordinary crabs have nothing to do with breathing: but it only needed comparatively small changes to adapt them to a respiratory function—less space between them, an increase of their length, and the enlargement of the hairs on their fore and aft margins.

The point I want to make is that practically all the characteristics of an animal are adaptive—in other words, have been moulded by natural selection so as to perform some special function. And this applies as much to an animal's appearance as to its construction or its inherited patterns of behaviour. The difference is that the appearance is generally adjusted to the sense-organs and habits of some other creature, either the prey that the animal needs to catch or the enemies from whom it needs to escape. And of course some adaptations are more curious and surprising than others—certainly the adaptation of Dorippe to not being eaten by Japanese is one of the most curious that we know.

However, there are plenty of other equally surprising examples of animals or plants acquiring a resemblance to other animals or plants, or to inanimate objects.

Most people know of walking-stick insects; but there are in reality many insects of many different groups, from grasshoppers to moth caterpillars, which look like twigs. As for leaf-insects, their number is legion. Some are like one big green leaf, others like scattered bits of foliage; some like just-dead leaves, others like dead leaves with mould-spots and holes in them, others like half-decayed leaves. And there are also leaf-frogs and leaf-toads, and, most curious of all, a leaf-fish in the Amazon, *Monocirrhus,* which gets within striking distance of its prey by looking precisely like a dead leaf drifting in the current.

Then there are the insects of the family Membracidae. These are all defenceless little plant-bugs which spend most of their time in exposed situations on the twigs or leaves of plants, sucking the sap, so that they are in considerable need of protection from hungry predators. Furthermore, they all have a large hood-like outgrowth on the fore-part of their thorax, whose primary function is not known, but which provides excellent raw material for developing a resemblance to various non-edible objects, often masking the whole body underneath. Thus in some membracids the outgrowth has been elongated fore-and-aft to look like a grass-seed; in others it has been moulded into one or more sharp hooks, so that the creatures appear exactly like thorns; in one it is orange-coloured, hollow, and enormously swollen, completely hiding the rest of the animal, and has achieved a striking resemblance to the chrysalis of a moth, whose brilliant orange colour is known to be a warning signal of nauseous taste; in another it has been flattened from side to side, expanded, and coloured green, so that the creature bears a strong resemblance to a leaf-cutter ant carrying back to the nest a piece of green leaf which it has bitten off a neighbouring tree; in some, it has been turned into the semblance of a bit of bark. In others, into a sweeping sickle-shaped structure, resembling nobody knows what; and finally, in the most curious case of all, *Heteronotus*, it has been enlarged and moulded into the semblance of a worker-ant, of a species which is abundant in the bug's surroundings. Of course it is only a hollow shell, concealing the animal's real body; but from above the resemblance to an ant is amazing, and, since ants, with their gregarious habits, their powerful bite, and their reservoirs of formic acid, are well protected against most insectivorous creatures, it must be of great biological advantage to the plant-bug.

Ants indeed are commonly mimicked by quite a number of ground-living insects besides plant-bugs—beetles, two-winged flies, and grasshoppers—and by spiders. I myself have been doubly deceived by a spider's ant-mimicry. On an island in Lake Victoria in Central Africa, I had my attention forcibly directed to the tree-ants which swarmed over the dense vegetation, because every time I accidentally got one on my person, it inflicted a painful bite. Suddenly I noticed one give a somewhat un-antlike jump; on inspection, it turned out to be a spider. This was the first example of ant-mimicry by spiders which I had seen, and I set about trying to find some more specimens. After some searching I discovered what I thought was another: but when I had got it safely into a glass tube it turned out to be an ant!

How is a spider to look like an ant when an ant has a pair of antennae on its head and only six legs on its body, while a spider has eight legs and no antennae? What is more, how is a spider going to acquire the long slender waist of an ant? What happens is very illuminating. In general, spiders that mimic ants first of all become more elongated. Secondly, the front pair of legs are placed farther forward than usual, and are not used for walking, but are held out in front so as to look like feelers. And thirdly, a waist is "painted in" by making the sides of the middle part of the body light-coloured so that they do not catch the eye, while a central narrow dark band with a dark oval patch behind gives an excellent imitation of an ant's waist and hind abdomen.

This sort of visual deception is very commonly employed to obtain a resemblance. The same trick of painting in a waist is often used by the beetles and grasshoppers which mimic ants, and equally by those numerous chunky-bodied insects which mimic wasps.

Among butterflies which escape detection by looking like dead leaves, patches of mould are often imitated by spots of special colour, and holes in the leaf by wing-patches which are transparent because no scales are produced on them. In the extraordinary *Draconia*, not only is this device used, but the wings grow with irregular edges, giving an exact imitation of a half-decayed leaf.

Similarly, fish that escape detection by looking like marine vegetation are generally beset with weed-like outgrowths. The Australian sea-horse *Phyllopteryx* has become quite fantastic in this way, looking like a surrealist's idea of a cross between animal and vegetable, with imitations of three quite different kinds of seaweed sprouting from various parts of its body.

Perhaps the most curious of such deceptions is shown in the resemblance of various insects and spiders to a bird's dropping. The creature often manages to imitate the viscid soft appearance of a dropping so perfectly that the eye is completely deceived, and it is easier to use touch to decide whether the object is an animal or a piece of excrement.

Such examples completely dispose of the idea that the protective resemblances of animals can be due to the direct effect of the conditions of the environment. This is also borne out by various facts of true mimicry, when a harmless and palatable animal gains a biological advantage by looking like some other animal which is relatively immune from attack owing to its possession of a formidable weapon, like the sting of a wasp or the bite of a poisonous snake or the jaws and formic acid of an ant, or to its having a nauseous taste, often coupled with general toughness and inedibility, as in the milkweed butterfly, various swallow-tails, and many other brightly coloured butterflies. Here it often happens that the two animals, mimic and model, owe their similar appearance to quite different means. Thus the pigments used to produce the sham warning colours of edible butterfly mimics are often chemically quite different from those used to produce the real warning colours of their models.

The converse proof is provided by the numerous cases where the biologically advantageous resemblance is only evolved where it will be seen, like the grasshopper which imitates a decaying green leaf, but not with those parts of its wings which are concealed when at rest. This is on a par with the fact that a white actor playing Othello blacks only his face and hands, and is what one would expect on a selective interpretation.

In butterflies and moths, an adaptive transparency of the wings has been produced in several quite different ways. In the Hornet Clearwing hawk-moth, the scales are only loosely attached, and fall off soon after the moth emerges from its chrysalis; but in other cases the scales are much reduced in number or in size, or are converted into thin hair-like structures, or are set up on end so as to let the light pass through.

The clearwing has an astonishing resemblance to a hornet, not only in its general form and its transparent wings and black-and-yellow colouration, but also in the way it flies, and the fact that it flies by day instead of by night. The resemblance not only deceives most human beings, but also the creatures that would otherwise eat the moth. Lizards, for instance, which have learnt the meaning of the yellow-and-black danger-signals so common in nature, refuse clearwings equally with wasps and hornets. Indeed, as Cott has shown in his fine book, *Adaptive Colouration in Animals,* the experimental evidence for the biological value of warning colouration and mimicry is now conclusive.

The diurnal habits of the Hornet Clearwing are a reminder that behaviour as well as structure or colouration usually needs to be changed to secure an effective resemblance. Thus the wonderful resemblance of the hawk-moth *Xanthopan* to the bark of a tree, based on its general colour and by the dark lines that simulate cracks in the bark, would not be achieved unless the creature always settled with its head pointing vertically upwards. On the other hand, the equally striking resemblance to bark of the Garden Carpet-Moth, *Xanthorrhoë*, depends on the animal settling horizontally.

Creatures that escape detection by their resemblance to twigs spend all the daytime grasping a branch, immobile and rigid, and only move about to feed when darkness falls.

Spiders that mimic ants walk and behave like ants as well as looking like them (indeed one South American species adds to the picture by walking around holding over itself the dead body of a real ant, so that it looks like a worker ant carrying a dead comrade); many insects which mimic stinging models like bees and wasps curve their abdomen round when seized, threatening their captor with a non-existent sting.

Even the highest vertebrates, like birds, may have their behaviour thus modified. The common nightjar escapes detection while brooding by crouching immobile, and so looking just like part of the floor of dead leaves on which its nest is placed. But the South American nightjar *Nyctibius* lays its eggs in the cavity of a broken stump; and the bird broods in a strange unbirdlike posture, rigid and erect, with eyes almost closed, in which it looks exactly like a continuation of the stump. Even when not nesting, it roosts during the daytime in this position, sometimes in full view on top of a fence-post; and even then is practically invisible.

The most extraordinary of all such cases is that of a kind of shrike, whose nestlings combine forces to produce a deceptive likeness. If a potential enemy comes near the nest while the parents are away, the nestlings all elongate themselves upwards, at the same time leaning together; the group, "frozen" immobile in this position, looks like a broken-off branch, the combined beaks simulating the angular edge of the break.

There is only one other example of combined mimicry known to me. When Professor Gregory, on his journey to the Rift Valley of Kenya, started to pick a specimen of a new plant, all its flowers flew away! These flowers were really Flatid plant-bugs of one of the species of the genus Phromnia, which have the instinct to perch in company on upright stems. What is more, they come in two colours, pink and green, so that the green ones look like buds and the pink ones like opened flowers. Other Flatids also escape detection by simulating flower-spikes, but this species has adopted the added refinement of imitating both buds and flowers.

Birds also afford examples of true mimicry. Thus the inoffensive orioles of the Malay archipelago mimic what Alfred Russel Wallace described as the "noisy and powerful" friarbirds of the region—each group of islands having a model and a mimic of identical appearance, the orioles always developing a ruff or cowl of feathers like their models. Though the black patches of bare skin round the friar-birds' eyes are counterfeited by black feathers in the orioles, the resemblance is so close as to have taken in professional ornithologists. The drongos of Central Africa are not only bold and powerful, but their flesh is unpalatable; and they are mimicked by several different kinds of birds—so successfully that when Swynnerton offered the mimics to his hungry cat, they were decisively rejected.

However, the most interesting examples of mimicry in birds concerns the eggs of cuckoos. As is well-known, some cuckoos, like cowbirds, are reproductive parasites, laying their eggs in the nests of other birds and leaving the young to be brought up by the foster-parents. And the eggs of such species are often extremely like those of the fosterer. Furthermore, when a species of cuckoo parasitizes a fosterer which is much smaller than itself, it lays eggs much smaller than is normal for a bird of its size, almost as small as those of the fosterer. Finally, when, as in the common European cuckoo, the species is divided into a number of strains, each parasitizing a different species of small bird, the eggs of the different strains are different, and are usually close mimics of the fosterer's eggs in colour and pattern as well as size. However, there are one or two exceptions: for instance, the Hedge-Sparrow lays pure blue eggs, but Hedge-Sparrow cuckoos lay spotted greyish eggs. That this is not due to an inherent inability to produce blue eggs is shown by a strain of cuckoos in Northern Europe, which lay unspotted blue eggs in the nests of blue-egged birds like Wheatear and Redstart.

To understand how these resemblances could have been brought about, we will jump for a moment to the plant kingdom. There is a variety (or possibly a distinct species) of the plant Camelina which is found nowhere else but in flax-fields. Its chief difference from its nearest wild relative is its small seeds, which are of the same size as flax seeds. Flax seed is harvested for sowing by sifting through a fine sieve: and so the Camelina seeds pass through too and are sown next year with the flax. What has happened is obvious. Quite automatically, in each generation, the bigger Camelina seeds were

The South American nightjar *Nyctibius griseus* nests on the top of a stump, out of reach of ground prowlers. To escape detection by other enemies, it broods throughout the day without moving, with its head pointing upwards, when it looks exactly like the continuation of the stump.

sifted out of the crop of flax seed, while the smallest ones were sifted in—until finally only those strains which produced small seeds were left, and the small-seeded variety became a reproductive parasite of cultivated flax, or it might be better to say a parasite of man, since it depends on man's agricultural labours.

In the case of cuckoos, the sifting is done by the host species, which is liable either to turn a strange egg out (or to desert), if it is too unlike its own. Thus a strain of cuckoos which lays smaller eggs will have a better chance of being perpetuated, and so will one whose eggs bear some resemblance to those of the host. However, different host species vary in discrimination, and only when they are very particular will selection see to it that the resemblance becomes really close. The Hedge-Sparrow is known to be highly tolerant of strange objects in its nest: so here there was no handle for selection to bring about a close resemblance.

In passing, though a defenceless mimic usually counterfeits the visual appearance of a model, it may sometimes imitate its sound. The rattling of the rattlesnake is an auditory warning which serves to scare away animals that might tread on it, as well as predators that might otherwise eat it. And one quite harmless species of snake has developed a small rattle that serves the same function as the counterfeit red, black, and white of the harmless False Coral Snake, which imitates the warning colouration of the highly poisonous true Coral Snake.

A great many snakes hiss by way of warning; and quite a number of harmless creatures make use of hissing to scare their enemies by pretending that they are snakes. The most curious example is that of the wryneck, a small European bird related to the woodpeckers, and like them nesting in holes. When an intruder tries to enter a wryneck's nest, the sitting bird flattens itself against the side of the hole, then presses up towards the enemy with a strangely snake-like motion, and finally shoots back, emitting a completely snake-like hiss. The first time I saw this performance, even though I was prepared for it and was actually seeing the bird after taking the lid off the nest-box in which she was brooding, it was quite startling and indeed disconcerting: it must have an overwhelming effect on a small egg-stealing mammal in the darkness of the bird's natural nest.

I shall come back to the imitation of snakes and other reptiles: but meanwhile I must just mention a few others of the more fantastic resemblances that natural selection has brought about.

One of the best is the reversed butterfly trick. Some little butterflies belonging to the family of the Blues, or Lycaenidae, have "tails" on their hind-wings which, when the creature is at rest, look like antennae, and are moved up and down to increase the resemblance. The angle of the wing is scalloped out to look like a butterfly's head, and on it is a conspicuous spot which simulates an eye. The real head with the real eyes and antennae is practically hidden by a forward curve of the fore-wings, and the underside of the wings bears a pattern of stripes which forces attention on the sham head by converging upon it. The biological reason for this elaborate deception is of course to ensure that if a hungry bird or lizard does find the butterfly, it should snap at the wrong end. If so, all it is likely to get is a dusty mouthful of scales, or possibly a dry bit of wing, while the insect flies off little the worse.

Many butterflies, including a number of Blues, are known to deflect the attack of their predators by means of conspicuous tails or "eye"-spots near the hind edge of their hind-wings, and the complete false head is merely an elaboration built on this foundation.

Most of my examples have had to do with the protection of edible animals from attack: but of course similar devices may be equally well employed by predators to help them secure their prey. The most wonderful of such aggressive deceivers are the flower-mantises and flower-spiders. These are all brilliantly coloured, but are not conspicuous because their colours match those of the flowers in which they sit all day waiting for unwary insect visitors. There are many different species of many colour-patterns, but the colour-patterns have always been adjusted by natural selection to the particular kind of flower that they frequent. For instance, in Manila there is a beautiful white spider with yellow legs which lies in wait in white lily flowers with yellow stamens. Again, the Malayan flower-mantis Hymenopus refuses to take up its station except in the flower-clusters of a particular kind of rhododendron, which it matches to perfection with its colouration of pale pink and pearl white, with a disruptive band of leaf-green across its thorax. Of course, these resemblances may, and generally do, have the second function of concealing the spider or mantis from its own numerous enemies.

Sometimes the animal even constructs a background for

itself. Thus Azilia, a Guianan spider, sits in invisibility on a little carpet of bits of bark and lichens that it has built in the middle of its web.

The example of Camelina shows that seed-size can be adjusted to that of another species by natural selection; but other plants have their whole visible appearance changed. Lithops is a succulent plant, related to the Mesembryanthemums, which lives in South-West Africa: and, like other succulents of the same region, it is practically indistinguishable both in form and colouration from the stones and pebbles of its desert habitat. (And so, by the way, are some of the desert grasshoppers.)

But the most remarkable plant examples are to be found among the orchids. The flowers of various smaller orchids are so like insects that the plants have been named after the resemblance, like the Fly Orchid in Britain. Until quite recently it was always supposed that this was something quite accidental, just a by-product of the general construction of orchid flowers, and of no biological advantage to the plant. However, it has now been proved up to the hilt that it is a device for securing cross-pollination. The flowers (or rather the lips of the flowers) of each of these mimetic orchids imitates the female of a particular species of insect, in appearance and sometimes also in smell. The male insects are taken in, and attempt to mate with the imitation females provided by the orchid. In the process, pollen is transferred from one flower to another, and the orchids are fertilized!

Archdeacon Paley in his celebrated *Evidences of Christianity,* which was for so long a set book for all students at Cambridge, maintained the thesis that all adaptations were evidences of deliberate design on the part of a Divine Designer. I cannot help wondering what he would have said about the Divine purpose behind the design of these bogus sexual attractions, and whether perhaps he would not have welcomed Darwin's great intuition, as having freed God from the responsibility for all the biological gadgets—some admirable, some monstrous, and some just queer—that the automatic mechanism of natural selection has ground out during the process of evolution.

I have kept to the last some counterfeit faces to show that even if Dorippe provides a unique case of an animal gaining a biological advantage by mimicking a man, there are other just as astonishing examples of a mimetic likeness to other animals.

It is a well-known fact that an eye-spot has a powerful psychological effect on animals as well as on people. Accordingly we find eye-spots used over and over again to focus attention on one part of the body, as on the wings of many butterflies, or on the display plumage of various male birds. But of course the effect can be strengthened and made more terrifying when the eye is in a fierce face. The terrifying effect of real eyes in a real face is utilized in the threatening displays of many birds, like owls, and many mammals, like baboons. In some of the latter, the horrifying effect is enhanced not only by the ivory colour of the gums, revealed as the creature bares its teeth, but by an ivory-white patch of skin that it exposes above its eye. Quite often, however, the same effect is achieved by sham eyes in a false face. Various large moth caterpillars, when alarmed, swell out the forepart of their body into an imitation snake's head, bearing on its sides two eye-spots which are concealed when the creature is in its normal position. The imitation is sometimes very close; but even a rough one, with the staring eye-spots and the threatening movements of the animal, is quite frightening enough to repel most potential enemies.

The caterpillar of the puss-moth produces a false face in quite a different way. It draws in and flattens its head in such a way that it presents a mask-like surface adorned with two little false eyes. The face is not the face of any particular animal, just a miniature vertebrate face. Meanwhile the animal adds to its terrifying qualities by sticking up its forked tail and protruding from it two waving scarlet threads.

However, one of the lantern-bugs of South America has produced a complete sham head whose resemblance to an alligator is just as astonishing as that of Dorippe to a Samurai. The counterfeit protrudes in front of the insect's real head. It is olive-brown in colour, with one protuberance serving for counterfeit nose, a pair farther back for eyes. The nose has a pair of black patches for nostrils, while the black "eyes" are painted in complete with a white patch to imitate light falling on the eyeball. Finally, there is a sham mouth, complete with sham teeth, ivory-white and actually standing out in relief! A marmoset or lizard which suddenly came upon this apparition would certainly get a good fright, and would not be likely to reflect that baby alligators would not be likely to be crawling about in the foliage of trees.

The natural question to ask is how did such a resemblance start? As with the Japanese crab, the answer is ready to hand: there existed a prior structure which could fairly easily be converted into the required resemblance. All the members of one sub-family of lantern-bugs have a huge hollow outgrowth on the front of their head. No one knows what its primary function is: but it has the general shape of a reptilian head, and needs only a little touching up to begin looking like a fierce face.

But the precision of the resemblance could quite certainly not have been attained without the operation of natural selection over many generations: the odds against anything so detailed and so accurate being due to chance are as astronomical as they would be against a monkey with a typewriter producing a Shakespeare sonnet. And that holds for Dorippe too—if its resemblance to the medieval Japanese idea of a savage warrior is mere accident, we can give up trying to find any sense or order in nature.

However, the resemblance is quite certainly not accidental, but brought about by natural selection, that blind, surprising and potent force implicit in the very nature of life itself. The results of natural selection demonstrate the unpredictability and the amazing potentialities of nature. Natural selection can only generate consequences of immediate biological utility: and yet over the generations it produces results of almost infinite variety and fantastic improbability—but still in the highest degree orderly, and comprehensible by those willing to make the effort to comprehend. The incredible resemblances which it brings into being are reminders of the basic fact that nature is miraculous—in the proper sense of the word, namely that it provokes our admiration and our wonder.

Nature is indeed orderly, but its order transcends our most disorderly imaginations: that is the lesson to be learnt from life's improbable resemblances.

NATURAL HISTORY IN ICELAND

IN Iceland, in the summer of 1949, a number of new facts and experiences, interesting and exciting to a naturalist, came my way—some of them through my own eyes, others through the mouths of the able Icelandic zoologists who put so much of their time and knowledge at the disposition of my companion James Fisher and myself.

Thus we saw various species that were new to us, and sometimes spectacular, like the harlequin duck. That was exciting enough; but the interest was multiplied when we remembered that it is an essentially North American bird, one of the rarest stragglers to Europe, and yet here breeding close to familiar British ducks like mallard, tufted duck, widgeon, and pintail. We found a meadow pipit breeding in a wood, like a tree pipit, instead of on the customary open heath; and what is more, singing a song halfway to a tree pipit's. We saw some local birds recognizably different from their British congeners, like the Iceland redshank, which is several shades darker than ours. We saw a Painted Lady butterfly in the northern half of the island—a truly astonishing sight, since its nearest permanent breeding-place is the south of France. We got evidence, from our own counts, of the increase of the gannet; and from our Icelandic colleagues of the fact that not only it but nine or ten other birds of the region have been rapidly extending their range northwards during recent decades.

But the modern naturalist is not content unless he can relate his facts, however valuable, and his isolated experiences, however exciting, to general principles; and the very vividness and novelty of the impressions made by an unfamiliar country will set his scientific imagination to work. Here is the result of my own case—some of the ways in which Iceland's natural history illustrates or illuminates general evolutionary biology.

The most obvious point is the paucity of bird species in general, and of song-birds and other passerines in particular. Thus the number of regular breeding species in Iceland is only a little over a third of that in Britain; but the number of breeding passerines is less than one-eighth of the British. In part this is due to the unfriendly climate and the barrenness of much of the island. Although Iceland barely touches the Arctic Circle, real trees cannot grow except in two small sheltered localities, and both vegetation and insect life have much less luxuriance and variety than with us in Britain, while the winter is such that very few species of bird could possibly live through it.

In Spitsbergen, farther poleward, we find a marked further

drop, both in the total and the passerine percentage. The best way to bring this home is by means of a table:

Country	Latitude	Regular breeding species	Passerines	
			Number	Per cent. of total
Britain	49° 57′—58° 40′ (mainland); 49° 51′—60° 51′ (with islands).	186	77	41.4
Iceland	63° 20′—66° 32′	69	9	13.0
Spitsbergen	76° 26′—80° 50′	25	1	4.0

There is also the fact that Iceland is an island, and a fairly remote one, lying over five hundred miles from the Hebrides (a little more from Cape Wrath, the nearest point of the British mainland), and close on three hundred miles from Faereo. Admittedly the distance north-westward to the Greenland coast is under two hundred miles; but Greenland, especially in these latitudes, is so forbidding that very few species can have used it as a stepping-stone to Iceland.

Now remote islands invariably show a fauna and flora which are impoverished compared to that of the nearest mainland. With birds this is mainly due to the difficulties presented by a long sea passage, especially to small terrestrial species or those with feeble flight. In addition, an island is likely to have fewer kinds of habitats than a mainland area, and this may cut down the number of species which can find a permanent niche in its biological economy, even if they manage to reach it.

It is difficult to say just what birds are lacking merely because they have failed to overcome the sea barrier. Some apparent candidates turn out, on reflection, to be ruled out for other reasons. Thus the fact that among the thrushes the redwing breeds in Iceland and the fieldfare does not is not so surprising when we remember how the fieldfare seems much more definitely wedded to tall trees to nest in, and (we may presume at least partly for that reason) does not exist so far north in Scandinavia as the redwing.

Then, with such a favourite as the meadow pipit to

parasitize, it is at first sight puzzling that there are no cuckoos. The reason is the low density of pipit population. A cuckoo has to keep about a dozen fosterers' nests under observation if it is to succeed in its parasitism, and this would be impossible in Iceland.

The absence of the rock-dove seems also surprising—until one remembers that the species seems to be dependent on weed-seeds and other by-products of human cultivation.

But I do find it puzzling that the ring ouzel, which likes rocky slopes and in Norway breeds as far north as the North Cape, has not established itself; and still more so that the dipper is absent, when its smaller relative, the wren, has been breeding in Iceland so long that it has evolved into a distinctive subspecies. Of course, the streams by which the dipper lives would be frozen over in winter, but part of the dipper population of northern continental Europe migrates southward in winter, and the same might readily have occurred in Iceland, while the rest might have done what all the Iceland wrens do, namely take to the seashore. And I am pretty sure that if the house sparrow ever reached Reykjavik, the capital of Iceland, it would flourish and multiply. The

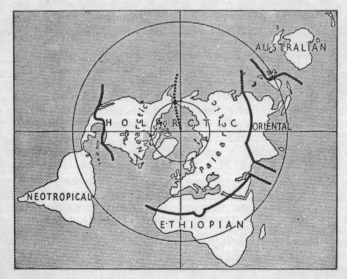

Distribution of land animals in the main zoo-geographical regions of the world

greatest puzzle is that posed by the Lapland bunting, which breeds in Greenland and north of the Arctic Circle in Norway, but not in Iceland, although it seems to traverse the island regularly on passage!

That for strong fliers the climate is the only obstacle is shown by the fact that since the beginning of this century the list of breeding species has been increased by nearly 10 per cent., undoubtedly owing to the amelioration of the climate—a fact to which I shall return. Conversely, swallows come to Iceland every summer (we saw some in the Westmann Islands), as do willow warblers, but neither species has yet been found breeding.

It seems that many species are all the time sending out scouts, so to speak, into areas where breeding is impossible but on the chance that one day they can establish themselves permanently. This seems a wasteful method, but natural selection always involves wastage. The most striking example is the Painted Lady butterfly (*Vanessa cardui*), which cannot reproduce itself regularly through the winter north of southern France, but in most years sends out vast numbers to Britain and other countries. The one we ourselves saw, by Lake Myvatn, was nearly fifteen hundred miles outside its permanent range.

Another interesting feature of broad geographical distribution is this—that Iceland is at the same time the western-most outpost of a number of Old World bird species and the easternmost of some (but fewer) New World ones. Lake Myvatn is the area of maximum overlap between the bird faunas of what zoologists call the Palearctic and Nearctic regions, northern Eurasia and North America respectively.

Thus Iceland is the western limit of breeding range for such Old World species as whooper swan, greylag goose, snipe, golden plover, whimbrel, redwing, white wagtail (and indeed the entire wagtail genus); but it is the eastern limit for those otherwise New World species, great northern diver, Barrow's goldeneye, and harlequin duck. The ducks, by the way, well illustrate the complexities of geographical distribution—Iceland shows us not only several Old World species at their western limit, like wigeon, teal, common scoter, and tufted duck, and several New World ones at their eastern limit, but also a number of circumpolar or Holarctic species such as mallard, pintail, gadwall, and shoveller.

All the New World species which breed in Iceland are hardy enough to inhabit parts of Greenland also. If the

Labrador Current did not cool the east coast of Greenland
and northern Canada so much below the temperature they
ought to enjoy by virtue of their latitude, and the Gulf
Stream did not warm Iceland and Spitsbergen and the north-
west coasts of Europe so much above it, the contribution from
the New World would presumably at least equal that of the
Old.

There is at least one plant in Iceland of New World origin.
The sea-rockets, *Cakile,* are shore-dwelling crucifers with
lilac flowers. Two Icelandic botanists, Dr. and Mrs. Löve,
have recently shown that the sea-rocket of Iceland does not,
as has been generally assumed, belong to the species found in
Scandinavia and Britain, *Cakile maritima,* but reveals itself,
both by its slightly different form and its double chromo-
some-number—thirty-six instead of eighteen—as the North
American species, *C. edentula.* This holds also for the sea-
rocket of the Azores: the Löves' conclusion is that the Gulf
Stream has been responsible for the appearance of the
American sea-rocket in these otherwise Old World islands, by
transporting the seeds in its slow, warm drift.

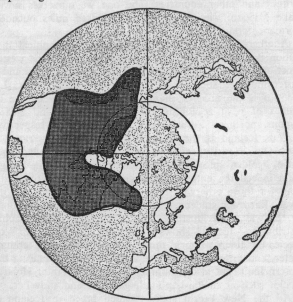

Breeding distribution of the Loon or Great Northern Diver

At various times in the geological past there was a land connection between the Old and the New Worlds across what is now the Bering Strait, and probably also, though not so often or so long, across the North Atlantic, along the line still indicated by the submarine ridges between Greenland, Iceland, Faeroe, and Shetland. The climate in the regions connected by these land bridges was then less rigorous, and there was more uniformity of animals and plants in the Holarctic region than now. But isolation and time saw to it that the inevitable differences were accentuated, and meanwhile the New World fauna received large additions from the Central and South American region, which were very different from the immigrants that the northern Old World received from Africa and south-western Asia. Thus eventually two quite distinct faunas and floras, the Palearctic and the Nearctic, were differentiated—distinct, but with a number of elements obviously of common origin, and with a considerable number of species still shared by both and therefore classed as Holarctic.

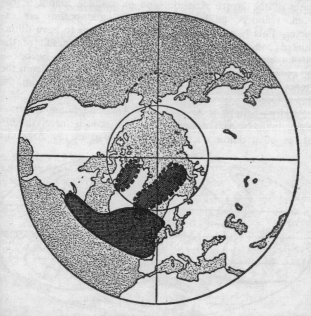

Breeding distribution of the Little Auk (arctic) and the Gannet (north temperate)

The greater isolation of the two regions to-day may possibly be due not only to the breaking of the land bridges between North America and the Old World, but to an actual increase of the distance across the Atlantic, caused by the slow drifting away of America from Europe. This was postulated by Wegener in his theory of Continental Drift. Iceland is well situated to test the theory. The position of certain points should be determined with great accuracy, so that afer a lapse of years even a few yards' shift could be detected. German scientists had begun on this project before World War II, and had set up a number of triangulation points in Iceland. However, the Icelanders were so suspicious that these might be camouflage for some military project that they destroyed them all—another of the innumerable minor casualties of modern war.

But there are other faunas represented in Iceland. An important one is the North Atlantic fauna, mainly of course of marine creatures, but emerging into the air in the form of a number of sea-birds which exist on both east and west coasts of the North Atlantic, and on suitable islands in between. Gannets, guillemots, razorbills, and puffins are examples. This North Atlantic bird fauna seems to have differentiated comparatively recently—perhaps as a result of the drifting apart of northern America and northern Europe—and consists of immigrant types from other regions—from the Arctic, from the Pacific round Cape Horn, and from the Indian Ocean.

Finally—believe it or not!—the Antarctic fauna is represented in Iceland. The bonxie or great skua is merely a subspecies of a dominant species widespread in the Antarctic

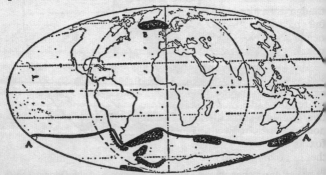

Breeding distribution of the Great Skua

and sub-Antarctic regions. Many high-latitude birds migrate to the other hemisphere after breeding, thus perpetually avoiding winter. Our bonxies must be descended from some southern hemisphere migrants which stayed to breed in their off-season area—one cannot say "in their winter quarters."

Thus we have in this one island representatives of five faunas—North Hemisphere Old World, North Hemisphere New World, North Atlantic, circumpolar South Hemisphere, and circumpolar North Hemisphere. This last includes two subdivisions—the true arctic fauna, with such Iceland birds as little auk and glaucous gull, and the sub-arctic and north-temperate forms shared by New and Old Worlds, such as wheatear, raven, mallard, and Slavonian grebe.

One of the interesting things that came to our attention was the frequent distinctiveness of the local Iceland race or subspecies of various species of birds. The Iceland wren is both larger and darker than ours in Britain, and the Iceland redpoll is also larger than our British subspecies, the so-called lesser redpoll, as well as having a recognizably different call-note. The redpoll, by the way, is an example of an Iceland bird which is small in size but yet is found in Greenland and North America, as well as in the Old World, so that it, like the wheatear, is Holarctic. But, unlike the widely spreading ducks, both these small birds have broken up into numerous well-marked subspecies. The wren is curious in this respect. Although it has produced separate and distinctive subspecies in Iceland, Faeroe, St. Kilda, and Shetland, it is uniform over the whole of western and central continental Europe. The separation of Britain from the Continent has not resulted in the evolution of a British subspecies, though this has happened with many other birds, of which our pied wagtail, so easily distinguishable from the continental white wagtail, is an example. Why this is so, is a real puzzle.

The fact that the Iceland redpoll and wren are larger in size than ours is an example of an interesting general rule —that warm-blooded animals tend to be slightly larger the nearer they live to the pole; further, in mammals, the relative size of ears, tail, and limbs tend to diminish—a phenomenon strikingly illustrated by the tiny ears of the arctic fox as compared with the huge flaps of the fennec fox from the scorching deserts. These changes are undoubtedly adaptations, working to reduce heat-loss in cold climates and to promote it in over-hot ones.

Thus some of the special characters of Iceland birds are adaptations to climate, while others, like the colour of the Iceland wren, seem to be non-adaptive consequences or accidental results of isolation. But there is a third class of difference, and perhaps the most interesting—difference in behaviour and song. Some of these differences, like the harsher song of the Iceland wren, are again aspects of the distinctiveness of the local subspecies. Others seem to be due to the birds being on the margin of their range, in surroundings quite different from the normal. Thus, as already mentioned, the Iceland wren out of the breeding season has to become almost exclusively a shore-bird.

Frequently, however, the reason is more subtle—the absence of competition from close relatives which have not reached this part of the species' range. Thus, in Britain, snipe are inhabitants of open country, so that it was surprising to find them quite common in the one of Iceland's two woods that we visited. James Fisher hit on what I am sure is the solution—namely that there are no woodcock in Iceland. With us, woodcock occupy the habitat provided by boggy woods. But where woodcock are absent, the snipe avail themselves of these as well as of their normal open habitats.

The absence of close relatives may have another effect. When two closely allied species come into contact in the same area, it is generally a biological advantage for them to proclaim their distinctiveness by some characteristic difference of plumage or voice. This will help to prevent actual or attempted cross-breeding, trespassing, and other waste of time and energy. In Britain, the closely related meadow and tree pipits are not only restricted to different habitats but sing quite distinctive songs. With us, the meadow pipit is exclusively a bird of moors and heaths and other open country, and its song is a rather feeble descending scale gradually accelerated into a little trill, given as the bird parachutes down after having flown up from the ground. The tree pipit, on the other hand, demands scattered trees and has a much more striking song; this also is given in the air while floating down, but the flight starts from (and often ends on) a high tree perch.

Here the need for distinctiveness cannot well be met by plumage differences, since both species are adapted to concealment by cryptic colouration; but the songs, given high in the air, are obvious trade-marks for the species. In the

Iceland birchwood where we found snipe, there were also meadow pipits. We would never have dreamt of finding meadow pipits in such a place in England, and their presence was clearly due to the absence of their close relative and competitor, the tree pipit. What is more, the song of one of them had a distinct tree pipit flavour, and it was begun from a tree perch.

Finnur Gudmunsson told us that in western Iceland he had once spent a couple of hours stalking the singer of a song which was wholly unknown to him: he eventually shot it for identification purposes—only to discover that it was an ordinary meadow pipit! This, too, was in a birch area, though the birches here were only scrub. Thus the relaxation of the need for distinctiveness seems to have permitted the song to change. The meadow pipits of open country in Iceland have so far not been heard to give any intermediate or markedly abnormal song (though one we heard in the Westmann Islands was exceptional for its brilliance). Possibly the woodland and scrubland birds are evolving into a distinct ecological race.

There remains to mention one amusing incident. In this same wood we found a redwing's nest quite high in a birch tree. Now, in Iceland the redwing, that attractive little thrush, is normally a confirmed ground-nester, though in Norway it frequently builds in trees, and Dr. Gudmunsson was quite impressed by this unusual event. Then on Myvatn we saw another tree nest, some eight feet up in a willow; and Dr. Gudmunsson grew really excited—until Sigfinson, the farmer-naturalist, reminded him that this had been the latest season in living memory, and that the ground had been deep in snow when the breeding urge took the redwings. Seeing that they thus so readily revert to ancestral habit under the stress of necessity, it is rather curious that they do not normally do so as a matter of convenience wherever trees or bushes abound.

Finally, I come to what to me is the most interesting point of all—the bearing of field natural history in Iceland upon the fascinating and basic question of a world-wide change in climate.

Professor Ahlmann, the well-known Swedish geographer, has summarized the evidence on this subject in the *Geographical Journal*. He concludes that in the northern hemisphere a widespread amelioration of climate, most extensive in higher latitude, is in progress. It began about a hundred years ago, but has been especially marked in the last two decades. The most likely explanation is that it is world-wide and due to increased heat from the sun, which in its turn operates by altering the world's great system of atmospheric circulation.

The evidence is of every sort—increased temperatures, spectacular regression of glaciers, changes in the position of main low-pressure and high-pressure areas, alterations in rainfall and snowfall, desiccation in lower latitudes (including the drying up of East African and South-East Russian lakes), enormous shrinkage of the polar pack ice, enlarged growth-rings of trees, and changes in the distribution of many animals and plants.[1]

On this last point Iceland provides a great deal of evidence, since it lies on the sensitive limit between sub-arctic and arctic conditions. We know from historical records that for over four hundred years the early colonists successfully grew barley, but that soon after A.D. 1300 this became impossible. To-day, to quote Ahlmann, "the present shrinkage of the glaciers is exposing districts which were cultivated by the early medieval farmers but were subsequently over-ridden by ice".

The ensuing cold spell of about six hundred years has been called the Little Ice Age; it was the coldest period since the retreat of the ice after the last major glacial period, while the warmest period since the end of the Ice Age seems to have been the few centuries just before our present era. About 1880 the Iceland glaciers reached their maximum extension for some ten thousand years.

As showing how sensitive animals may be as climatic indicators, Finnur Gudmunsson told me that in the warm spell just before the Christian Era, the dog-whelk (*Purpura*) was found all along the north and east coasts of Iceland, while to-day it stops dead at the north-west and south-east corners. (The slightly hardier whelk, *Buccinum*, still occurs all round the island.)

To come down to the present, the last few decades have seen drastic changes in the fish which are Iceland's prime economic support. Herring, haddock, halibut, and especially cod have extended their range northward in Greenland (the

[1] This was written in 1950. Dr. Dunbar, of the Arctic Institute in Canada, tells me that in the last few years there is some indication that the trend has passed its peak and that a reversal of the process may be setting in.

cod at the rate of about twenty-four miles a year for over thirty years); and cod and herring are moving north from Iceland, so that anxiety is beginning to be felt about the future of the fisheries.

As a result of the amelioration of climate, there have been extraordinary changes in the bird population of the island. No less than six species—nearly 10 per cent. of the previous list of breeders—have only started to breed in Iceland during the present century. There is the tufted duck, which arrived in 1908, and has spread so fast that now it is the second commonest species on Myvatn; three gulls—the black-headed, herring, and lesser blackback; the coot and the starling, both only after 1940, the latter still confined to cliffs near its presumed landfall in the south-east. Further, the oystercatcher, previously confined to the south-west, has a spectacular spread northward. The blacktailed godwit and the gannet have also pushed up the northern limit of their range, the latter having established three new colonies on the north and east coasts.

Meanwhile, the little auk, the only truly arctic species in Iceland, has entirely deserted one of its two breeding colonies in the north-east, while the other has dwindled to almost nothing; apparently Iceland seas are no longer cold enough for it, or more probably, for the marine crustacea on which it mainly feeds its young. Some plants, too, are moving north, notably the bilberry (*Vaccinium myrtillus*), which has colonized areas previously reserved to dwarf willows; and there have been similar shifts in some of Iceland's insects.

All these changes have become much more pronounced within the last ten to fifteen years.

We in Britain have had numerous examples of bird species spreading northward in the present century, including some birds which have been doing the same thing in Iceland, like the tufted duck, and others like the black redstart, which are quite recent invaders of our islands.

All such observations take on new interest when it is realized that they can contribute to our understanding of a world-wide and secular change of immense significance for our future; and one which is unique, since, in Ahlmann's words, "It is the first fluctuation in the endless series of past and future climatic variations in the history of the earth which we can measure, investigate, and possibly explain."

POPULATION AND HUMAN
FULFILMENT

POPULATION is the problem of our age. The increase of
population, and its relation to resources and to fulness of
life, inevitably obtrudes itself on anyone who, like myself,
happens to travel round the world in the middle of the
twentieth century. The traveller is struck by sheer numbers
as in China, high density as in Java, attempts to control increase as in India, the effects of immigration as in Ceylon
or Fiji, large vacant spaces in Australia, and erosion, deforestation and destruction of wild life almost everywhere.
But the experiences of travel merely highlight and illustrate
in greater detail something that is already obtruding itself
on the world's consciousness—the fact that the increase of
human numbers has initiated a new and critical phase in
the history of our species.

The most striking symbol of this new phase was the
United Nations' Conference on World Population, held in
Rome in 1954—a milestone in history, as being the first
occasion when the subject of human population was surveyed as a whole, and under the aegis of an official international organization.

In point of fact, this was the second step into the new
phase. The first step had been taken in 1949, with the holding of the U.N. Conference on World Resources in Lake
Success—the first attempt to survey the world's material
resources as a whole. When this Conference was being prepared, I was Director-General of Unesco, which, in common
with other specialized agencies of the U.N., such as F.A.O.
and W.H.O., was asked to collaborate in the project. In
formally accepting this invitation, I took it on myself to
suggest informally that a survey of resources would lose
half its value if it were not supplemented by a similar survey
of the population which consumed and used the resources. I
was told that there were political and religious difficulties;
then, as the months passed, that the demographic experts
insisted on the mid-century censuses first being held; and

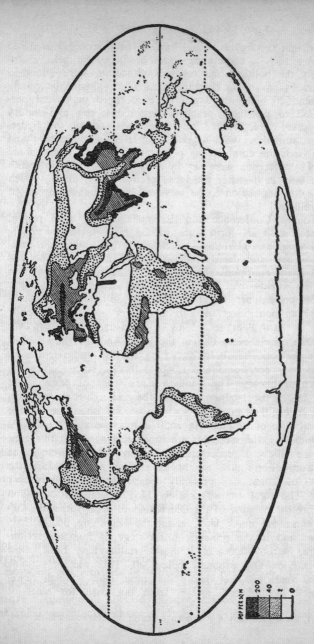

World population density (about 1940-41)

then that the figures would have to be thoroughly analysed before such a conference could profitably be held. Eventually the political and religious difficulties were smoothed over, by arranging that the Conference should be purely "scientific" and should not be encouraged or indeed permitted to pass any practical resolutions; the mid-century censuses were, with a few exceptions, taken; the figures were, sometimes with a good deal of delay, assembled and analysed; the cumbersome preparations for an international U.N. conference were set in motion; and the Conference was duly held—after the lapse of five years, during which time the population to be surveyed had increased by about 30 millions!

To the Conference and its implications I shall return. First I shall set forth some of the facts—often surprising and sometimes alarming—which justify our calling the present a new and decisive phase in human history. The first fact is the enormous absolute size of the present population of the world—over 2½ billion.[1] The second is the amount of its present net increase—some 34 million a year, nearly 4000 an hour, over 60 a minute, over one every second: this is equivalent to adding a good-sized town of over 90,000 people every day of the year. And the third fact is that the total has been increasing steadily and relentlessly, with only occasional and minor setbacks, since before the dawn of history. The 2-billion mark was not passed until the 1920s, the 1-billion mark in the mid-eighteenth century, the half-billion mark somewhere around the time of the Great Fire of London (in 1650 it was about 470 million). Before this, the estimates are much less accurate; but even if we allow a considerable margin of inaccuracy, the quarter-billion mark cannot have been passed before the birth of Christ, and probably not before the third century A.D. The total cannot possibly have reached 100 million before the collapse of the Old Kingdom of Egypt, and probably not till much later, about the beginning of the Iron Age: and in the pre-agricultural stage of human development, before 6000 B.C., it must certainly have been below 30 million and probably below 20. This was only some 8000 years ago, yet before that time, man (though represented by different species from our own for most of

[1] I use billion in the American sense of a thousand million—10^9.

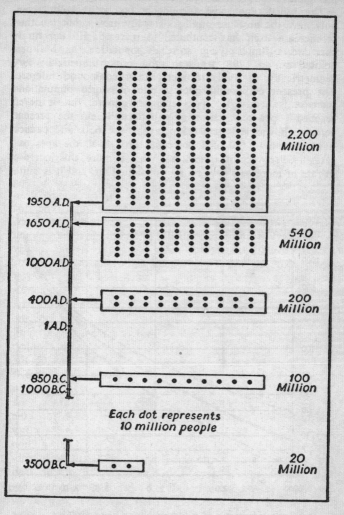

Estimated increase of world population since the dawn of civilization

the period) had existed for at least half a million years.

The fourth and most formidable fact is this—that not only have the absolute numbers steadily grown, but the rate of increase itself has continued to increase. Human numbers are self-multiplying, so that population, as Malthus pointed out in 1798, tends to grow not arithmetically but geometrically: it tends to increase by compound interest. The present compound interest rate of world population-increase is nearly 1⅓ per cent. per annum. But it never reached 1 per cent. per annum until well into the present century. It was less than 0.5 per cent. in 1650, and cannot have exceeded 1/10 of 1 per cent. through all the ages before the discovery of agriculture. What is more, this increase in rate of increase shows no sign of falling off, and it is quite

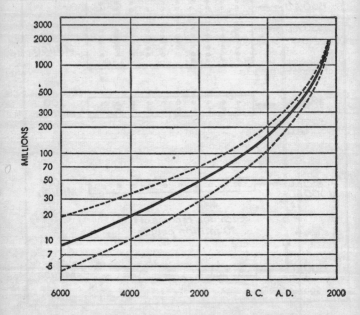

Estimated growth of world population since 6000 B.C.

Note.—The estimated growth is traced in this chart by the heavy curve. The curves above and below it represent upper and lower limits of the estimated growth. The population curve is on a semi-logarithmic scale, so that the slope of the curve is directly proportional to the rate of increase.

safe to prophesy that it will continue to go up for at least several decades, and probably into the twenty-first century.

With this, the prospect becomes really alarming. Let us first remember that, even if the *rate* of increase stayed the same, the absolute *net* increase would still go up each year, for obvious arithmetical reasons.[2] Population increase, in fact, proceeds—or at least has in the past proceeded and is now still proceeding—not at a constant velocity, but by acceleration, and the result has been to convert an early state of virtual stability into one of slow but appreciable growth, then into a rapid expansion, and finally into an explosive process.

The acceleration has not been constant. It has proceeded in a series of upward steps, each step resulting from some new discovery or invention. The essential discoveries are

[2] If the present world population be taken at 2600 million, and its rate of increase at 1 1/3 per cent., its absolute net increase in the course of the next twelve months will be 34 2/3 millions. If the resultant 2634 2/3 million people continue to increase at the same rate, the net increase for the next twelve months will be just over 35 1/8 millions. Since the rate too is increasing, the actual net increase will of course be still larger.

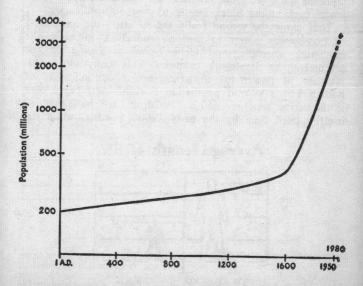

Rate of increase of world population since 1650 (semi-logarithmic scale)

those which provide subsistence for more people. The chief stages in this process are broadly as follows. First, the food-gathering stage, as typified by the Australian aborigines before contact with white civilization. During this stage of human evolution, the maximum world population could not have exceeded a few millions. The invention of organized hunting, as practised by Upper Paleolithic man or by the Plains Indians in their pristine state, would have allowed perhaps a doubling or trebling of maximum human numbers, though never any high density of population: the total population of North America east of the Rockies in pre-Colonial times is estimated at only about one million. The discovery of agriculture had a much bigger effect, and the two or three millennia of the neolithic revolution were marked by a great expansion in human numbers and by great movements of peoples.

The next major step was the step to civilization, with writing and large-scale organization of production, trade, and administration, but still relying for its energy on man-power and beast-power, with a little tapping of wind and water. This permitted population to rise again, in spite of constant wars, recurrent famines, and occasional world pestilences such as the Black Death, to over 500 millions.

Then came the second really radical step—the harnessing of non-human power to human production, initiating the industrial, scientific, and technological revolution of the seventeenth to nineteenth centuries. This many-fold multiplication of power led to a spectacular multiplication of human beings. World population doubled itself twice over in the period between 1650 and 1920, and will have doubled itself a third time by the early 1980s. Further, while the

Average length of life

Average length of life in North America and Britain, and in Asia first doubling took nearly two centuries, the second took well under one century, and the third will have required only about 60 years. Unless something wholly unforeseen happens, the world's present population will be doubled again within half a century.

The excessively rapid acceleration during the present century is due to yet another decisive set of discoveries—the discoveries of physiology, scientific medicine, and hygiene, whose result we may call death-control. Where these discoveries have been fully applied, the expectation of life at birth has more than doubled. This was only about 30 years in Imperial Rome, and did not increase much even in Western Europe until well on in the nineteenth century, but is

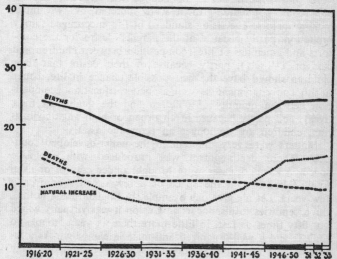

Birth, death and natural increase rates in the United States of America
(1916-1953)

Note.—The figure shows a combination of a low and steady death-rate with a birth-rate which declined by about 1935 to the low level normally associated with Western countries towards the end of their population cycle. Then came the sharp increase which brought births up to the high rate of twenty-four a thousand by 1947, since when it has remained roughly constant. So high a birth-rate and therefore so high a natural increase is a new phenomenon in Western countries which had apparently reached the end of their population cycle.

now about 70 for the people of Britain. The process is just setting in in Asian countries. Thus in India the expectation of life in the decade 1911-21 was only 20: in three decades it had increased to 32. Death-rates dropped from their traditional heights of 35 to 40 per 1000 to less than 10 per 1000 in the more advanced countries, with 7.7 in Holland as the present lowest figure; and infant mortality, during the first year of life, which may reach 30, 40, and even 50 per cent. in primitive communities, has shown the most spectacular fall, to 2.8 per cent. in the U.S.A., with a present minimum of 1.9 per cent. in Sweden. In Britain it was still over 15 per cent. in 1900, but is now only 2.75 per cent.

This differs from all the other previous major steps: it permits people to escape death longer, rather than to support life more efficiently.

In the Western world the change was gradual, and its effects on population-growth were buffered by two interlocking factors. The rising standard of life encouraged family limitation, partly because of the parents' desire for the comforts and amenities of life (competition between children and cars or TV sets), partly because of their desire that their children should have the best possible chance in life, better health and enjoyment as well as better education (competition between quantity of children and the quality of their lives), and partly because in an urban or high-wage civilization, children are no longer an economic asset.

Matters were very different in the under-developed countries. There death-control was introduced with explosive speed. Ancient diseases were brought under control or even totally abolished in the space of a few decades or even a few years. Let me give one example. In England malaria took three centuries to disappear: in Ceylon it was virtually wiped out fifty times as fast, in little more than six years, thanks to D.D.T. and a well-organized anti-malaria campaign. As a result of this and other health measures, the originally high death-rate has fallen to the Western level—from 22 to 12 per 1000—in seven years, a fall which took exactly ten times as long in England. But the birth-rate has not even begun to drop, and so the population is growing at the rate of 2.7 per cent. per annum (nearly twice the highest rate ever experienced in Britain), which if continued will mean doubling in thirty years—about a ninefold increase in a century!

The Reverend Thomas Malthus, a century and a half ago, alarmed the world by pointing out that population-increase

Some crabs, like *Corystes cassivelaunus*, happen to show a crude resemblance to a human face

Starting from such crude accidental resemblance, the Heike crabs from Japan have achieved a startling likeness to the face of a Japanese Samurai fighter—so startling that they are regarded as reincarnations of dead warriors, and are never eaten.

Shape, colouration and pose combine to turn the caterpillar of the Peppered moth into a perfect imitation of a side-twig on a branch.

Butterflies and grasshoppers are among the many insects which escape detection by looking like the leaves among which they live.
Photographs S. Beaufoy

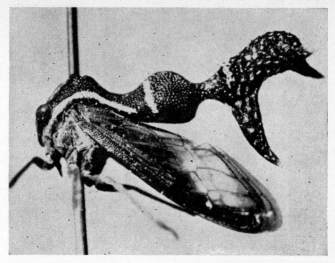

7   8   9

Ants are left alone by most insect eaters; accordingly, they are mimicked by various harmless insects and spiders.

a) This little Membracid plant-bug *(Heteronotus)* is completely concealed from view by a hollow excrescence on its thorax which from above looks exactly like an ant.

b) Spiders may mimic ants by elongating their body, growing a waist and holding their front legs in the position of an ant's antennae.

Left. The harmless clearwing moth has lost the scales on its wings, tapered its abdomen, and becomes coloured in black and yellow circles so as to resemble a hornet.
Photograph S. Beaufoy

Right. This small butterfly has developed a false front at the hind corner of its wings, complete with false head, false eye and false antennae, to deflect the attacks of predators from its true head, which is concealed between the protruding anterior margins of its fore-wings.
Photograph S. Beaufoy

The leaf-fish *Monocirrhus* escapes detection by its prey by looking like a dead leaf drifting in the current. Note the imitation stalk, leaf-tip and mid-rib.

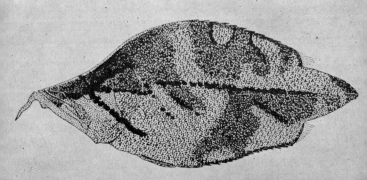

The colour and markings of the hawkmoth *Xanthopan morgani* exactly match the bark on which it rests, but only if it aligns itself in the right direction.

The position adopted by the garden carpet moth *(Xanthorrhoe fluctuata)* also makes it virtually indistinguishable from the lichen-patched surface on which it spends the day.

Most desert plants protect themselves from being eaten by growing formidable spines; but in stony deserts some, like *Lithops*, do so by imitating stones or pebbles.

Some animals show the same adaptation. The grasshopper *Eremocharis* from the Algerian desert resembles a weathered fragment of stone in form, colour, and texture. The outline of the leg is disguised by a frilly flap which is pressed against the body, and at any threat of danger it freezes and the antennae, which might otherwise give it away, are tucked out of sight.

Above. All lantern-bugs have a hollow outgrowth in front of their head. In the alligator bug *Laternia lucifera* this has been moulded into a striking likeness of a miniature alligator's head, with sham eye, sham nostril and a convincing set of sham teeth—quite sufficient to scare off its insect-eating enemies.

Left. The reproduction of the Fly Orchid is assured by its growing flowers that look like female flies. Male flies attempt to mate with them, and so transfer the fertilizing pollen from one flower to another.

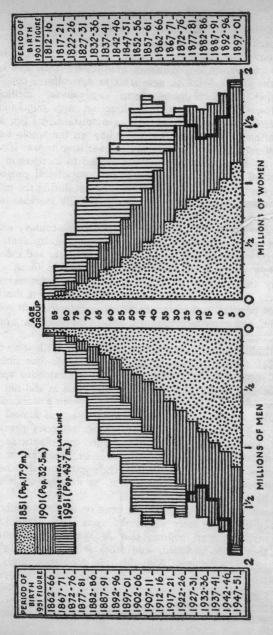

Distribution of the population of England and Wales by age-groups; 1851, 1901, 1951. The period of birth for the 1851 population (dotted area) can be read by subtracting 100 from the figures in the left-hand column, which shows the period of birth of the 1951 population.

Note.—The period of birth for the 1851 population (dotted area) can be read by subtracting 100 from the figures in the left-hand column, which shows the period of birth of the 1951 population.

Legend:
- 1851 (Pop. 17·9 m.)
- 1901 (Pop. 32·5 m.)
- 1951 (Pop. 43·7 m.) AND INSIDE HEAVY BLACK LINE

PERIOD OF BIRTH 1901 FIGURE:
1812–16, 1817–21, 1822–26, 1827–31, 1832–36, 1837–41, 1842–46, 1847–51, 1852–56, 1857–61, 1862–66, 1867–71, 1872–76, 1877–81, 1882–86, 1887–91, 1892–96, 1897–01

PERIOD OF BIRTH 1951 FIGURE:
1862–66, 1867–71, 1872–76, 1877–81, 1882–86, 1887–91, 1892–96, 1897–01, 1902–06, 1907–11, 1912–16, 1917–21, 1922–26, 1927–31, 1932–36, 1937–41, 1942–46, 1947–51

AGE GROUP: 85, 80, 75, 70, 65, 60, 55, 50, 45, 40, 35, 30, 25, 20, 15, 10, 5, 0

MILLIONS OF MEN — MILLIONS OF WOMEN

was pressing more and more insistently on food-supply, and if unchecked would result in widespread misery and even starvation. In recent times, even as late as the 1930s, it had become customary to pooh-pooh Malthusian fears. For one thing, the opening up of new land to agriculture, coupled with the introduction of better agricultural methods, had allowed food-production to keep up with population-increase, and in some areas even to outdistance it. For another, attempts were being made to impugn the whole basis of Malthus' argument. It was pointed out that he was incorrect in saying that food-production tended to increase in an arithmetical progression, as against the geometrical progression of population-increase: food-production during the nineteenth and early twentieth century did actually increase in a more than arithmetical progression.

Now, however, we realize that the nineteenth-century spurt in food-production was a temporary historical incident: it cannot be expected to continue at the same rate, and indeed must slow down as it approaches an inevitable limit; and secondly that, though Malthus' particular formulation was incorrect, there *is* a fundamental difference between the increase of population, which is based on a geometrical or compound-interest growth-mechanism, and of production, which is not.

In primitive societies, population-growth is kept low by the checks of famine, disease, and war, which Malthus noted, and by some form of "birth-control", in the extended sense of deliberate control of population-size, which he did not. It was reserved for Carr-Saunders in his pioneering work, *The Population Problem* (1922), to demonstrate that almost all savage and barbaric and some civilized societies practise some form of population-control—either by infanticide or abortion, or by anti-conceptional drugs or practices, or by long periods of sexual abstinence. Only exceptionally, in a few advanced cultures, has there been no socially recognized system of population-control.

However, during the nineteenth century, artificial methods of family limitation were widely practised in the technologically most advanced culture, that of Western civilization, where they were invented, and from it are beginning to spread to other cultures. With this, the population problem has entered on a new phase. It is no longer primarily a race between population and food-production, but between death-control and birth-control.

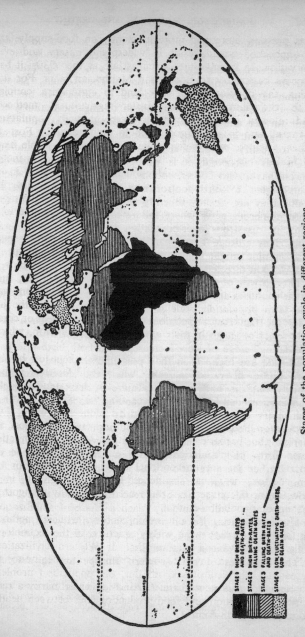

Stages of the population cycle in different regions

STAGE 1 — HIGH BIRTH-RATES AND DEATH-RATES
STAGE 2 — HIGH BIRTH-RATES FALLING DEATH-RATES
STAGE 3 — FALLING BIRTH-RATES AND DEATH-RATES
STAGE 4 — LOW FLUCTUATING BIRTH-RATES, LOW DEATH RATES

Some cultures and groups go so far as to offer vehement opposition to birth-control on ideological grounds. By a strange irony of history, the Catholics and the Communists find themselves united on this point. The Roman Catholic Church lays down that birth-control is contrary to the will of God, while Russian Communism during the Stalinist era went further and asserted that over-population is non-existent, a figment invented by the economist "lackeys" of capitalism to justify "imperialist" and "colonialist" exploitation!

On this last point, it is worth noting that the colonial powers have, with few exceptions, avoided giving official encouragement to birth-control measures even when, as in Malta, they are already urgently needed, and still less in the more numerous cases where failure to apply them now will result in disastrous over-population in one or two generations. This attitude has apparently been due to a fear that local opinion might regard any policy of population-control as a weapon directed against an "inferior" race.[3]

The growth of world population is not uniform, for different countries are in different stages of the population cycle. The term *population cycle* is used by demographers to express the fact that populations usually pass through a definite series of stages in their growth. They begin with a "high fluctuating" stage of slow increase, when both birth-rate and death-rate are high. Then they pass into the "early expanding" phase of rapid increase, when the death-rate falls sharply but the birth-rate stays more or less steadily high. This is succeeded by the "late expanding" stage, during which death-rates continue to fall towards a limiting value and birth-rates show a rapid decline: the population continues to increase, but not so rapidly as in the preceding stage. Finally, both birth- and death-rates reach a low figure and show little further sharp variation. This introduces the "low fluctuating" phase, when increase is still taking place, but is very slow. Once this stage has been reached, we may expect that the population will eventually reach a phase of stabilization unless new sources of food-production are discovered, or new outlets are acquired through conquest or colonization, or new ideas and values begin to operate.

The countries of north-western Europe are in the low

[3] Since this passage was written, Family Planning Schemes have, I am glad to say, been implemented in Jamaica and in Puerto Rico, and the official attitude towards population-control has become more favourable.

fluctuating phase of near-stabilization, while the under-developed countries have now almost all entered on the early expanding stage, a number of them so explosively as to be increasing at rates of 2 or even 3 per cent. per annum, whereas the maximum reached by Europe in its slower cycle was less than 1⅓ per cent. When we remember that an annual increase of 2 per cent. doubles a population in about thirty-five years, and one of 1½ per cent. in under forty-seven years, and then recall that rates of this order are at work in about half the world's 2½ billion inhabitants, we cannot but feel alarmed. If nothing is done to control this flood of people, mankind will drown in its own increase, or, if you prefer a very mixed metaphor, the world's economy will burst at the seams, and mankind will become a planetary cancer.

There are still some optimists who proclaim that "science will find a way out"; or that the situation can be taken care of by taking new land into cultivation, combined with emigration; or by improved agricultural techniques; or by tapping the food resources of the ocean; or by industrialization, which it is hoped will have the same effect as in the advanced countries, of bringing down the birth-rate in correlation with a rising standard of living—or of course by a combination of some or all of these methods.

These arguments seem plausible—until we begin to look at matters quantitatively. Then, it becomes painfully clear to all but incurable or pathological optimists that they just won't and can't achieve the results claimed for them—of stimulating the rate of food-production so that it overtakes or even keeps up with human reproduction. To achieve that result, skill, capital, and time are needed—skilled experts to direct projects, capital to finance them, and above all time—time to clear tropical forests, construct huge dams and irrigation projects, drain swamps, start large-scale industrialization, give training in scientific methods, modernize systems of land tenure, and, most difficult of all, to change traditional habits and attitudes among the bulk of the people. Quite simply there is not enough skill and capital and time available. Their effects will always lag behind the increase of population. Population is always catching up and outstripping production. Since, for instance, the great Lloyd Barrage on the Indus was built, it has brought over 4000 square miles of the earth's surface into cultivation: but within one generation this huge area of new land was fully settled, without in the slightest reducing the density of population in the rest of the Indian sub-continent.

The fact is that an annual increase of 34 million mouths to be fed needs more new food than can possibly go on being added to production year after year. Population-increase to-day has reached such enormous dimensions and acquired such speed that population cannot help winning in a straight race against production. The position is made worse by the fact that the race is not a straight one. Production is severely handicapped, because it starts far behind scratch: according to the latest estimates of the World Health Organization, nearly two-thirds of the world's people are under-nourished. Production has to make good this huge deficiency as well as keeping up with the mere quantitative increase in human numbers.

Is there then no remedy? Of course there is. The remedy is to stop thinking in terms of a race, and to begin thinking in terms of a balance. We need a population policy, and any practical policy involves a pattern of rational compromise.

We must give up the false belief that an increase in the number of human beings is necessarily desirable; and the despairing belief that increase is inevitable; and the fatuous over-optimism that shuts its eyes to the grievous effects of over-population; and the airy assertion that "science" will surely find a way out.

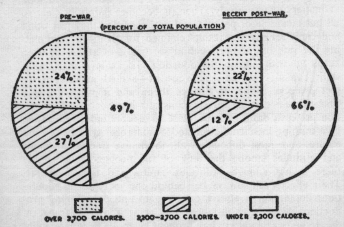

Distribution of world population according to average daily supply of calories

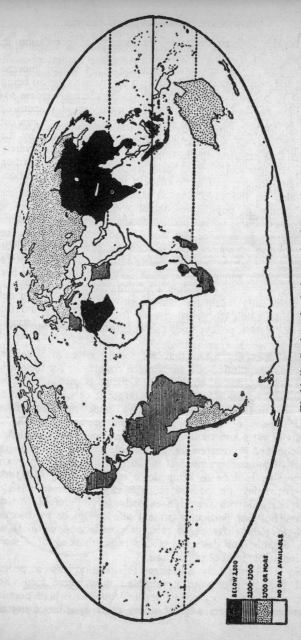

BELOW 2200
2200-2700
2700 OR MORE
NO DATA AVAILABLE

World distribution of calories per head

The production of people, like the production of food, is a fact of nature, using nature comprehensively as it should be used, to include human nature. Like other natural phenomena, both can be studied, understood, and to some extent controlled, though by different methods. Put in another way, if science can and should be applied to increase the rate of food-production, it can and should also be applied to reduce the rate of population-growth or people-production. And for that, as for all scientific advance, we need both basic research and practical application.

In this particular case, basic research is needed not only on new, simpler, and more efficient methods of birth-control, but also on the psychological attitudes of different nations and groups to population-control and family limitation, as well as of course on the precise details of demographic trends in different sections of the world. And practical application will involve measures for overcoming psychological resistances and ensuring popular participation, and for the building of proper administrative machinery and information services, as well as for providing a quantitatively adequate supply of technically adequate contraceptives. But the essential step is to admit the pressing need for a clear-cut and scientific population policy: once this is agreed, the rest will surely follow.

This does not mean that we should envisage a definite optimum population-size for a given country or for the world as a whole. Indeed, to fix such a figure is probably impossible, and to use it as a definite target is certainly unpractical. In matters of population we must get away from static figures of absolute number and think dynamically in terms of rates and trends. For the time being our aim should be confined to correcting undesirable trends. The danger-point of human increase lies in the next thirty or forty years. If nothing is done to bring down its rate during that time, the succeeding period will be exposed to disastrous miseries and charged with the high explosive of billionfold frustration. Thus our particular present aim should be to discover how to reduce over-rapid rates of population-growth. If we can do this, our descendants can begin thinking of a more or less stable level of population.

So far, I have only considered this relation between people and food, and only in its simplest quantitative form. But over-population—or, not to beg any questions, high population-density—affects a great many other spheres of human life, some of which have repercussions on food-production. Thus, to take this last point first, in England agricultural land is being steadily devoured and permanently lost by the growth of towns, of necessary communications—roads, railroads, and aerodromes—of new large-scale industry, and, temporarily at least, by open-cast mining and defence. In many countries, deforestation, even when carried out to provide new land for cultivation, often results in erosion, with an eventual reduction of food-production instead of the hoped-for increase. Wherever population outruns food—as it does now in the billion-and-a-half of the world's population who are undernourished—it reduces human energy and initiative and so impedes higher productivity.

But man does not live by bread alone, nor should he live for bread alone. He needs power and shelter and clothing, and in addition to all material requirements he needs space and beauty, sport and recreation, interest and enjoyment.

Excessive population can erode all these things. Up till now, rapid population-increase has led to hypertrophied cities, so big that they are beginning to defeat their own ends; they are producing discomfort, inefficiency and nervous strain as well as cutting off millions of people from any real contact or sense of unity with nature.

Population-increase also threatens the world's open spaces and the beauty of unspoilt nature. In small countries with high population-density, like England, the pressure on mere space is becoming acute. But even in newer and less densely inhabited countries the process of erosion and destruction is going on, often at an alarming rate. Everywhere, even in Africa, wild life—not merely big game, but wild life in general—is shrinking and often being exterminated: the world's mountains are being invaded by hydro-electric projects, its forests cut down or commercialized, its wildernesses infiltrated by farmers and miners and tourists and other invaders. Even the cultural richness of the world is being impoverished. The pressure of population is being translated into economic and social pressures, which are forcing mass-produced goods into every corner of the globe, pushing people into Western dress and Western habits, sapping ancient cultural ideals and destroying traditional art and craftsmanship.

Indeed, once we start looking at the population problem as a whole and in all its implications, we find ourselves being pressed into a reconsideration of human values in general. First of all we must reject the idea that mere quantity of human beings is of value apart from the quality of their lives. Then, after realizing that all existence is a process of transformation or evolution, that the human species in its cultural evolution is continuing and extending the process of biological evolution from which it arose, that the well-rounded and developed human personality is the highest product of the evolutionary process of which we have any knowledge, but that the human individual cannot achieve full development except in the environment provided by an adequate society, we find ourselves inevitably driven to the ideal of fulfilment—greater fulfilment for more fully developed human individuals.

Accordingly, the values we must pursue are those which permit or promote greater human fulfilment. Food and health, energy and leisure are its necessary bases: its value-goals are knowledge and interest, beauty and emotional expression, inner integration and outer participation, enjoyment and a sense of significance. In practice these values often come into competition and even conflict; so to achieve greater fulfilment we need a pattern of compromise and mutual adjustment between values.

The space and the resources of our planet are limited. Some we must set aside for the satisfaction of man's material needs—for food, raw materials, and energy. But we must set aside others for more ultimate satisfactions—the enjoyment of unspoilt nature and fine scenery, the interest of wild life, travel, satisfying recreation, beauty in place of ugliness in human building, and the preservation of the variety of human culture and of monuments of ancient grandeur.

In practice this means limiting the use to which some areas are put. You cannot use ploughed fields to land aircraft on, you cannot grow crops in built-over areas, you cannot permit exploitation or unrestricted "development" in national parks or nature sanctuaries. In the long run, you cannot avoid paying the price for an unrestricted growth of human numbers: and that price is ruinous.

It is often asserted that science can have no concern with values. On the contrary, in all fields of Social Science, and (in rather a different way) wherever the applications of Natural Science touch social affairs and affect human living, science *must* take account of values, or it will not be doing its job satisfactorily. The population problem makes this obvious. As soon as we recall that *population* is merely a collective term for aggregations of living human beings, we find ourselves thinking about relations between quantity and quality—quantity of the human beings in the population and quality of the lives they lead: in other words, *values*.

Though I may seem to have painted the picture of world population in gloomy colours, there is hope. Just as the horrible destructiveness of atomic warfare is now prompting a reconsideration of warfare in general, and seems likely to lead to the abandonment of all-out war as an instrument of national policy, so I would predict that the threat of over-population to human values like health, standard of living, and amenity will prompt a reconsideration of values in general and lead eventually to a new value-system for human living. But time is of the essence of the contract. If before the end of the century the rate of human increase is not lowered, instead of continuing to rise, so many values will have been damaged or destroyed that it will be difficult to re-create them, let alone to build a new and better system. It has taken ten years for the atomic threat to affect world thought and action: how long will it take for the less spectacular but more insidious reproductive threat to do so?

So far I have been dealing with the problem of world population in general. Now I shall take some individual cases, as illustrating particular aspects of it.

Let me begin with Indonesia. The outstanding fact is the extraordinary difference between different parts of the Republic. Java is the most densely populated large island in the world, with over 50 million people on its 50,000 square miles. In spite of its being almost entirely an agricultural country, the density of its population is nearly twice that of the highly industrialized United Kingdom. Though its area is under a tenth of the whole Republic, it carries over two-thirds of the population. The contrast with the adjacent island of Sumatra is especially striking. Sumatra is well over three times the area of Java, but has a population well under a fifth as big, giving a density of less than one-seventeenth. Indonesian Borneo is even larger in area, and has an even lower population-density.

In Java, the cultivable land is very fertile, but there is less than two-fifths of an acre per head. Though rice is the staple diet, so much land is devoted to exportable products that rice has to be imported to feed the people, even at the insufficient level of about 2000 calories per head per day. Death-rates have dropped somewhat in recent decades, but birth-rates hardly at all, with the result that the population—

universally recognized as already excessive—is increasing at a compound-interest rate of at least 1½ per cent., with some three-quarters of a million people added each year. The proximity of large under-populated areas like Sumatra and Borneo has fostered the idea that Java's over-population could be solved by transfers of people within the Republic. But this facile suggestion has proved to be quite impractical. With considerable difficulty, the Indonesian authorities have settled a number of Javanese in Sumatra. But their total was only a fraction of Java's annual increase, and even so, many of the settlers could not stand the hardships of pioneering agriculture and have drifted away into a depressed urban life on the coasts of Sumatra, or found a way to return to Java. The fact is that to convert a region of dense equatorial forest to agricultural production is a formidable undertaking, demanding as much capital and technological skill as any large hydro-electric or irrigation project—and considerably more in the way of experts, administrators, and leaders. Indonesia simply does not have the necessary financial, material, and human resources.

This is not to say that settlement should not be attempted. Of course it should be, and on the largest possible scale. But the largest possible scale cannot possibly cope with more than a small part of Java's annual surplus of people. Improved agricultural practice is also necessary, and better marketing methods, and some degree of industrialization, not to mention political stability—but, in addition, birth-control. Unfortunately there is no sign yet that the Indonesian Government recognizes this last necessity.

If the necessity for birth-control has not been officially recognized where over-population is starkly obvious, as in Java, it has naturally not been recognized in islands like Bali, where population-density is only a little more than half that of Java (though even so it exceeds 500 per square mile). The Balinese too live mainly on rice, grown on the lovely rice-terraces which add so much to the island's beauty. The planting and harvesting of the rice are community affairs, carried out under careful regulation and to the accompaniment of shared rituals and ceremonies. Bali still just about feeds itself: but if population continues to grow at its present high rate, it will seriously outstrip food-production in two or at most three generations.

Bali provides an extreme illustration of another problem stemming from the general expansion of world population

—the erosion of cultural variety. The Balinese have a rich and vital cultural tradition, in which beauty and significant participation are part of everyday living. Every aspect of life is marked by some celebration or embellished with some form of decoration. Every Balinese participates in some form of creative activity—music, dance, drama, carving, painting, or decoration. What is more, the tradition is not rigid, and the culture is a living and growing one, in which local and individual initiative are constantly introducing novelty and fresh variety.

But the Balinese are afflicted with many preventable diseases: they are largely illiterate (though far from uncultured); their religion is now being undermined by the Christian missionaries who have at last been allowed to work in Bali; growing economic pressure forces them to take advantage of the flood of cheap mass-produced goods, originating from Western technology, to which they are now being exposed; their mounting population demands some adaptation to modern industrial life if living standards are to be raised or even maintained; and this in turn is imposing a Westernized scientifically based system of compulsory education.

Most foreign residents prophesy that Bali's vital culture is doomed, and will wither and die within ten or fifteen years. This may be over-gloomy, but certainly Balinese culture is in danger, and will die out or be debased by bastard Westernization unless something is done to check its decline. The question is what, and how? I can only hope that the Indonesian Government will realize the value, to their own country and to the world, of this rich product of the centuries, and that Unesco will justify the C in its name— C for Culture—and do all in its power to help. No one wants to keep the Balinese in a state of ill-health and ignorance: but instead of being pushed by the well-meaning but ill-considered efforts of over-zealous missionaries and administrators and "scientific" experts to believe that their traditional culture is a symbol of backwardness, to be sacrificed on the twin altars of Christian doctrine and technological advance, they could be encouraged in the truer and profounder belief in the essential validity of their indigenous arts and ceremonials, and helped in the task of adapting them to modern standards. A traditional culture, like a wild species of animal or plant, is a living thing. If it is destroyed, the world is the poorer; nor can it ever be artificially re-created. But being alive, it can evolve to meet new conditions. It is an urgent but a sadly neglected task of the present age to discover the means whereby the flowerings of culture shall not be extinguished by the advances of science and technique, but shall co-operate with them in the general enrichment of life. And in coping with this task we must not forget that population-increase can make it more difficult, by forcing people to think more of how merely to keep alive, less of how to live.

The situation of Siam, or Thailand as it is now officially called, is in some ways not unlike that of Bali. It is not yet over-populated; it is in the fortunate position of producing enough rice not only to feed its own people but to export a considerable amount to less fortunate countries. Its people are well fed and look cheerful. The general impression of happiness is in strong contrast with the depressing atmosphere of much of Indian life (though the stimulating feeling of devoted national effort and scientific leadership is also absent). Thailand is proud of its past, and especially of the fact that it alone of South-East Asian countries has never lost its independence. There is a traditional culture in which the bulk of the people are content to find fulfilment, though there is not so much active participation or artistic creativeness as in Bali.

Thailand is crowded with various foreign organizations and agencies, international and national, which are giving advice and assistance on every possible subject—health and agriculture, democracy and scientific development, administration and industry, education and fish-ponds and rural community life. As a result, the traditional culture is being eroded or undercut. Food-production is beginning to go up and death-rates to fall; but unless birth-rates also fall, Thailand will lose her happy distinction among Asian countries and will become seriously over-populated well before the end of the century.

A partial remedy would seem to lie in the better co-ordination of the various departments of Government and the motley collection of foreign agencies, and the framing of a comprehensive plan which would take account of population and traditional culture as well as of food-production and industry, science and education.

Fiji is another group of islands with another problem. Its population of about a third of a million is made up of two separate populations, which at present are about equal in numbers—the indigenous Fijians and the immigrant Indians —together with a handful of Europeans, Chinese and others.

The history of the two populations is instructive. The impact of white intrusion caused, or at least was correlated with, a decline in Fijian numbers. These must have been nearly 200,000 in 1850, but only about 150,000 when the islands were taken over by the British in 1874. A succession of epidemics, beginning with measles, which in 1875 killed 40,000 people, and going on through whooping cough, influenza, dengue, and cerebro-spinal meningitis, steadily reduced the population, which numbered 115,000 at the first census in 1881, to a low point well under 100,000. The health measures introduced by an alarmed administration then began to take effect. In the first decade of the twentieth century the decline was reversed, and a slow increase set in which, in spite of a bad setback from the Spanish flu at the end of World War I, has continued to bring the Fijian population up to its present figure of around 140,000.

Indian immigration started in 1879, and has continued to the present day; but now nearly 90 per cent. of Indians in Fiji are native-born, and their rate of increase has gone up to a figure well above that of the Fijians. As a result the Indian population outstripped the Fijian during World War II, and is now over 150,000. If there is no change in the trends, Indians will in the space of two or three generations constitute a large majority of the islands' people.

The two groups are very different in cultural background, interests, and work-habits as well as in physique. The Fijians have the finest physique I have ever seen: they make good soldiers and wonderful athletes. But their athletic and warlike propensities have induced no very great keenness for Western education, and a definite dislike of regular agricultural work. As the economy of Fiji depends primarily on its sugar crop, labour for the sugar plantations had to be found: and the Indians have provided it. They make excellent labourers and small farmers and traders, and have a notable thirst for education. Deeming the Government's educational provisions inadequate, they have even started secondary schools on their own initiative and at their own expense.

There is little intermarriage between the two groups, and indeed little liking. The Indians tend to regard the Fijians as barbarian and backward, while the Fijians (who still take a sneaking pride in their cannibal past) find the Indians effeminate and affect to despise their laborious way of life. However, there are now signs of a rapprochement, and some of the younger Fijians are realizing that they must change their attitude to work and to education if the Fijian community is not to lapse into a sort of living fossil, cushioned by the protective measures of the colonial government.

The fact of rapid Indian increase has had various repercussions. It has largely contributed to bring about this new Fijian attitude. And once this new attitude is realized in practice, and the Fijians accept Western standards more whole-heartedly, their death-rate is bound to fall and their numbers to jump rapidly up. Since the Indian rate of increase shows no signs of falling, a demographic crisis looms ahead: Fiji will become over-populated within the lifetime of its younger inhabitants. This appears inevitable—unless something is done about it, something in the way of introducing the people, Fijians and Indians alike, to the necessity and desirability of family limitation, and of providing birth-control facilities as an integral part of the health services. We can only hope that too much economic distress and social misery will not be required to force the action that present intelligent foresight could undertake—and could now undertake with much less difficulty than when the cohorts of the yet unborn have swelled the population to disastrous proportions.

Australia is a storm-centre of demographic controversy. She is an entire continent (albeit the smallest of the seven), with an area of close on 3 million square miles—almost the size of the U.S.A. and nearly 2½ times that of India—but with only 9 million human inhabitants.

In spite of this low density of population—a mere three people to the square mile—she is committed to a White Australia policy, and admits no Asians or Africans (or I presume Amerindians) as immigrants. Yet she is on Asia's back doorstep. Australia lies only a few hundred miles from the eastern outpost of Indonesia, less than a thousand from its grossly over-populated heartland of Java, which has to carry six times Australia's number of people on a sixtieth of its area; and the three great swarming countries of Asia —India, China, and Japan—have for decades been casting longing eyes on Australian space as a possible outlet for their surplus people: if the Axis Powers had won the war, large-scale settlements of Japanese would undoubtedly have been imposed on Australia.

However, Australia's open spaces are, from the point of view of human occupation, largely a mirage. Most of them are destined to remain indefinitely open, demographic blanks on the world's map. Three-quarters of Australia is desert with under ten inches of rain a year, or semi-desert with under twenty. And even this pittance of rainfall cannot be counted on: it comes in cycles. Again and again settlers have hopefully taken up marginal land, only to have their hopes dashed by a succession of rainless years at the low point of the cycle.

At the present time, only 2½ per cent. of the land surface is being cultivated. It is true that big irrigation schemes are being planned, and that the discovery that much poor land could be enriched by adding trace elements is heartening the farmers and vine-growers and pastoralists. But heavy additions of fertilizers would also be needed, and these, like irrigation schemes, are expensive.

Never is a big word: but it looks as if much of the land can never be brought into cultivation. Either there is no water at all for irrigation; or the only water available is salty; or the soil is lateritic or otherwise wretched and wholly unworkable. I was driven down from Darwin to Alice Springs, three days and a thousand miles—a thousand miles of increasingly sparse bush on increasingly stony and barren soil, miserable and for the most part quite intractable to human effort. The best estimates put 7½ per cent. as the maximum area of Australia's surface which can be brought into cultivation, and even to achieve this will demand great effort and great expense.

Australia *is* under-populated, in the double sense that it could support a larger population, and that a larger population would benefit its economy. How much larger is the question. Some say 50 million more people; but this seems very over-optimistic. A total of 25 or at most 30 million seems more reasonable. And this would absorb less than one year's increase of Asia's population, less than five years' of that of India alone.

Furthermore, though the Australian Government recognizes that Australia is under-populated, and encourages immigration by assisted passages and settlement schemes, the country is hard put to it to cope with the problem of keeping up living standards in face of the present rate of population-growth. This, when immigration is added to natural increase, is one of the highest in the world—some 2½ per cent. per annum; and living standards can only be maintained if considerable capital and energy is diverted into industry and the exploitation of mineral wealth. Thus as soon as the

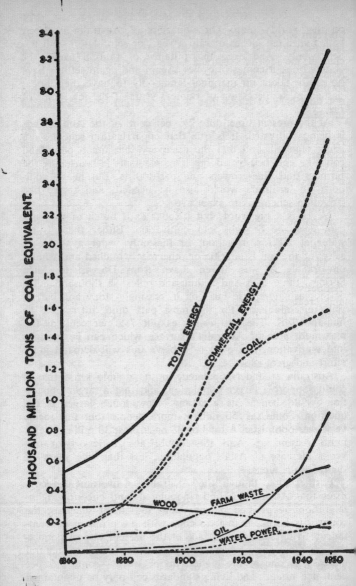

Growth of world consumption of energy, 1860-1950.

problem is looked at not in the static terms of existing population-density and production but in terms of relative rates of change, the idea of Australia as an outlet for the spillover of Asia becomes chimerical. The highest rate of human absorption possible without jeopardizing economic health could not take care of more than a tiny fraction of Asia's annual increase.

The White Australian policy remains as an affront to Asian sentiment. But this too has strong arguments in its favour. Certainly it cannot and should not be justified on racial grounds. There is no such thing as radical or permanent racial superiority or inferiority: all races and ethnic groups are capable of a high level of development and of participating effectively in human progress.

But it can be justified on cultural grounds. It is an empirical fact that cultural differences can create grave difficulties in national development. They often do so when cultural and racial differences are combined. A large minority group which clings to its own standards and its own cultural and racial distinctiveness inevitably stands in the way of national unity and creates all sorts of social, political, and economic frictions. And if it multiplies faster than the rest of the popula-

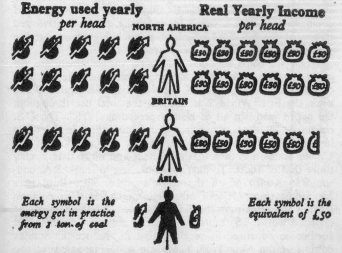

Energy used yearly
per head

Real Yearly Income
per head

NORTH AMERICA

BRITAIN

ASIA

Each symbol is the energy got in practice from 1 ton of coal

Each symbol is the equivalent of £50

Annual consumption of energy and annual income in North America, Britain and Asia.

tion, the problem is aggravated, as we have seen in Fiji.

It is probably true that the introduction of brown, yellow, or black labour would in the short run give a boost to the exploitation of Australia's hot tropical northern areas. But in the long run it would almost certainly result in complications and difficulties which would far outweigh its immediate advantages.

It should be put on record that there is little colour prejudice in Australia. The watchword for the aborigines, the only non-white permanent inhabitants of the continent, is now assimilation—a policy of gradually incorporating the blackfellows into the country's social and economic life. Under the Colombo Plan, and similar international schemes, Australia is now not only admitting a number of Asians as students or trainees, but giving them the best of opportunities and a very friendly welcome. What Australia seeks to guard against is the creation of permanent racial-cultural minorities.

Resources and their consumption are the obverse of the population problem. Like population, consumption shows alarming differentials as between different regions and nations. Even in food these are serious enough. The daily calorie intake of some countries, like Ireland, with 3500 per head, or the U.S.A., is more than double that of others, like India's with only 1590. And these figures are of course only averages: the under-privileged groups of the under-privileged countries will have a much lower intake, the over-privileged classes of the favoured countries a much higher one, giving nearly a fourfold instead of a twofold range.

When we come to other resources, the contrasts are far more startling. The Paley Report found that "the quantity of most metals and mineral fuels used in the United States since the First World War exceeds the total use throughout the entire world in all of history preceding 1918". The U.S. consumes 80 times more iron per capita than India, while in the field of energy the per capita consumption of the United States is double that of Britain and more than twenty times that of India. To-day, space-heating in the U.S.A. consumes one-third of all the world's oil; another third goes for motor transport and other internal-combustion engines; leaving the remaining third for the needs of the rest of the civilized world. The fantastic disparity between countries can further be visualized by recalling that to produce the Sunday edition of the *New York Times* alone during one year one must cut down a forest roughly the size of Staffordshire.

As facts like these seep into the world's consciousness, they affect the world's conscience. Such inequalities, once brought into the open, appear intolerable. The underprivileged are feeling an increasingly strong sense of injustice, while the over-privileged are beginning to experience a sense of shame. This guilty feeling finds a partial outlet in the various international schemes for Technical Assistance and Aid to under-developed countries. But these schemes are not nearly bold or big enough. We need a World Development Plan on a scale at least tenfold greater than all existing schemes put together, a joint enterprise in which all nations would feel they were participating and working towards a common goal. To achieve even the roughest of justice for all peoples, the favoured nations of the world will have not merely to cough up a fraction of their surpluses but voluntarily to sacrifice some of their high standard of living; and to qualify for aid and indeed for membership in the international development club, under-developed countries would have not only to pledge themselves to hard and intelligent work, but also to be willing to restrict their populations by initiating effective policies of birth-control and family planning.

Nothing short of this will ensure a reasonable and enduring balance between population and resources, and transform the present atmosphere of frustration into one of fulfilment.

Since the end of the war, a small but hopeful beginning has been made. A new phenomenon has occurred in the world's history: the first official policies of population-control have been launched. What is more, they are not the desperate gestures of small countries helplessly seeking relief from overcrowding, but the deliberate instruments of two large and powerful nations, India and Japan.

Japan I was unable to visit, but its demographic plight is so extreme and so illuminating that I will take it first. It is not only over-populated, but technically highly developed. It is an island country, with 90 million people crowded into an area only one and a half times as great as that of Britain, and so mountainous that there is only one-seventh of an acre of cultivable land per head. And its population is increasing by over 1 per cent. per annum, so that within ten years it will easily overshoot the 100 million mark.

The Japanese are not well-nourished: the average daily calorie intake is only 2000. They have, however, developed agricultural methods so efficiently that the rice yield per acre (rice is of course their staple food) is far the highest in

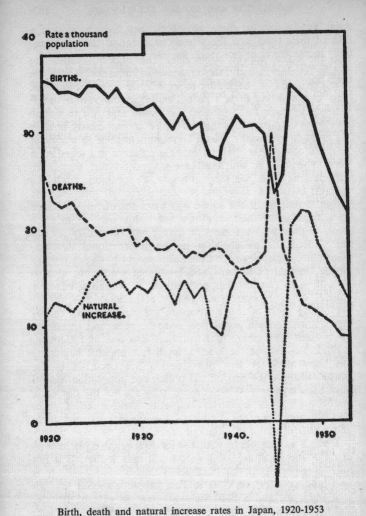

Birth, death and natural increase rates in Japan, 1920-1953

Note.—From 1920 till the early 1940's, birth- and death-rates irregularly declined with a wide gap between them, resulting in a large natural increase. In 1945 the war came to an end following the explosion of the first atom bombs and Japan was plunged in confusion. The death-rate rose sharply and became higher than the birth-rate, which decreased abruptly. Thereafter death-rates fell sharply, reaching a figure below nine a thousand in 1953. At the same time the birth-rate briefly shot up to the level of the early twenties, when the rate of natural increase exceeded 2 per cent a year. Later it fell sharply.

Asia. Yet in spite of these two facts, they have to import a fifth of their food, and there is no prospect of their substantially increasing their rice yields further.

The war has lost them their empire, and robbed them of their hopes of new outlets for settlement or emigration, while the fact that China has become Communist has, for the time being at least, deprived Japan of its biggest market. It is only through United States aid that post-war Japan has been able to secure enough food to live and enough fuel to keep its industrial economy active. As the P.E.P. Report on World Population and Resources says, "Japan is undoubtedly the most over-populated great country there has ever been."

In his *Human Fertility*, Robert C. Cook states the fourfold possibilities before Japan: (1) continued and increasing subsidization by the U.S. or other foreign powers; (2) immensely increased industrial and commercial development; (3) drastic population control; (4) a miracle. Both miracles and indefinite foreign aid are, to say the least of it, highly improbable, and an increase of industry and trade sufficient by itself to take care of population-increase is quantitatively impossible. So the Japanese Government have embarked on a firm policy of population-control. There are only three ways of limiting population—by destroying the life of children after birth, of embryos and foetuses before birth, or of gametes before conception: in other words, infanticide, abortion, and conception-control. In Japan, infanticide persisted later than in any other civilized country, for it continued to be widely practised up till some eighty years ago, when it was dropped under the influence of the new policies of imperialism and population-expansion. These, however, eventually brought not only disaster but a violent aggravation of the demographic problem, through the enforced repatriation of 5 million people from the mainland of Asia after the war. Faced with this desperate situation, the Government took desperate measures. To implement a contrary policy of self-sufficiency and population-control, it turned to abortion. In 1948, under the euphemistically titled "Eugenics Protection Law", termination of pregnancy was legalized and indeed encouraged. As a result, the number of induced abortions rose from a quarter of a million in 1949 to well over a million in 1953. As was to be expected, the results on the health of Japanese women were serious and often deplorable—and yet the annual percentage rate of population-increase has not even been reduced to the pre-war level.

With these stark facts in mind, in 1954 the Japanese Minister of Health's Institute of Population Problems passed a strong resolution urging Government encouragement of conception-control, with widespread propaganda and the provision of birth-control facilities as part of the Health Services, as well as ample research and the inclusion of family planning in the medical curriculum, and with the duty of medical men who have induced an abortion to provide the woman with information about birth-control. There are no recommendations for a family welfare service as in India; and in the following resolution—"in relation to wage payments as well as the taxation system, measures should be taken to avoid provisions which may be interpreted as encouraging large families"—the Council seem even to suggest the penalisation of couples who produce too many children.

Drastic though these recommendations are, they or something very like them are necessary, and it is much to be hoped that they will be speedily and thoroughly implemented. If not, within a very brief space of time Japan will have been pushed into a state of explosive misery and frustration. If, on the contrary, they are successfully put into practice, they may not only save Japan from disaster but will provide valuable lessons for other countries.

India's problem is rather different. The demographic situation is not so desperate (though if nothing is done to remedy it, it will become desperate within a few decades). Then India is not a small and insular country, but the best part of a sub-continent, with large resources waiting to be developed. Here again, however, complacent optimism is out of place: it is difficult to see how enough new capital and new skill could be made available fast enough to overtake existing population-increase and raise the general standard of living. Yet without this, there will be no automatic fall of the birth-rate, and the inexorable pressure of population will continue.

Again, India's rate of increase is not notably high. It is only just under 1⅓ per cent. per annum, which is lower than that in the U.S. (which is 1.6 per cent., excluding immigration). But there is an immense amount of leeway to make up before the barest minimum of decent living is achieved. The average daily calorie intake is a mere 1590, and at least two-thirds of India's 380 million people are under-nourished. Methods of cultivation and systems of land tenure are primitive and will need a painful and difficult process of improvement before they begin to satisfy modern requirements. Tradition, ignorance, and illiteracy are grave obstacles to progress; and so are superstitions like the sanctity of cows, unjust social systems like caste, and ancient habits like child marriage and the ban on the remarriage of widows.

There is relatively little land which can fruitfully be brought into cultivation, even with the aid of large-scale emigration projects, and the outlets for emigration (which at the best of times could take care only of a small fraction of population-increase) are being steadily restricted. Deforestation has brought about a vicious spiral of decreasing fertility, through forcing the use of cow-dung as fuel, and so progressively robbing the soil of necessary ingredients. The influence of Gandhi's hostility to mechanization, though diminishing in face of obvious necessity, is still making itself felt.

Above all, the mere size of the problem is formidable. Even at the present rather modest rate, 5 million people are added each year: the net increase of India's population in the last decennial period between censuses was greater than the total population of Great Britain.

The size of this human flood was forcibly brought home to me by the Kumbh Mela, which I visited in 1954. The

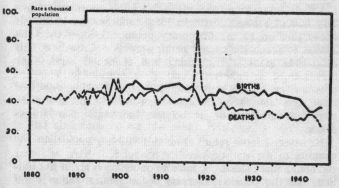

Estimated annual birth- and death-rates in India, 1881-1946

Note.—Until about 1900 birth- and death-rates fluctuated above and around forty a thousand. Shortly after 1900 the birth-rate assumed an ascendency which, with the exception of a short period about 1919 during which death-rates soared to a sharp peak, has been maintained since. The peak in death-rates was caused by the pandemic of influenza, and was accompanied by a decline in the birth-rate. In the mid-thirties the birth-rate began to fall slightly, the decrease becoming temporarily more pronounced in the early forties.

Kumbh Mela is a religious festival held at the junction of the two great rivers, the Jumna and the Ganges, at Allahabad. The assembled pilgrims acquire merit and salvation by bathing in the sacred waters. Every twelfth year, the festival is especially sacred: and the Kumbh Mela of 1954 was uniquely important as being the first of these twelfth-year high points to occur after India's independence.

Pilgrims had come from all over the sub-continent—some walking hundreds of miles on foot, a few by plane or car, others by bullock-carts, others in convergent streams of special trains. The festival lasts for a couple of weeks, and anyone dying there during this period is believed to obtain great advantages in the later progress of his soul. But one day is especially holy, and to bathe on that day especially efficacious. Allahabad has not much more than a quarter of a million inhabitants: yet when we visited it, there were 2½ million pilgrims encamped on the flats by the river, and three days later, on the great day of the festival, the number had grown to 4¼ million! Such quantities, though all drawn from one nation, dwarf the international gatherings of Rome's Holy Year or Islam's Mecca, and make the most famous pilgrimages of earlier centuries, like Compostella or Canterbury, seem small indeed.

I shall never forget the spectacle of this enormous transitory human ant-heap, with its local condensation of crowds converging on to the temporary pontoon bridges over the Jumna to reach the sacred bathing-grounds. Crowds of this magnitude made a frightening and elemental impression: they seemed so impersonal and so uncontrollable. This impression was all too well justified by the shocking events of three days later, when the crowd got out of hand and trampled four hundred of its helpless individual members to death.

However, I must return from this visible manifestation of quantity to the statistical reality behind it. I have said that the net annual increase of India's population is about five million. But the potential increase is far greater. India is still in the early expanding stage of the population cycle. According to the latest available figures the birth-rate is high—about 40 per 1000, well over double that of north-western European countries—and shows few signs of dropping; and though the death-rate has begun to fall (it is now about 27 per 1000) it has a long way to go yet before it approaches the level of advanced countries. The point is, however, that it has begun to fall, and is certain to fall considerably further in the next few decades, thanks to the policy of the Ministry of Health. A recent official report concluded that the adoption of quite elementary health measures, such as are well within the reach of an energetic Health Ministry, could save another 3 million lives a year. This, if nothing is done to control births, would bring India's net annual increase of population up to 8 million—roughly the equivalent of adding a new London each year!

Calcutta was another manifestation of India's mere bulk. The hypertrophic overgrowth of cities has been a constant accompaniment of the growth of population: the hypertrophy of Calcutta has been exceptionally rapid and severe. In 1901 the population of greater Calcutta was under 1 million: in 1941 it was about 2¾ million: to-day it is over 5 million. In spite of the notorious overcrowding of its appalling slums, at night the pavements are strewn with people who have nowhere else to sleep—just how many, nobody seems to know, but probably near 100,000—and are forced to share the streets with the miserable roaming cattle. I shall always remember, as I drove through the busiest part of the city on the evening of my first day there, seeing a man and a cow approach a traffic refuge in a busy street from opposite angles, and compose themselves for the night on either side of the policeman directing the traffic. This urban hypertrophy was temporarily accentuated by floods of refugees after partition: but it will continue as long as over-population sends poor landless villagers crowding into the city in search of work.

The Government of the new, independent India born in 1947 showed a refreshing courage in grasping this formidable nettle. Recognizing that superabundance of people was one of the major obstacles to Indian prosperity and Indian progress, they made the control of population a major plank in their first Five Year Plan. The Census Commissioner of India, in his report on the 1951 census, put the problem starkly in quantitative terms. Efforts to keep pace with the existing rate of population-growth by increasing food-production were bound to fail, he said, when the population passed 450 million (which with existing trends will happen in less than fourteen years). If, however, India could "reduce the incidence of improvident maternity to about 5 per cent", an increase of 24 million tons a year in agricultural production would be sufficient to feed the people and bring "a visible reduction of human suffering and promotion of human happiness".

Population-control was assigned to the Health Ministry, which set up a representative and quite strong Committee to advise the Minister (who, improbably enough, was and is a woman and a Christian). Some valuable work is being done. Thus this last year grants were made for research on new contraceptives and on the effectiveness and acceptability of existing ones; for the study of demographic problems such as the relation of high birth- and death-rates to social and economic conditions; for the establishment of a training centre for workers in the field of family planning and maternal and child welfare; for educating public opinion about family planning and the need for population-control; and to help the existing family planning ventures of State governments and voluntary organizations.

It is encouraging that a great country like India should make population-control part of its national policy. But it must be confessed that the effects are as yet small, and that to the outside observer the execution of the policy seems somewhat half-hearted.

Let me take an example. The one large-scale experiment initiated by the Government itself has been a pilot study of the so-called rhythm method of birth-control or conception-avoidance, carried out at the Government's request by the World Health Organization. The Roman Catholic authorities, realizing that some means of family limitation are essential, but committed to the doctrinal thesis that ordinary birth-control methods are immoral because they involve the destruction of life and are allegedly "unnatural", have sanctioned the rhythm method as being "natural", since it takes advantage of the fact of human nature that women are infertile during part of each monthly period. (In parenthesis, the method does involve just as much destruction of life as any other, since the man's living spermatozoa are all doomed to die, and the woman's living ovum will perish unfertilized.) However, there is so much variation in the "safe period", both between individuals and between the period of one individual, that it is notoriously unreliable.

I had the opportunity when in India of visiting the chief centre of the project near Mysor (there was a second in Delhi), and of a long talk with the capable and attractive woman in charge, a Negro social scientist from the U.S.A. The results were interesting. In the first place, the encour-

aging fact emerged that when the situation was properly
explained, about three-quarters of the married people in the
village said they would like to learn some method of limiting
their families—though in many cases their marriage partner
said no. Then came the staff's task of discovering the individual cycles of the women who wanted to learn, and then
the women's task of practising the method. To facilitate this,
each woman was given a kind of rosary, with the number of
beads equal to the number of days of her usual cycle, and
different-coloured beads for "safe days" and "baby days".

A number of women managed to avoid pregnancy during
the ten months of the experiment. The social scientist in
charge thought about 20 per cent. of Indian villagers might
learn to practice the method successfully: but this was a
maximum, and in any widespread campaign the figure is
more likely to be 15 or 10 per cent. Thus the general result
of the study was what could have been expected—that the
natural irregularities of the cycle, combined with the practical difficulties of adjusting sexual behaviour to the rhythm,
conspired to make the method quite inadequate as sole or
main means of population-control.

Methods used in Western countries are difficult to apply in
India, partly because of the cost of appliances and materials,
partly because of the lack of privacy and hygienic facilities
in the vast majority of Indian homes. In addition, there is the
persistent influence of Gandhi. Gandhi, as he narrates in his
autobiography, indulged excessively in sexual pleasure after
his marriage: indeed he considers that he was only enabled to
continue his intellectual development by the abstinence enforced on him by the custom which sends the young Indian
bride to her parents' home for a considerable part of each
year. As a result of his self-disgust at his own indulgence,
coupled with his general dislike of anything he considered
as scientific materialism, he pronounced against all mechanical or chemical methods of birth-control, and solemnly rec-
ommended abstinence as the cure for India's population
problem. In spite of the obvious absurdity of believing that
this could possibly be effective, Gandhi's prestige is still so
great that his views still influence those of many people,
notably by stiffening their resistance to the official use of
normal methods of birth-control.

The ideal solution would be the discovery of what laymen
(to the annoyance of scientific and medical experts) persist in
calling "The Pill"—something cheap and harmless which

when taken by mouth will temporarily prevent conception—either by preventing ovulation or perhaps by rendering the ovum unfertilizable. A number of promising substances are being investigated, including some extracts of plants used by primitive peoples. But so far nothing satisfactory has emerged: one substance turns out to be an early abortifacient, others have unpleasant side-effects, or are not fully reliable.

However, our knowledge of reproductive physiology on the one hand and of biochemistry on the other has been so enormously increased in the last few decades that I would bet heavily that a solution can be found. But we must work for it. It is no good relying on isolated or casual researches: a large-scale concerted programme is necessary, as it was for the atom bomb. If we were willing to devote to discovering how to control human reproduction a tenth of the money and scientific brain-power that we did to discovering how to release atomic energy, I would prophesy that we would have the answer within ten years, certainly within a generation.

But I must return to India. One of the facts that prompted the Government to undertake the task of reducing population-increase was the ghastly recurrence of famine—not merely chronic under-nourishment or even hunger, but real famine, in which tens of thousands of human beings die of starvation. The last great Indian famine occurred quite recently, in 1952, when the rains had failed for two or three years over wide areas, and a major tragedy was only averted by large-scale importations and gifts of wheat and other foodstuffs. While modern rapidity and efficiency of distribution can thus alleviate local starvation, famines will continue to recur in India so long as population is not brought down into reasonable balance with food-production.

The Government have made heroic efforts to increase food-production, and for the first time in modern history India has recently had a surplus of home-grown food. But, perhaps unfortunately, this has only been made possible by two good seasons of abundant rain: when the climatic cycle brings the bad years round again, as it inevitably will, food will again fail, and hunger once more stalk the land. The long-term prospect is blacker: if population goes on increasing by 5 or more millions a year, food-production cannot possibly continue catching up with the mouths to be fed.

Meanwhile the Indian Government are devoting more and more attention to industrializing the country, both by way of small-scale village industries and large-scale technological projects. They apparently consider that industry will be able not only to absorb much of the surplus population from the land but also to raise the general standard of living. However, while industrialization is highly desirable, it is chimerical to suppose that it alone can cope with the problem. A radical reduction in the rate of population-increase is also necessary. Money and energy spent on birth-control, through the provision of free advice and free contraceptives, backed up by intensive propaganda, would be a better investment than a corresponding sum devoted solely to promoting industrialization.

One simple administrative change would be of great value —the creation of a separate Ministry of Population. So long as population problems are assigned to the Ministry of Health, as at present, they will be regarded as a subsidiary nuisance, hindering rather than helping the Ministry in its main enormous task of creating a healthier India. Although over-population of course creates its own problems of ill-health, and although family planning and birth-control services are best operated as part of a comprehensive Health Service, population and health demand very different approaches: furthermore, to make population-control the prime task of a separate Ministry would be a spur to ministerial ambition and departmental zeal.

In conclusion, let me return to where I began—the world situation. As I emphasized before, the crux of the problem lies in establishing a satisfactory balance between the world's resources and the population which consumes or uses the resources.

The resources consumed fall under two main heads—agricultural and non-agricultural. Food is the prime agricultural resource, but fibres and wood are also necessary, and their production often competes with food-growing. Non-agricultural resources include mineral and other inorganic raw materials on the one hand, and energy sources on the other.

The careful survey made by P.E.P. discusses the prospects of the world's main resources in some detail for the next twenty-five years, and in more tentative fashion up to the year 2000. For the many interesting specific points, I must refer my readers to the P.E.P. Report. Meanwhile I quote its broad summary of the situation: First, "there is no need to take account of the probable rapid increase of population to predict a world food-deficiency: one of appalling magnitude already exists". The general conclusion is "that, considered simply on a global basis, the requirements of energy, minerals, and raw materials can probably be met [during the coming twenty-five years], but that supplying the necessary foodstuffs to feed the expected newcomers and also to bring about substantial and lasting improvement in the position of the many millions now underfed is likely to prove exceedingly difficult and increasingly precarious. Several economic difficulties, notably in capital formation, must also be expected." For energy resources, the prospect continues reasonably bright up to the end of the century, but for food it appears increasingly gloomy, though the difficulties of accurate forecasting are greater.

This forecast, it must be repeated, applies only to global consumption. Actually, of course, individual countries differ enormously both in productivity and in consumption, as well as in rates of population-increase, and there are many obstacles to easy diffusion of any surplus resources to where they are most needed. Accordingly, when we take regional and local differences into account, the situation appears more serious and the prospect much blacker.

I have already mentioned the almost grotesque differences in consumption that exist between various countries. The exaggerated consumption by a few favoured nations of such resources as oil, newsprint, and various important minerals shows little sign of decreasing, while for food, the general trend at present is "making the distinction even greater between the well-nourished and the under-nourished regions of the world". The rise in domestic living standards in food-exporting countries is reducing the amount of food they have available for export, for instance of meat in Argentina.

Everything points to one conclusion. While every effort must be made to increase food-production, to facilitate distribution, to conserve all conservable resources, and to shame the *have* nations to a fairer sharing of the good things of the world with the *have-nots,* these alone cannot prevent disaster. Birth-control is also necessary, on a world scale and as soon as possible.

The portentous threat of atomic warfare has brought humanity to its senses and the Big Four to Geneva, and opened up the prospect of a world without major war. It has been so horrible and so urgent that it has overshadowed the equally portentous threat of over-population. If the political détente persists, population problems could begin to receive the attention they deserve. Their urgency might again bring the leaders of the peoples together, and open up the prospect of a world without major over-population.

But time presses. New year will add nearly 34 million people to humanity's total, and certainly for two or three decades to come, each successive year will add more. If nothing is done soon, world over-population will be a fact well before the end of the century.

It has taken just one decade from Hiroshima for the world to face up resolutely to the implications of atomic war: can we hope that it will take no more than a decade from last year's World Population Conference in Rome for the world to face up equally resolutely to the implications of over-population?

WHAT DO WE KNOW ABOUT LOVE?

THE opening scene of that glorious satire, *Of Thee I Sing,* reveals a party caucus with an admirable presidential candidate but no ideas. They accordingly ask the hotel chambermaid, as representative of the People, what most people are most interested in, and are unhesitatingly answered "Love". And so love becomes the chief plank in their platform.

The first thing we know about love is what the chambermaid's answer implied—that for most people it is the most absorbing and interesting subject in existence. (In 1954 the Russians, at the Second Congress of Soviet Writers, officially rediscovered this important social fact.) Love can send young people eloping to Gretna Green, break up families, reduce strong men to love-sick slaves, even lead to murder or make kings lose their thrones; it can also energize human lives, induce the writing of a great deal of verse, including some of the finest poetry, induce states of ecstasy otherwise unattainable by the great majority of men and women, and provide the substance for most of our emotional dreaming.

This statement needs two qualifications. While it applies to contemporary Western peoples and doubtless to many others, it is not true for all cultures: sometimes war or hunting may take first place. Secondly, love as a plank in the chambermaid's personal platform and as an engrossing subject of popular interest means only one kind of love—the romantic sexual kind, the fact of "being in love".

It is almost impossible to give a formal definition of anything so complex and general as love. All I can do is to indicate some of the range of meanings comprised in this one little word. There is mother-love and self-love, father-love and grandmother-love, and children's love for their parents; there is brotherly love (which gave Philadelphia its name) and love of one's country; there is being in love, and making love; one can say that a man loves his food, though good manners dictates that he should not say it himself (when I as a small boy said I would love some chicken, my great-aunt rebuked me with the Victorian rhyme "You may love a screeching owl; you may not love a roasted fowl").

Many people love dancing; there are music-lovers, art-lovers, sport-lovers, dog-lovers, bird-lovers, sun-lovers, mountain-lovers; most of us have an intense and deep-rooted love of the surroundings in which we grew up; ministers assure us that God loves us and insist that we should love God, while Jesus adjured us to love our enemies; and there is love of money and love of power. . . .

All these are legitimate and normal usage: in its comprehensive sense, *love* clearly includes all of them. But equally clearly, the love in which one can be or into which one can fall is for most of us somehow pre-eminent over all other kinds.

Being in love is a special case of love as a general human capacity. It is love at its most intense, and love personally focused and directed in a very special way. Our common speech reflects this fact. We talk of *falling in love,* as if it was something outside us, into which we are precipitated suddenly, accidentally and against our will, like falling into a pond. We say that X is infatuated with Y, or bewitched by her, or madly in love. Classical mythology expressed the suddenness and the sense of compulsion in the symbol of Cupid the blind archer, whose arrows inflict a magic wound on our emotional being.

Love at first sight (though of course not universal or indeed usual) is a frequent occurrence, surprising as a fact for scientific consideration as well as to those who experience it. But even when we are in love with someone we have known for months or years, the actual falling in love has been often, perhaps usually, not a gradual process but a sudden moment. Being in love, whether we fall suddenly or grow gradually into it, always has an element of compulsion, a sense of being possessed by some extraneous and magical power. Lovers are obsessed by an image of the loved one, to whom they ascribe every virtue and merit. Outside observers of the phenomenon speak of the lover's madness; and love is proverbially blind.

The lover experiences a sense of heightened vitality and finds a new significance in life. Mere contemplation of the beloved becomes a wellspring of the highest enjoyment. The lover seeks the presence of the beloved. Merely to see her (or him) from a distance is to feast the soul as well as the eyes; and to touch her is an inspiring bliss. But when, through two hands and two pairs of eyes, the two souls can interpenetrate, an even more magical state is achieved, as described in Donne's poem *The Ecstasy*.

> . . . Our hands were firmly cémented
> By a fast balm which thence did spring;
> Our eye-beams twisted, and did thread
> Our eyes upon one double string. . . .
>
> As 'twixt two equal armies Fate
> Suspends uncertain victory,
> Our souls—which to advance their state
> Were gone out—hung 'twixt her and me.
>
> And whilst our souls negotiate there,
> We like sepulchral statues lay;
> All day the same our postures were,
> And we said nothing, all the day.

Modern psychology has rightly abandoned the term *soul*, because of the philosophical and theological implications that have become attached to it; but we can translate it as meaning the unitary inner core of our conscious selves and this sense of the going out of our essential being and of its interpenetrating or uniting with another being is one of the hallmarks of being in love.

This is embodied in one of the loveliest epigrams of the Greek Anthology:

> Τὴν ψυχὴν Ἀγάθωνα φιλῶν ἐπὶ χείλεσιν ἔσχον·
> ἦλθε γὰρ ἡ τλήμων ὡς διαβησομένη.

As I kissed Agathon, I had my soul in my lips; for the rash creature came thither as if to pass across.

For true lovers, the act of physical union is actuated not merely or indeed mainly by the desire for pleasure but for the transcendent sense of total union which it can bring. William Blake rightly rebukes the puritans who

> Call a shame and sin
> Love's temple that God dwelleth in . . .
> And render that a lawless thing
> On which the soul expands its wing.

And Robert Bridges reminds us how the lower is necessarily incorporated in the higher

> We see Spiritual, Mental and Animal
> To be gradations merged together in growth, . . .
> . . . And that the animal pleasure
> Runneth throughout all graces heartening all energies.

Even children may fall in sudden love, long before puberty and its hormones have actuated the full sexual urge. The classical example is Dante, who fell in love with Beatrice when she was just eight and he nearly nine. In his *Vita Nuova* —The New Life—he has left an immortal description of the event which coloured all his later existence. "At that instant, the spirit of life which dwells in the heart's most secret chamber began to tremble so violently that all the pulses of my body shook; and in trembling it said these words: 'Here is a god stronger than I, who is come to rule over me.' "

He only saw her a few more times, and she died at the age of twenty-five. But his love dominated the rest of his life, and inspired his great work. The distinction between love and sex is very obvious here. Dante reserved his fullest and highest love for a woman whose hand he had never even touched, but had four children by the excellent wife he later married. However, before dealing further with this question, I want to say something about the evolution and development of love—its evolution in nature apart from man, and its development in individual human beings.

People sometimes ask what purpose love serves in nature. But a biologist cannot answer a question framed in terms of purpose, for purpose implies deliberate design for a conscious end, and there is no evidence of that in the natural world. To be biologically answerable, the question should run, "What functions does love perform in living organisms?" Even so, the biologist cannot give a nice simple or single answer, for among animals there are various different kinds of love, expressed in various different ways, and manifested in different degrees of clarity and intensity. There has been an evolution of love, as of every other property of life, and we must supplement our question by asking how the different kinds of love have evolved.

In many young mammals, like kittens, some adult mammals, like otters, and various adult birds, like penguins and rooks and swifts, we find something closely akin to our love of play or sport—the enjoyment of bodily performance for its own sake, irrespective of its practical utility. Among birds there is the beginning of a love of beauty, manifested in the collection of bright objects by jackdaws and magpies, and in bowerbirds by a preference for certain colours and by their deliberate painting of their bowers. The roots of love of country are shown in the attachment of many kinds of birds and mammals to their home territory, and of love of nature in such rituals as the high aerial dawn-chorus of swallows and martins.

Finally, animals show several different types of love in the restricted sense—love focused on other individuals. There is parental love, of parent for offspring; there is offspring love, of offspring for parent; there is sexual love, between actual or potential mates; and there is social love, for other individuals of the same species. The roots of social love are found in gregarious animals, and are manifested in the distress caused by solitude and the impulse to seek the company of their fellows.

Parental love is in most species only maternal. In many mammals and in all polygamous birds, the mother alone is concerned about the young—think of bears or sheep or the domestic hen. But in some fish and toads and a few birds, like emus and phalaropes, it is the male alone that looks after eggs and young; and of course in all our familiar songbirds the cock bird helps to feed the young once they have been hatched by the hen, while in birds like grebes and gannets, auks and petrels and penguins, both cock and hen share equally in incubation too. Comparatively few insects show parental love (the female earwig is one), and in those where it is most developed, namely bees and ants, it is not strictly speaking parental love but maiden-aunt love (or nurse love if you like), for it is only the neuter females, the so-called workers, that have the instinct to look after the eggs and grubs.

This brings up an important point. In animals, parental (and nurse) love is purely instinctive; not only the urge to care for the young, but also the detailed ways in which it manifests itself, depend on inborn nervous mechanisms, and do not have to be learned. Furthermore, like all instincts, parental love, though doubtless associated with strong emotions, is blind and automatic. It is a psychological mechanism which works admirably in normal conditions, but is apt to go astray in abnormal ones. Thus a worker wasp which was kept from access to food for the young was seen to satisfy its nurse-instinct by biting off the hind end of a grub and offering it to the front end!

The same blind imprisonment of instinctive behaviour within a limited situation is seen even in birds and mammals. Thus song-birds only pay attention to their young so long as they are in the nest. When a cuckoo has ejected its foster-brothers and -sisters, the parents take no notice of their cries of distress, even if they are hanging on a twig just outside the nest. And even in normal circumstances it is not the sight of the young bird as an individual that impels the parents to feed it, but merely the colour and shape of its gaping mouth: they will feed an artificial gape of painted wood (if properly made) just as readily as their own nestlings. And a cow distressed by the removal of her calf can be comforted by its skin.

The same sort of things hold for the sexual instinct. Certain orchids get pollinated by looking and perhaps smelling like female flies: the male flies try to mate with them, and in so doing transfer the fertilizing pollen from flower to flower. Similarly many birds will attempt to mate with a stuffed dead female as readily as with a real live one—provided that it is set up in a certain pose; and the sperm for artificial insemination in cattle and horses can be obtained because the mating urge of bulls and stallions is aroused by suitable dummies as well as by live cows or mares.

But the mental life of birds, for instance, is a curious mixture, in which some types of emotional behaviour are carried out blindly, crudely, and wholly instinctively, while others depend on detailed learning. A cock robin, for instance (not the fat American robin, which is really a thrush, but our little European robin redbreast), will be automatically and irrationally stimulated to his threat-display by the sight of a red breast, whether on a live rival, a stuffed bird, or a headless and tailless dummy; but he learns the difference between his mate and all other hen robins and can recognize her individually afar off.

The robin's red breast and the gape of nestling birds are examples of what are called *releasers*—they are visual sign-stimuli which release the action of innate impulses and chains of activity, in the one case of hostility or aggression, in the other of service or affection—the beginnings of hate and of love.

In polygamous-promiscuous species like ruff and sage-grouse and blackcock, the sexes never meet except on a communal display-ground, and the males' sexual "love" is merely the urge to physical mating, expressed in violent antics serving to intimidate rivals or stimulate mates by showing off the exaggerated masculine display-plumage.

In most birds, however, there is an emotional bond between mates, and the pair stays together, either for the brood, or for the season, or, in a number of species, for life. Life-mates like to be close together even in the winter, as you may see with jackdaws. This emotional bond is clearly one of the forerunners of human married love.

In some water-birds, such as grebes, where male and female share equally the duties of incubating the eggs and feeding the young, there are elaborate ceremonies of mutual display, participated in by both mates together, and obviously highly stimulating to the emotions. What is more, some displays are not confined to the period of courtship or physical mating, but continue right through the breeding season, until the young are full-grown. Here I would say the rituals of animal love find their fullest expression.

Though from the standpoint of the species this emotional bond has been evolved for the utilitarian function of keeping the mated pair together while their joint efforts are needed for the successful rearing of their young, from that of the individual birds the ceremonies are clearly very satisfying and have emotional value in themselves.

Emotional life in animals is essentially a patchwork. Particular urges or emotions arise in particular circumstances, and usually stay in separate channels. Fear may dictate behaviour for a period, then suddenly hunger steps in, then perhaps sexual desire. Animals lack man's capacity to bring together many different urges and emotions, memories and hopes, into a single continuity of conscious life. The main exception to this, interestingly enough, concerns love. Both in the parent-offspring relation and in that between the two sexes, attraction and hostility are often combined. The primary reaction of a nestling or a brooding heron to the appearance of an adult at the nest is fear and hostility: before the arriving bird is accepted as parent or as mate, it must be recognized as such; and recognition is effected by a special "appeasing" display. This in turn forms the basis for the elaborate ceremony of nest-relief, which finally serves as an emotional bond between the mated pair.

In many birds' species, during the "courtship" period, the sight of a bird of the opposite sex often acts as a sign-stimulus releasing both hostility (as an alien intruding individual) and attraction (as a potential mate). Thus the unmated male house-sparrow in possession of a nest-site endeavours to attract passing females, but if one tries to enter the nest he will attack her, and even after they have accepted each other as mates, it may be two or three days before she is allowed into her future home.

The courtship-displays of many species turn out to be ritualizations of this ambivalent emotion compounded of attraction and either hostility or fear (and show many parallels with human courtship, especially in young people). The male bird's aggressivity may be transformed into a stimulating display of masculinity and desire, and female timidity often expresses itself by reverting to infantile dependence, with adoption of the nestling's food-begging attitude.

Thus love, in the sense of positive attraction between individuals, has arisen during biological evolution in the form of a patchwork of distinct urges or drives, each serving a distinct biological function. The mechanism of each separate kind of love is largely built in to the species by heredity. For the most part, each drive is automatically activated by a sign-stimulus functioning as a releaser, a distinctive pattern of sight or sound (like the gape of the nestling for stimulating the parental feeding drive of its parents, or the "song" of male grasshoppers for the sexual approach of the female); and is expressed in a genetically predetermined set of actions (like the displays of amorous male birds). Learning by experience plays only a secondary role, or sometimes no role at all.

Further, there is little synthesis of the separate drives into a coherent or continuous mental life. However, desire is often frustrated, and attraction often compounded with hostility or fear, and the resultant conflict is reconciled in the performance of some ritualized ceremony of display. This may then be further specialized during subsequent evolution to provide more effective stimulation of the female, or be converted into a mutual ceremony serving as a bond to keep the mated pair together; and such ceremonies, especially the mutual ones, may come to have emotional value in themselves.

" 'Tis love, 'tis love that makes the world go round," sang the anonymous ballad-monger. And certainly love, in its dawning manifestations among animals, secures the perpetuation of the species and the care of offspring, lays the foundations of more or less permanent marriage unions, and may even emerge as a value in itself.

When we come to our own species, we find a certain general parallel between the process of individual development of love in man and that of its evolution in animals, but also many important differences. There is more reliance on learning by experience, less on inborn genetic mechanisms. However, two or three inborn sign-stimuli do seem to exist. One is the smile. Even a crudely grimacing model of a smiling face will elicit from an infant a smile (and the positive mood which goes with smiling and is one of the bases of enjoying and loving). And women's breasts (though, as Dr. Johnson pointed out, not feeding-bottles) will act as a powerful sign-stimulus to male sexual love.

Non-sexual loves of many kinds appear and develop in the growing child. At the outset are the simple basic desires for food and warmth and protection, soon transmuted into love of enjoyment and contentment, general satisfaction and fulfilment. Then the personal focusing of love on to the individuals that provide what is desired—first mother or nurse, then father, brothers and sisters, and other children. Then the widening of the circle of love and of personal attachment (Walt Whitman speaks of the "fluid and attaching character" that some people seem to exude); and finally, love for the beautiful or the strange, the thrilling or the significant.

These more complex loves may sometimes attain the intensity of passions. The full force of a child's emotions may be bound up with some shell or curious stone that he has found: or the experience of beauty may change his whole emotional attitude to life. Let Wordsworth speak:

My heart leaps up when I behold
　　A rainbow in the sky:
So was it when my life began;
So is it now I am a man;
So be it when I shall grow old,
　　Or let me die!
The Child is father of the Man;
And I could wish my days to be
Bound each to each by natural piety.

Or again, in his famous Ode:

There was a time when meadow, grove and stream,
The earth, and every common sight,
　　　　To me did seem
　　　　Apparell'd in celestial light,
The glory and the freshness of a dream.

"The hour of splendour in the grass, of glory in the flower" may pass and fade, but the experience of love for natural beauty, of enhanced vitality and the upleaping heart, of self-transcendence in loving union with something outside oneself, may change a growing human being permanently, and can enter later into his love for God, for someone of the other sex, for ideals. As one of Truman Capote's characters says, apropos of a jay's lovely blue egg that she had kept from childhood, "love is a chain of love. . . . Because you can love one thing, you can love another."

The growing child comes to love many different kinds of things in many different ways—sometimes with the self-centred desire for possession; sometimes with the self-transcending desire for unity with the object of desire, or the outgoing sense of communion in the act of experience, as with Richard Jefferies' or Thomas Traherne's mystical experiences of the beauty and wonder of nature; sometimes with the enriching of enjoyment in the full and free exercise of his faculties, physical or psychological.

And then, at puberty, there is the intrusion of the sexual impulse. The sex impulse appears as an alien power, strong, new and often frightening. The experience is all the more upsetting because the new power, though alien to our past life or present make-up, is yet within us, a part of ourselves. The central problem of adolescence is, in general, how to incorporate this intruding force into the developing personality; and in particular, how to integrate sex and love. This is especially acute because of the disharmony between man's biological nature and his social arrangements, the fact that there is a gap of years between the time when the sexual impulse emerges (and emerges at maximum strength, at least in boys, as Dr. Kinsey has shown) and the time when marriage is possible.

Adolescence is also the time when love, as distinct from sexual desire, alters its character. At puberty romantic idealism raises its head as well as sex: and another problem of adolescence is how to integrate this idealism with the hard facts of existence, and romance with the practical business of living.

Man, however, differs from all other animals in having a brain which can and largely does bring all the various elements of experience into contact, instead of keeping them in a series of wholly or largely separate compartments or channels. This not only provides the basis for conceptual thought, and so for all man's ideas and philosophic systems, ideals and works of art and creative imagination, but also for his battery of complex sentiments unknown in animals, such as reverence and religious awe, moral feelings (including hate and contempt arising from moral abhorrence), and love in its developed form.

It also, however, provides the basis for emotional or psychological conflict on a scale unknown in animals. One of the unique characters of man is his constant subjection to mental conflict, with the resultant necessity for making moral decisions. Man's morality, indeed, is a necessary consequence of his inner conflicts.

Nowhere is this better illustrated than in love. Strong sexual desire, as well as the reverent worship of beauty, self-fulfilment, and ideal aspiration, plays a part in human love. But crude sexual desire in itself is merely lust and is universally regarded as immoral, and to many people the sexual act appears as something dirty or disgusting.

However, love at its truest and fullest and most intense can include in its single embrace an enormous range of emotions and sentiments, and fuse them all, even those of baser metal, in its crucible. It can combine humility with pride, passion with peace, self-assertion with self-surrender; it can reconcile violence of feeling with tenderness, can swallow up disgust in beauty and imperfection in fulfilment, and sublimate sexual desire into joy and fuller life.

It can, but it does not always do so. Sometimes the inhibitions of morality or romantic idealism are too strong, and the fusion is imperfect, the reconciliation remains incomplete. This is especially so in puritan cultures and religions imbued with a sense of sin. St. Paul's attitude to sexual love is expressed in his dictum that it is better to marry than to burn: tormented souls like St. Augustine and Tolstoy came to regard sexual love not as fulfilment but as sin, and Gandhi's autobiography tells us how his early indulgences drove him later to prescribe—for others!—self-control and abstinence instead of the ideal of pure enjoyment, of joy disciplined and transformed by tenderness, reverence, and beauty.

Sometimes, indeed, love involves contradictory and unreconciled emotions. In one of his most famous poems, Catullus wrote

> Odi et amo: quare id faciam, fortasse requiris.
> Nescio, sed fieri sentio et excrucior.

"I hate and love: how can that be, perhaps you ask? I know not, but so I feel, and am in torment." The hero of Somerset Maugham's *Of Human Bondage* is intellectually aware of the imperfections and indeed the unattractiveness of the girl he is in love with, but remains emotionally enslaved by her.

In love, indeed, the conflict between reason and emotion is often at highest pitch. However, though falling in love is irrational, or at least non-rational, yet love can be (though it is not always) later influenced by reason and guided by experience. Emotion in general is non-rational; it tends to all-or-nothing manifestations and is naturally resistant to the critical and balanced spirit of reason. And the emotions involved in love are so violent that this uncritical or anti-critical tendency readily overrides reason. That is why love is called blind, why it may become a kind of madness or sickness. But reason can play a part later. With time, as the emotional violence of love diminishes and rational experience accumulates, a point may suddenly be reached at which reason gains the upper hand, the deluded lover's eyes are opened, he realizes that he has been blind, and he falls out of love as he once fell in. Such experiences are useful though harsh reminders of the sad fact that emotional certitude alone is never a guarantee of rightness or truth, in religious or moral belief any more than in love: sudden religious conversion resembles falling in love in many ways, including its non-rationality.

Luckily for the human race, love often chooses aright. And then reason and emotional experience may give it eyes to see and may transform a transient madness into the highest and most enduring sanity. This rationally guided transformation and development of love have been immortally described by Wordsworth in his poem, *Perfect Woman*. It is too long for me to quote in its entirety, but you will recall how it begins with a magical, altogether non-rational moment—

> She was a Phantom of delight
> When first she gleam'd upon my sight;

how experience altered the vision—

> I saw her upon nearer view,
> A Spirit, yet a Woman too!

and how it finally transformed sudden magic into permanent serenity—

> And now I see with eye serene
> The very pulse of the machine . . .
> A perfect Woman, nobly planned,
> To warn, to comfort, and command;
> And yet a Spirit still, and bright
> With something of angelic light.

Often, however, love does not choose right the first time. I should rather say, first love often does not choose permanently right. Many teen-age "pashes" and "crushes", however violent at the time, and many cases of adolescent calf-love, though often valuable and indeed "right" in the sense of providing necessary experience to the callow personality, are soon outgrown.

Even when it comes to marriage, many first choices are wrong, and later ones may be much more right. The relation between love and marriage urgently needs reconsideration. For one thing, in our Western societies, we have become too credulous about romantic love, just as earlier ages were too credulous about religious faith. Both can often be blind, and then both can mislead us. For another, we have become obsessed with the rigid moralists' stern insistence on the inviolability and indissolubility of marriage—a religious doctrine imposed on a social bond.

The emotional certitude of being in love with someone does not guarantee either its rightness, or its uniqueness, or its permanence, any more than it ensures that the love shall be reciprocated. And the undoubted general desirability, both social and personal, of long-enduring monogamous marriage does not preclude the occasional desirability of divorce and change of marriage-partner, nor justify the branding of any extra-marital love as a grave social immorality or personal sin.

Our reconsideration should be related to the idea of greater fulfilment. Of course conflicts will inevitably arise between greater fulfilment for oneself, for one's partner, one's children, and one's community; but they will then be better illuminated and more readily soluble than in the light of romantic illusion, religious dogma, or static and absolute morality.

It must be remembered that love and its manifestations differ in different societies and cultures. We find a differentiation and development of love as part of the general cultural evolution of man. Margaret Mead and other anthropologists have shown to what a surprising extent cultures may differ in their general attitude to love, both sexual and parental, and in their expression of it. Masculinity may be valued either higher or lower than femininity, ardour and passion higher or lower than coolness and acceptance; parental love may be either indulgent or strict to children, or its expression, warm and full in early years, may be suddenly withdrawn from the child at a certain age; the attitude of society both to pre-marital love-making and post-marital love-affairs may differ enormously.

A striking example of the evolution of love is the rise of the idea of romantic love in medieval Europe. This found an exaggerated expression in the ballads of the troubadours and the rituals of chivalry, but has left a permanent mark on our Western civilization.

Love presents, in intensive form, man's central and perennial problem—how to reconcile the claims of the individual and of society, personal desires with social aims. The problem is perhaps most acute in adolescence, for this involves a disharmony of timing: our sexual desires arise, and in males arise in fullest force, several years before marriage is desirable or possible. Different cultures have met this problem in very different ways. Thus in eighteenth-century England and nineteenth-century France it was the acknowledged thing for upper-class young men to take a mistress, while this was frowned on in Geneva and New England. In twentieth-century America, dating and petting have superseded "bundling" as the recognized formula.

Many primitive societies go further, and institutionalize adolescent love. Thus among the Masai of East Africa the boys after initiation become Moran or Warriors and live in communities with the initiated girls, sharing what seems to be a very agreeable love-life. Only after some years do they marry, and from then on, extra-marital love is severely frowned on. Their neighbours, the Kikuyu, had a somewhat similar system, in which, however, full sexual intercourse was not permitted. The same sort of arrangement prevails among the Bontocs of the Philippines, as recorded by Stewart Kilton in his *Dream Giants and Pygmies*. Here, as among country-folk in England until quite recently, adolescent love-making serves also as a try-out of fertility. A girl can only marry if she conceives; and sterile girls become "a sort of educational institution" for young boys.

In modern civilization the problem is very real and very serious. On the one hand, clearly both undisciplined indulgence and complete promiscuity in love are individually damaging, or anti-social, or both; but on the other hand, complete repression of this most powerful of impulses is equally damaging, and so is the self-reproach that the indulgence or even the mere manifestation of the impulse arouses in sensitive adolescents who have had an exaggerated sense of sin imposed on them. From another angle, it is tragic to think of millions of human beings denied the full beauty and exaltation of love precisely while their impulses are strongest and their sensibilities at their highest pitch.

No civilization has yet adequately harmonized the disharmony or provided satisfactory means of resolving the conflict. Indeed there can be no solution in the sense that there is a single definite solution to a mechanical puzzle or a mathematical problem. The problem of love, as of any other aspect of life, must be solved *ambulando*, or rather *vivendo*, in living; and the correctness of the solution is only to be measured by the fulfilment achieved, the degree to which desirable possibilities are realized and conflicting elements and interests harmonized. What is more, we can rarely ex-

pect to arrive at a satisfactory solution at the first shot: fulfilment is a process, and we have to learn it, to achieve it
step by step, often making mistakes, often precipitated into
new and unforeseen problems or conflicts by the solution of
previous ones.

Love between the sexes can provide some of the highest
fulfilments of life. It also provides an important means for
the development of personality: through it we learn many
necessary things about ourselves, about others, about society, and about human ideals. We must, I think, aim at a
moral and religious climate of society in which the adolescent
experiments of love, instead of being branded as wicked or
relegated to furtive and illicit gropings, or repressed until
they collapse in neurosis or explode in lust, or merely tol-
erated as an unpleasing necessity, are socially sanctioned and
religiously sanctified, in the same sort of way as marriage
is now. Adolescent affairs of the heart could be regarded as
reverent experiments in love, or as trial marriages, desirable
preparations for the more enduring adventure of adult marriage. Young people would assuredly continue to make mistakes, to be selfish or lustful or otherwise immoral; but
matters would I am sure be better than they are now, and
could not well be much worse.

In considering love we must not leave out hate, for in one
sense love and hate are the positive and negative aspects of
the same thing, the primary emotional reaction to another
individual. This can either be one of attraction, desire, or
tenderness, or one of repulsion, fear, or hostility. In this light
it is easy to understand how love, especially when ardent
and blind, can so readily turn into equally uncritical hate.

From the evolutionary angle, however, love and hate must
be thought of as distinct. They have independent origins and
are canalized and expressed in different ways. As we have
seen, love in animals may have a number of separate and
specific manifestations—parental, sexual, and social. The
same holds for hate: it may manifest itself in fear, in avoidance, or in aggression. We have also seen how love and hate
may be simultaneously aroused, as in the combination of desire and hostility in the sexual life of birds, and may then
be compounded and the conflict reconciled in a new expression, in the form of a ritual display.

For the most part, however, psychological conflict is
avoided in animals by means of an automatic nervous mechanism similar to that which prevents conflicting muscles from

coming into action simultaneously. When, for instance, a nervous message is sent to the flexor muscles to contract and bend our arm, it is accompanied by a second message inhibiting and relaxing the extensor muscles which would straighten it. The same sort of thing often happens with more complicated reflex activities, and, as already mentioned, with animal instincts: when the fear instinct is switched into action, the hunger or the sex instinct is switched out.

It may also operate in man's emotional conflicts: one of two conflicting patterns of feeling and thought may be either voluntarily and temporarily suppressed into the sub-conscious, or wholly and permanently repressed into the unconscious. There, however, as Freud discovered, it can still continue its nagging and produce a sense of guilt. Total and unremembered repression naturally occurs most often in infancy and early life, before experience and reason have had time to begin coping with the paralysing conflict between contradictory emotions and impulses.

The primal conflict which besets the human infant is between love and hate. He (or she) inevitably loves his mother (or mother-surrogate) as the fountainhead of his satisfactions, his security, comfort, and peace. But at times he is also angry with her, as the power which arbitrarily, it seems to him, denies him satisfaction and thwarts his impulses: and his anger calls into play what the psychologists call aggression—his battery of magic hate-phantasies and death-wishes and destructive rage-impulses.

But his hate soon comes into paralysing conflict with his love, and must be repressed. It also gives him a sense of guilt or wrongness, even from its lair in the unconscious; and this charge of primal guilt continues to exist and is built into his developing personality. When an action or impulse arouses this sense of guilt, it is automatically felt as wrong. Thus the infantile conflict between love and hate generates what we may call the individual's proto-ethical mechanism, the rudiment around which his conscience and his truly ethical sense of right and wrong are later built, rather as his embryonic notochord provided the basis for the future development of his backbone.

Of course, reason and experience, imagination and ideals also make their contributions. But the basis of conscience and ethics remains irrational and largely unconscious, as shown by the terrifying sense of sin and unworthiness which besets those unfortunates on whom a too-heavy burden of personal guilt has been imposed.

Consciences, in fact, are not genetically predetermined and do not grow automatically like backbones, but need the infantile conflict between love and hate for their origination. This is demonstrated by recent studies like those of John Bowlby and Spitz, on children who have been brought up in impersonal institutions or otherwise deprived of the care of a mother or personal mother-substitute, during a critical period between one and three years old. Many of them never develop a conscience, and grow up as amoral beings, creatures without ethics.

The mother is thus the central figure in the evolution of love. For one thing, maternal love always involves tenderness and devoted care, which sexual love does not. Only when the different kinds or components of love become blended, as they do most thoroughly in man, though to some extent in some birds and mammals, does sexual love come to involve tenderness as well as desire. As Robert Bridges writes in his *Testament of Beauty*, "In man this blind motherly attachment is the spring of his purest affection, and of all compassion." And again, "Through motherhood it [selfhood] came in animals to altruistic feeling, and thence-after in man rose to spiritual affection."

But the mother also provides the focus for the human infant's personal emotions, both of love and hate, and in so doing unwittingly lays the foundations of conscience, and starts the child on its course towards high morality and spiritual ideals.

I have no space to discuss many other aspects of love—the problem of homosexual love, for instance; or the interesting differences found by Dr. Kinsey between the development of sexual love in men and in women; or the relations between married love and conjugal fidelity.

But I would like to close with an affirmation of the unique importance of love in human life—an affirmation which seems to me essential in a tormented age like ours, where violence and disillusion have joined forces with undigested technological advance to produce an atmosphere of cynicism and crude materialism.

Mother-love is indispensable not only for the healthy and happy physical growth of young human beings, but for their healthy and happy moral and spiritual growth as well. Personal love between the sexes is not only indispensable for the physical continuance of the race, but for the full development of the human personality. It is part of education: through love, the self learns to grow. Love of beauty and of all lovely and wonderful things is equally indispensable for our mental growth and the realization of our possibilities. It brings reverence and a sense of transcendence into sexual and personal love, and indeed into all of life. In general, love is a positive emotion, an enlargement of life leading on towards greater fulfilment and capable of counteracting human hate and destructive impulses.

Let the final word be that of a poet who was also a man of science—Robert Bridges.

He [Aristotle] hath made Desire to be the prime mover of all.
I see the emotion of saints, lovers and poets all
To be the kindling of some personality
By an eternizing passion; and that God's worshipper
Looking on any beauty falleth straightway in love;
And that love is a fire in whose devouring flames
All earthly ills are consumed.

THE BEARING OF SCIENTIFIC KNOWLEDGE ON BELIEF IN A FREE SOCIETY [1]

WHEN I saw my title in print I realized its ambiguity. It could mean either "The Bearing of Scientific Knowledge on Belief, in a Free Society" or it might mean "The Bearing of Scientific Knowledge on Belief in a Free Society". However, I am very glad that that ambiguity is there, because in the development of my theme I hope that both meanings will emerge, and will emerge as significantly related to the general theme of this Charter Day, namely, "The University's Responsibility in the Tradition of Freedom".

First of all, let us remember that freedom is one of those general terms which has the rather unfortunate property of meaning several different things. First of all, it can mean *freedom from* as well as *freedom of:* and that, as you re-

[1] Charter Day address to the University of Oregon, 1954.

member, was a great headache to those who had to translate President Roosevelt's Four Freedoms into other languages. *Freedom from* is of course exceedingly important. It includes freedom from restraint, freedom from tyranny, freedom from want, freedom from fear, and from many other undesirable things. But *freedom of* is equally important: freedom of opinion, belief, opportunity, assembly, and so forth.

Then in common parlance freedom is sometimes used in another sense as meaning simply the absence of all restraint, freedom to act as you will or to do what you like. That, however, is a very inadequate and indeed incorrect definition of freedom: it denotes licence and not liberty, or, in relation to the freedom of the will, a completely arbitrary power of choice. You will find that all the great thinkers of the world agree that all such definitions are false and misleading. *Freedom from* is never freedom from *all* restraint, but from arbitrary power or from some restraint (which may be an internal restraint in our own minds or souls, just as much as an external restraint by an outer authority) which impedes or prevents freedom for the full and rewarding realizations and enjoyments of our life-enhancing activities and creative faculties, or, in a word, for our richer fulfilment. Again, as all great philosophers agree, to speak of freedom of choice as purely arbitrary is essentially meaningless. Choice can never be wholly arbitrary. The fullest freedom is the expression of an inner compulsion of our being, of a choice which we have come to feel as inevitably necessary. When the poet says "we needs must love the highest when we see it", that is a poetical and perhaps rather idealized expression of a profound truth. In general, once we manage to "see things steadily and see them whole", the choice is made for us.

After this brief semantic introduction let me come to the question of belief. What do we mean by freedom or belief? If we Westerners look at the subject historically, we find that it first meant freedom to believe in different versions of the Christian faith. That had become a political necessity in order to put an end to the devastating religious wars and persecutions of the sixteenth and seventeenth centuries. Then it was extended to mean freedom for other faiths—first Judaism and eventually Islam and Buddhism and other Asian religions: and *pari passu* with this, freedom or at any rate reasonable absence of persecution for so-called freethinkers, atheists, and the like. However, in the twentieth century a serious diminution of this freedom has occurred. First there was the quarrel between Fascism and Catholicism, between Mussolini and the Pope, over the education of young Italians. Then there was the restriction of freedom in Nazi Germany, involving the extraordinary claim that there was a distinction between Aryan science, which was good and sound, and Jewish science, which was wrong and wicked. Meanwhile the same sort of trend, only on a larger scale, developed in Communist Russia. From the beginning there was no freedom of belief for "deviationists" like Trotsky. Then came the vilification and prohibition of all so-called "bourgeois" or "capitalist-imperialist" thought and science, which culminated in the strange dogma leading to the exaltation of "Marxist science" which is inevitably correct and good, as against "bourgeois science" which somehow is always wrong. This came to a head in the amazing phenomenon of Lysenko and the rise of Michurinism, accorded official status when the so-called truth about genetics was laid down by the Central Committee of the Communist Party. The same kind of thought-control was also applied in many fields of literature and art. Finally, we are seeing in the West, and perhaps particularly in the United States, the tendency to impose uniformity by public opinion, to crack down on heterodoxy and even difference, to introduce thought-control under the pretext of combating Communism.

This results from the fact that beliefs are again getting mixed up with power politics and with questions of national security, as they were in the religious wars of the seventeenth century. From another angle, the authoritarians have been confirmed in their resistance to full freedom of ideas by the anthropologists' demonstration of the relativism of beliefs and systems of morality.

However, though in one sense men in any truly liberal society are free to believe anything, however absurd—that the moon is made of green cheese, or astrological nonsense, or that measurements of the Great Pyramid can tell us something about the future—yet there must be practical limits to such freedom. For, after all, beliefs have practical consequences. An obvious example concerns beliefs about health. Now that scientific and medical discovery has given us a knowledge of the true causation of infectious disease, we can no longer afford to tolerate the belief that disease is not due to germs, but to divine visitation, or punishment for sin, or some other supernatural or moral cause. More accurately, though we may tolerate the beliefs, we cannot tolerate the actions that spring from them, such as permitting people suffering from infectious diseases to be free to spread them. Similarly, in no society is it possible to allow freedom to the beliefs of those whom we class as insane. The beliefs of the insane endanger themselves and often threaten others. This is especially true if they indulge in the belief that they are reincarnations of Napoleon, or have a divine mission to scourge the universe, but is still true if they are too different from the other human beings in their community to take sufficient account of the facts of reality or to draw sufficiently rational conclusions from the facts. When basically insane men, like Hitler, attain political and military power, we have to destroy them or their power.

We men are not truly free to believe nonsense, even when nonsensical beliefs involve no immediate or obvious practical consequences. A belief, after all, though in one sense it is a crystallization or fusion of emotions and feelings and knowledge into a system of ideas, is always in some degree operative or effective; it always has a dynamic aspect, always tends to issue in action of some sort.

Beliefs may have immediate practical effects on action. For instance, the belief of the early Mohammedans that they would go straight to Paradise if they died in battle for the Islamic faith had an enormous effect on human history. Again, the Nazis' belief in Aryan superiority and Jewish inferiority led to a very practical and quite appalling effect, namely gas chambers for over a million Jews.

A belief also may have less immediate, but in the long run equally serious, effects: because a belief often involves a set of the mind and the entire personality, and determines men's general attitude or approach to life. Beliefs always have a potential operative effect on behaviour. Thus, the belief which I have cited, that pestilence and plague are a divine visitation and may be mitigated by prayer, stands in the way of public health and discourages medical research and practice. Too strong a belief in salvation in the next world has often led to a despising of this world—to exaggerated asceticism, to tolerance of dirt and disease, to campaigns against beauty and enjoyment, and in general to neglect of the duty of building the kingdom of heaven upon earth. Again, a belief in miracles discourages a belief in the order of nature and so in science and the value of scientific research and the scientific spirit. A belief in predestined fate, such as we find in superstitions like astrology or palmistry, discourages the belief in free will and the power of creative activity. And finally, a belief in revelation or dogmatic authority, whether religious or political, encourages authoritarianism and intolerance and is therefore opposed to democracy, to science's progressive discovery of truth, and to freedom of opinion.

Yet, as I indicated earlier, the fullest freedom is always in a very real sense the fullest necessity, in matters of art and morals as well as in matters of inquiry and belief. In matters of morals, we know that we must act in a certain way and that, if we do not, we are not fully moral, or are even immoral or sinful. In the arts the great artist or writer is one who knows and feels the necessity of his vision, and then knows or learns how to employ the technical means necessary to express it satisfactorily. He feels the necessity of full and true expression and only so becomes truly and creatively free.

In science we are free to inquire into anything of relevance to scientific inquiry; but we are not free to discover anything except some fragment of the truth or some approximation to it. We scientists may make mistakes in interpretation; we may make errors of omission or commission; but in the long run the cumulative process of scientific discovery, the free creation of new knowledge and new organizations of knowledge, is subject to the necessity of truth, truth to external fact and truth of internal coherence.

Beliefs are ultimately subject to necessity; in the long run man cannot believe what is false. As the Romans said, "magna est veritas et praevalebit". It has been cynically observed that truth sometimes takes a very long time prevailing; but the statement is essentially true—truth will eventually prevail. Its lag in prevailing is due to obstruction by vested interests, like the Roman Catholic Church's resistance to the ideas of Copernicus and Galileo or the Fundamentalists' resistance to the idea of evolution. But even then it is partly due to psychological resistances—what one of our leading psycho-analysts, Dr. Ernest Jones, describes as "man's blind resistance to the forces making for higher and fuller consciousness". These resistances include sheer intellectual laziness, and the fear or dislike of new facts and ideas as against the comfortable assurance of the old. They also include inner resistance to changing our primitive methods of resolving conflict. For instance, a frequent infantile method of resolving our primal conflicts is to project our own inner aggression on to some external scapegoat or enemy, as was dramatically and horrifyingly illustrated by the history of Nazi Germany, and is now being exemplified by the mutual projection of scapegoatery from the United States to Communist Russia and vice versa. Again, men and women may cling to infantile modes of thought—to the idea of magic, to the craving for the support of external and absolute authority, to the desire for punishing others as an outlet for their own sense of guilt or insufficiency, for instance the dislike and envy by the common man for the intellectual, which is such a common and distressing feature of modern democratic societies.

In psycho-analytic jargon, beliefs are introjections of external fact. Beliefs incorporate the facts and forces of human nature and social nature, and result in the orientation of man, both the individual personality and the common consciousness of society, in a more or less significant relation to the facts of nature; beliefs are thus essentially dynamic, and give an orientation to potential action and a directional set to the personality. They are part of the directive mechanism of the human microcosm; thus it is important, and in the long run essential, that their direction shall be right— in other words, that our beliefs shall be correctly oriented relatively to the directional movement of the macrocosm, the single universal process of transformation. There is thus a constant and necessary interaction between our beliefs and the facts of the universe, or rather between our beliefs and our knowledge of the facts. A classical example is the change in our beliefs about the position of the earth and of man in the universe, in relation to our increasing knowledge of the facts of astronomy since the sixteenth century; another is the change in our beliefs about the origin of man in relation to our increasing knowledge of the facts of biology.

Furthermore, there is a reciprocal reaction; our beliefs may actively influence the facts of our social life and evolution. Thus a belief in divine mission or special status of a nation or group may have political or military results; for instance, in Islam, in Nazi Germany, in the behaviour of the Spaniards to the Indians of the New World, or finally, and of most immediate relevance, in the belief of Communism that the end which it envisages justifies any means.

Further, new knowledge may even affect our beliefs about beliefs themselves. For instance, the knowledge which we have gained in the last fifty years from biology and anthropology, from history and prehistory, that man alone is capable of taking the evolutionary process to greater heights; that he can only do so by means of advance in his cultural evolution, and that beliefs are important organs of cultural evolution, is leading to a quite new belief about our beliefs.

Let me amplify this point, about beliefs necessitated by new knowledge. We can no longer believe that man was created in his present form at some comparatively recent date; for we now know that he has a fantastically long and complicated evolution behind him. We believe that he evolved from some sub-microscopic origin about two thousand million years ago, up through a single-celled form, a primitive multicellular form, and on through more complex types, through fishlike, amphibian, reptilian, mammalian, ape-like creatures, eventually emerging in human form. Second, we now believe that during that vast period evolution was not merely change, but also involved a type of transformation that we must call progress or advance—advance in complexity and level of organization, as revealed in increasing speed, size, power, efficiency, in increasing capacity for self-regulation and inner physiological harmony, and, most significant of all, in increasing level and organization of awareness, as revealed in increase of sensory capacity, of complexity of behaviour, of capacity for learning, remembering, and profiting by experience. Third, what has been emerging more and more clearly in recent years is the belief that major biological evolution seems to have come to an end, that life has by now exhausted its material possibilities, and that its purely physiological capacities have reached their limit. Man has attained his new dominant position in evolution by exploiting life's mental capacities.

Our ancestors believed that mankind was very old. They referred to the period of classical Greece and Rome as antiquity, as if a mere two thousand years was a very long time, whereas in the perspective of biological time it is negligible. We now know that, biologically speaking, man is exceedingly young. He has only become a fully dominant type since he invented urban civilization some five thousand years ago. Sir James Jeans in one of his books gives a very illuminating comparison. If we take the height of Cleopatra's Needle as representing the length of time that elapsed from the first origin of life on this planet to the first beginnings of civilization, and then want to include the amount of time since the origins of civilization till the present day, all that would be needed would be to put a postage stamp on its top.

Frankly, when I read that I didn't feel like believing it; it seemed impossible. I figured it out for myself with pencil and paper, and after doing the sum about five times I concluded that Sir James Jeans was perfectly correct. If I recollect rightly, I think that the postage stamp would have to be slightly thicker than ordinary, but you wouldn't have to add a second postage stamp.

To-day we can project our time-scale into the future. The geologists and geophysicists and astronomers now believe that the future time available to man before life ceases to be possible on our planet is at least as great as that which has elapsed since the original life until now—at least another two thousand million years, another Cleopatra's Needle of time compared to the postage stamp from the pyramid to the present. Thus we can be assured of a reasonably long and, we may hope, a reasonably fruitful future for mankind.

Another fact which must inevitably colour our beliefs is the fact that knowledge has been decisive in promoting human evolution. Both man's new dominant position in the world of life and his subsequent advance in culture and civilization only became possible through the increase and improvement of his awareness, in the broad sense of that word—his factual knowledge of the external and the internal world, his organization of that knowledge, his understanding, his will and purpose, his feelings and the modes of their expression. His advances became possible through the discovery of more facts, a better interpretation of facts, the formulation of better ideas, a better resolution of internal conflicts—and, finally, more adequate beliefs.

As an extension of this, we are driven to a belief in science, or rather in the scientific method. History demonstrates that the best method for securing advance and improvement in awareness, and so for securing human progress in general, is the scientific method—in other words, going to the facts, questioning them, framing hypotheses about them, testing the hypotheses against the facts. It is through this dialectic exchange between brute fact and human reason that we discover new facts and new regularities which lead on in their turn to new hypotheses and new discoveries, and to a gradually increasing body of ever more firmly established truth. Anti-rationalists sometimes decry science for constantly changing its views—Einstein as against Newton, Freud as against the classical psychologists, atomic physics as against nineteenth-century atomic theory, pre-Mendelian heredity versus modern heredity, etc. However, though interpretation may change, the great body of established fact and principle remains; for instance, Newtonian mechanics is still perfectly adequate for immediate practical purposes in spite of the radical changes in interpretation we owe to Einstein.

The scientific method can be utilized in any subject, not only in natural sciences like physics or biology but in anthropology, psychology, social science, archaeology, or history. The scientific method is the best and most efficient method of utilizing man's curiosity and interest, his desire for comprehension and explanation and logical coherence. Mere idle curiosity will not produce a satisfactory body of organized knowledge. On the other hand, too much concentration on logical coherence, with insufficient observation and inadequate testing of the facts, will produce purely speculative or metaphysical word-spinning in place of scientifically and practically profitable theories.

Thus we come to a belief in man's mind—Pascal's "thinking reed". Man is the agent or instrument of further evolution, whether he likes it or not; but he can best perform his cosmic function if he becomes a conscious instrument, a conscious agent of fufilment, with the deliberate aim of realizing further possibilities of the evolutionary process.

And that brings me to what I think is destined to prove the greatest change in our beliefs. Lord Bryce was struck by America's belief in the future. This foreshadows an essential characteristic of the new age for which we are heading; we are becoming increasingly interested in the possible future as against the actual past, in possibilities rather than in origins, in descendants rather than in ancestors.

When I say possibilities, I *mean* possibilities, not impossibilities; many people advance what they claim are possibilities, but are really wish-fulfilments or unbridled speculations. We need a science of possibilities. Such a science will take account of the limitations of reality as well as of its immense potentialities. As an immediate step, we need a new science directed to the investigation of unrealized human possibilities. Furthermore, that must eventually be matched with a religion based on the idea of fulfilment of possibilities. Christianity took the first great step towards this in proclaiming that all men have the possibility of salvation. Our modern formulation would be that all men have the possibility of greater fulfilment.

Let me now return to the problem of freedom of belief. When we survey the cultural history of mankind, we find that the largest advances, whether in science, in the arts, in writing, in architecture, in religious and moral insight, or in what Walt Whitman called the progress of souls—the largest advances have taken place when there have been the greatest outbursts of free, creative activity of the human mind and spirit, of human personalities free from artificial restraints and subject only to the necessities imposed by their own nature and the nature of things.

Another clear lesson of history is that beliefs cannot be imposed by force. The attempt to do so damaged the whole structure of society, since society has a psychological as well as a material basis. We have two examples from our own times. It has become clear that the Nazis' belief in the superiority of so-called "Aryan" science over "Jewish" or "non-Aryan" science led to a degeneration of science in Nazi Germany, because so many of their leading thinkers and scientists were not "Aryans" and were either suppressed or fled into exile. And I can testify from my personal, professional experience that the enforced rise of Michurinism and Lysenko in the U.S.S.R. in about 1935 brought about a degeneration of Soviet biology, especially in the field of genetics.

Again, authority cannot just forbid beliefs, though it can forbid or restrain action flowing from false beliefs, as in regard to public health or in regard to subversive actions (as opposed to belief in Communism). On the other hand, it is possible to encourage or promote right beliefs. This cannot be done by force, or by mere moralizing, or by the setting up of orthodoxies, still less by encouraging uniformity and discouraging originality. It must be done with the aid of another belief—the belief in human possibilities, in the value of free creative activity, whether intellectual, scientific, artistic, practical, or moral, or concerned with the development of one's own personality. We must believe in this, and in the eventual rightness of its results; that is the long-term lesson of history.

Take an example from education. We are beginning at long last to realize that the best results are obtained not by just telling boys and girls what they ought to know, not by making them learn it by heart unintelligently, still less by trying to beat it into them *a posteriori* as was the practice all through the Middle Ages; but by making them interested, showing them things, stimulating their curiosity and their natural desire to know and understand, their desire to find and to create significance.

Again, in regard to society as a whole, the lesson is that we must not merely be tolerant of differences, but should manifest an active encouragement of creative diversity.

Finally, we have to believe in keeping our own lives open, "open to novelty and change", as Charles Morris says, "and not close them down against progress". Man is unique as an organism in that his individual development, because it is more than merely physiological, so largely mental and aesthetic and spiritual, can continue until death. Thus we should aim throughout life at the realization of fuller possibilities, including possibilities of larger understanding and more adequate and more comprehensive beliefs. If I recollect right, it was Edmund Burke who said, "For the triumph of evil it is only necessary that good men shall do nothing." This applies to intellectual evil just as much as to moral evil. For the triumph of falsehood and ignorance it is only necessary that men shall do nothing with their intelligence. And the converse is also true, that for the triumph of right, including intellectual right, it is necessary that we should do something with our intelligence.

In conclusion I would say that the most important belief now emerging from our new knowledge is the belief in human possibilities, including the belief that they can be realized to a far larger extent than now, but only by providing opportunity and example, coupled with intellectual and moral effort. To realize this fact, to grasp this belief, and to put it into practice seems to me to be the chief responsibility of a university in the tradition of a free society.

KNOWLEDGE, MORALITY, AND DESTINY[1]

OUR Western world, in this year 1951, is psychologically in a bad way. Our thinking is chaotic, our nerves are jumpy, we are a prey to pessimism and depression, we seem frightened of our human selves. Our half of the world lacks

[1] The third William Alanson White Memorial Lecture, 1951.

a common faith; the other half has had imposed upon it a domatic faith which can never satisfy free men. We in the West have lost our sense of continuity, our long-term hope, and seem only able to concentrate on prospects of immediate disaster or immediate methods of escaping from it.

Never was there greater need for a large perspective, in which we might discern the outlines of a general and continuing belief beyond the disturbance and chaos of the present. Yet, paradoxically enough, never was there a greater possibility of attaining so large a perspective, and attaining so firm and enduring a belief.

Every society, in every age, needs some system of beliefs, including a basic attitude to life, an organized set of ideas round which emotion and purpose may gather, and a conception of human destiny. It needs a philosophy and a faith to achieve a guide to orderly living—in other words a morality.

Any such system of beliefs must of necessity contain both short-term and long-term elements. It must be relevant to the immediate business of living here and now, to the development of existing individual lives, to the social and political problems of the time; but it must also be capable of reaching out beyond the particular to the general, beyond the immediate to the enduring, so as to put men in touch with what is universal in reality, or at least with what they feel as being universal. And of course (though the fact is not always recognized) our beliefs are in the long run based upon, or at least correlated with, our knowledge and the organization of our knowledge.

In many belief-systems there is often a break between the elements concerned with the present and the particular, and those concerned with the permanent and the universal. This is especially marked at the present day. Thus, for many people, beliefs based on science have only immediate relevance, while long-term relevance is reserved for beliefs rooted in idealist philosophy or traditional religion.

However, the present epoch is the first in which our knowledge, and the beliefs which it could support, is adequate to do justice to both these aspects of our life—our immediate business of living and acting, and our relations with the long-term and the universal. For the first time in history there is available a general picture of mankind, of the universe in which mankind exists, and of the relations between them. The human species can see itself as a process in time, a small but decisive element in the universal process of evolution. An earlier generation could speak of man's place in nature: this static formulation is now outdated; to-day we must speak rather of man's destiny in the world-process.

Elsewhere I have attempted to analyse the general process of evolution more fully, and to point out some of its implications. Here I must confine myself to the brief mention of a few essential points.

Evolution in the comprehensive sense is a unique, one-way, irreversible process in time, generating novelty and variety. During the process, an immense increase in organization has been produced, but only in a few sectors in which conditions have been favourable.

In the universe at large, evolution has remained on the inorganic level; its rate has been exceedingly slow, and the degree of organization it has produced has usually not exceeded the atomic, though here and there it has reached a simple molecular level.

On our earth (and possibly on a few other planets of other stars), conditions permitted the formation of complex organic molecules capable of self-reproduction and therefore what we call alive. With this, a new mechanism of change automatically became available, in the shape of natural selection, and the biological phase of evolution was thereby initiated. The process of evolutionary transformation was much accelerated, and incredibly complex organizations were produced, from cells with their thousands of different genes and other biochemical parts, up to avian and mammalian individuals with their thousands of millions of such cells, and to communities like beehives and termitaries, with their hundreds of thousands of such individuals, existing in a highly complex social pattern. As for variety, it will suffice to recall that there exist some three-quarters of a million separate species of insects alone, and probably one and a half million species of living organisms in all. But the most remarkable feature of biological evolution was the emergence of mind—the increasing importance of the capacities of living matter for knowing, feeling, and willing.

Finally, after about two billion years, biological improvement reached its limit, except along this one direction—of improved organization of mental capacities. This led to a radically new phase of evolution, the human or psycho-social phase.

Pascal gave expression to the unique value of mind in the

pattern of things when he wrote, "All bodies, the firmament, the stars, the earth and its kingdoms, are not equal to the lowest minds. For mind knows all these and itself; and these bodies, nothing." But we have had to wait over two hundred years for the further illumination provided by evolutionary biology that the mindless universe has generated mind, and, through the mental capacities of man, can now begin to contemplate and even to comprehend itself.

It is no coincidence that within a decade of Darwin's *Origin of Species* Walt Whitman wrote "Passage to India" with its unitary vision of the cosmos:

> O, vast Rondure, swimming in space,
> Cover'd all over with visible power and beauty,
> Alternate light and day and the teeming spiritual darkness,
> Unspeakable high processions of sun and moon, and countless
>   stars, above,
> Below, the manifold grass and waters, animals, mountains,
>   trees,
> With inscrutable purpose, some hidden, prophetic intention,
> Now first it seems my thought begins to span thee.

Through the mental capacities of man, organizations of a new quality and degree of complexity arise in the universe. Human mind is capable of organizational construction and synthesis on an unexampled scale, and can impose unity on a virtually unlimited variety. In one act of consciousness, a man can hold together elements of the present and past, projections into the future, particular experiences and general concepts, emotions and intellectual ideas, facts and fancies, fears and hopes. And a single human mind in the course of its development comprises an unlimited number of such complex organizations of thought.

On this new level, the rate of evolution again becomes much more rapid, and the process becomes concerned mainly with transformations of ideas, cultures, and societies. It leads to new heights of complexity and variety of organization, not merely in such distinctively human products as machines and buildings and social systems, but in individual organisms. During man's growth, individuality becomes personality.

Here I would like to stress the importance of the organization of our knowledge, as opposed to mere increase in its amount. Experience is organized anew in each one of us.

So far as organization of experience is concerned, the infant starts with a *tabula rasa*—but a *tabula rasa* endowed with predispositions, potentialities of building up the raw materials of experience into organized systems. The experience of those who recover their sight after having been blind from infancy, together with the work of physiologists and psychologists on illusions and perceptual assumptions (like that of Ames and Cantril with distorted rooms), shows that even our perceptions, far from being the automatic and immediate product of the impact of the world of sense on our brains, are elaborate though unconscious creations, built up and organized by a selective synthesis of sense-data: and the same is true of all but our most elementary emotional states.

We first organize our experience into what we call "objects" and "events"; the words of our languages, our concepts, and abstractions are constructions for organizing the chaos of experience into order; so are scientific laws, works of art, philosophies, and systems of religion.

The development of knowledge is the most important aspect of evolution on the human level. Not only does the amount of available knowledge increase, but the methods of obtaining it and of organizing it for use are improved. Even in the earliest civilizations of Egypt and Mesopotamia there was no organized philosophy, as has been emphasized by Henri Frankfort and his collaborators in their book *Before Philosophy;* the idea of a single universal god, one of the most powerful organizing concepts of all time, did not emerge until much later; and modern science, the most efficient method to date of obtaining and organizing knowledge, is a product merely of the last three centuries.

Man is a microcosm, though in a sense different from that of earlier ages. Medieval thinkers essayed to find correspondences between the structure and working of man and of the rest of the universe, or macrocosm; to-day we concern ourselves with the correspondences which man establishes between the universe and his thoughts about it, until the macrocosm acquires a new unity and significance in the microcosm organized by human mind.

Man constructs within himself some sort of picture of the universe; a miniature model housed in what Blake called the crystal cabinet of his mind. And this present century is the first period in which that picture could be even approximately accurate, or approximately complete in its extent. Furthermore, man now sees himself in a new light, as solely responsible for continuing evolutionary advance: for this planet at least, he *is* further evolution. His microcosm thus comprises not only a picture but a purpose.

To-day the different elements and parts of the universe, however distinct or separate, however distant in space or remote in time, may be brought together in a single pattern within the unity of human knowledge, and its multifarious and often conflicting processes may be envisaged in relation to a single line of action within the unity of human purpose.

For here, as always, knowledge is related to action. It was only through centuries of scientific labour that man could come to know that the entire universe is a process of evolution and only in virtue of that new knowledge can he now begin to frame a purpose and a course of action consonant with the nature of that universal process. The dispersed and material macrocosm is concentrated and unified in the mental microcosm.

From a somewhat different angle, the process of evolution in all its phases can be envisaged as a trend towards the actualization of potentiality, the realization or fulfilment of inherent possibilities. However, this trend is constantly confronted by obstacles to its advance. Each situation imposes certain limitations on the possibilities to be realized, or distorts their form: the degree of realization attained is conditioned by the opportunities of time and space. Thus, over the vast majority of the universe, conditions are such as to prevent the attainment of any level of organization above the atomic, and higher potentialities, such as those of life or mind, are quite ruled out.

Again, it took over a thousand million years of biological evolution to overcome the limitations set to the self-reproduction of mind and so to reveal the potentialities of life for accumulating organized experience. And it took all of human history until the seventeenth century to overcome the limitations set by primitive social structure on the organization of thought and to develop the scientific method as a tool for increasing knowledge.

L. L. Whyte has put the matter in a nutshell by defining the essential property of all natural processes as the tendency of systems, when conditions permit, to develop their characteristic forms without arrest or distortion. And various modern psychiatrists, such as Erich Fromm, concentrating on the particular process of human development, have pointed out that true freedom consists in the overcoming of the limitations and distortions imposed by external conditions and internal conflict on the fulfilment of our inherent potentialities. In the free employment and enjoyment of our capacities, we attain the particular fruition which is the "characteristic form" of the system we call human personality.

The first and obvious implication of this new picture of human destiny is that man must try to understand more about the process of evolution, about himself as an essential operative part of it, and about the relations between himself and the whole. He must accept what is given in the universe.

If we are truly to accept the universe, we must not deny the reality or validity or significance of any elements in it. The Marxists, and the Behaviorists try to deny the validity of the mental and spiritual elements in the universe; conversely, some mystics and idealists and theologians try to deny the importance of the material ones.

We must accept reality as unitary, and so must reject all dualistic ways of thinking. We must accept the fact that it is a process, and so must reject all static conceptions. The process is always relative, so we must reject all absolutes. And it tends to a fuller realization of inherent potentiality, so we must study what facilitates fulfilment and what hinders it.

For this we must develop new methods of thinking. We must learn how to think in terms of organization and pattern, and in those of trend and process—what one might call pattern-process thought. We must learn to think in terms of organizations-as-wholes, as well as in terms of elements-by-analysis. We have to adjust our thinking to deal with one-way directional processes as well as with static situations or reversible systems.

There are four possible main ways of thinking about the universe. We may think in dualistic and at the same time in static terms. This has been the characteristic mode of European thought, of Plato and Paul, of Dante and Aquinas, of Descartes and Newton. We may think dualistically, but at the same time in terms of process and movement. This combination characterizes Hegel, and also the Marxist system. We may have a unitary system, which however is static. This is exemplified by the thought of Buddhism, and of a few Western philosophers, such as Spinoza. Or we may think in unitary terms, and at the same time in those of movement, trend, and process. Such a system seems certainly to be the one which now needs to be developed.

Of course, you can subdivide these main brands or modes of thinking according to their dominant components at any one time. Thus absolutist philosophies constitute one branch of static thinking, based on absolutes as limiting values of static concepts. Again, during the last hundred years, scientific thought has been dominated by the concept of quantity, and this has spread into many other fields of thought, such as economics.

Looked at from the angle of history, each type of organization of thought can be regarded as a broad adaptation to the situation and the conditions of the times. Thus the emergence of the dualist idea was probably necessary to make man conscious of himself and his possibilities as an independent agent, who could hope to understand and deal with the natural forces by which he was beset. The absolutist approach was an adaptation to provide man with some basis of permanence from which he could operate in the flux of events, before its apparent chaos could be more properly comprehended as a definable continuing process. And the quantitative mode of thought was an adaptation permitting the fuller control of nature and the rise of precision technology. Finally, it seems that the unitary-process type is that which is appropriate to our time to-day, to permit the fuller control of the processes of human development, alike of individuals and of societies and cultures.

An apparently progressive advance may turn out ultimately to be a limitation. For instance, the insects successfully conquered the land by developing a method for breathing with the aid of fine air-tubes penetrating every tissue of the body. This constitutes an admirable mechanism so long as the creature remains small, but makes large size impossible. An insect as big as a rat just wouldn't work properly: actually no insect is bigger than a mouse. This limitation of total size naturally sets a limit to the size of the brain, and so to the number of cells in the brain, which in turn sets a low limit to the degree of intelligence and the flexibility of behaviour. That is why insects are never very intelligent, but have to depend mainly on the often marvellous but always rigid and limited behaviour-mechanisms we call instincts. This limitation of insect size is very lucky for us, because without it, man assuredly could never have evolved.

However, there are certain types of advance, namely advances in all-round organization, which do not limit future possibilities but leave the way open for further advances and therefore can be called progressive. Biological progress in this sense takes place in a series of separate steps, each of them taking a finite time for its achievement, and each making some new and different step possible. To take a few obvious examples, one of the earliest steps in progress was the differentiation of life into plants and animals. Another one was the attainment by life of the cellular level of organization, which in turn provided the basis for the further step constituted by the organization of separate cells into multicellular organisms. And a very decisive step, but one taken only in a few lines, was the evolution of a central nervous system and brain, together with organs of special sense like eyes. Again, the step to accurate regulation of internal temperature provided the foundation for a new possibility—the possibility of a unified continuity of mental life.

With the taking of this next step of progress, to the human type of brain and mind, we pass into the third main phase of evolution; and here too this same step-by-step process of advance occurs. As an obvious example, before a certain period in human history, man had not learned to domesticate animals and plants. In the brief space of a few millennia before the beginning of urban civilization, he achieved this step. He has made a few later refinements, but in all major essentials the process was over before the dawn of history; since then no important species has been added to the list of man's domesticated animals or cultivated plants.

Biological evolution leads to the transformation of actual organisms, via the struggle for existence and natural selection. Human evolution leads to the transformation of cultures (including of course the types of personality which are permitted or fostered by particular cultures) via cultural and mental selection.

Thus in man the transaction of the real business of evolution has been shifted from the domain of matter to that of thought. This gives a new dimension and a new flexibility to evolution and makes possible much quicker and fuller adaptation. However, the adaptation is not primarily to the environment in the limited static sense of the external physical environment alone, nor even to that together with the social environment, as some sociologists would like us to believe, but to the business of transformation and realization of inherent potentiality: that is to say, adaptation to the process of evolution itself. Furthermore, since thought is potential action, its organization must be adapted to the particular problems of each cultural stage or situation in human transformation, though of course always also to the longer-term aspects of the process, as in giving hopeful continuity and an over-all relation of man to his destiny.

The most decisive of the steps in human advance are those introducing new modes of organizing thought, new ordering concepts, new attitudes, which help to determine the set of conduct and the pattern of culture.

Thus magic was once the chief dominant concept. Millennia later, that was transcended—not wholly superseded, but transcended as a dominant concept—by that of a single universal god.

The ideas of salvation and of universality crystallized the chaos of beliefs and the welter of misery in the late Roman Empire into a wholly new transformation, leading to a new dominant idea-system, in the shape of Christianity. The organization of thought about social order, expressed in codes of law applicable to all alike within the community, beginning with Hammurabi in ancient Babylon and culminating in the Roman Empire, served as a foundation for all later advance in civilization. Another but much later step was the organization of thought in terms of scientific method and scientific knowledge.

During this last process, one development is particularly illuminating. The eighteenth century was characterized by a remarkable series of technical advances: coal mining, cast iron, the steam-engine, the spinning-jenny, the power-loom, improved communications like canals and better roads, new methods of agriculture, the factory system, and so forth. It is tempting to regard these as the beginnings of applied science. But when one considers the people responsible for these transformations, men like Watt, Arkwright, Benjamin Franklin, Thomas Jefferson, Coke of Norfolk, the Duke of Bridgewater, Boulton, Count Rumford, or McAdam, it becomes clear that the movement was not in any real sense applied science, but what may be called applied scientific attitude. Science had not yet developed to the pitch at which its results could be directly applied to practical problems, as they can now; and the men responsible for the technological advances were not scientists or the products of scientific training, but practical men of business, or aristocrats, or public men interested in affairs. They were applying not the findings of science, but the outlook of science. The primary idea of science that Bacon and the founders of the Royal Society put forward and stuck to in spite of ridicule—the idea that by investigating natural phenomena, however apparently insignificant, men could attain new realms of knowledge and acquire new possibilities of control over nature—together with the general idea resulting from Newton's great work —the conception of the physical universe as a machine— those ideas so dominated the general attitude and so transformed the intellectual climate that it was natural for people to think technologically, in terms of inventing new techniques for the better handling of old problems, and of a general extension of man's control over nature.

This shows how the organization of knowledge round a broad general idea can, through constructive imagination and correct insight, come to have force and effect long before the idea has been worked out in detail. The idea of science became practically effective well before the time when science itself could be so. Key concepts like this stand at the top of the hierarchy of the organization of thought; they impose a pattern on it and pull other less dominant ideas into place, modifying them in relation to the whole pattern.

As an example of the organizing and transforming properties of dominant ideas, we see that the broad pattern of thinking derived from the developing humanist, protestant, and scientific traditions, gave a new twist to the idea of the intrinsic value of the human individual, earlier established by Christianity, and transformed it so as to lead to the nineteenth-century ideas of universal political democracy and individual enterprise.

Many interesting parallels could be drawn between the evolution of organisms and the evolution of organizations of thought. Thus in the evolution of thought, new key concepts may develop and become dominant either by transcending the previous dominant concepts, in the process assimilating what of the old is relevant to the new; or by the extinction of the old. This latter process may be due to the old concepts simply disappearing, or at any rate falling from a dominant to a very inferior position, since they are no longer workable in the new situation; or the new may have to compete with the old, eventually ousting it. Thus monotheism transcended polytheism, but took from it the idea of personal divinities behind phenomena; the idea of sympathetic magic has for all practical purposes ceased to count in Western civilization, leaving the field open for the rise of unitary thought; Christianity fought and extinguished polytheism and emperor-worship within the Roman Empire.

A detailed historical study of the evolution and transformation of human thought would also bring out many interesting points. For instance, the fact that individual thinkers may be in advance of history, and therefore unable to translate their thought, albeit true in essence, into formulations appropriate to the times and capable of exerting practical effects on the process of human transformation. Thus Goethe's unitary approach was too far in advance of the analytic temper of his age to have much effect on science or philosophy; Mendel's work had to wait for thirty years before it found its place in the process of science; Roger Bacon was a premature scientist, and the Emperor Frederic II a premature humanist (phrases which recall that shocking distortion of the idea of being before one's time—the smear use of the phrase "premature anti-Fascist").

But I must pass on to my main topic. How are we to take the new bold step which clearly seems necessary, of transforming our system of thought in a way appropriate to the problems of to-day? How best to act as midwife to deliver the world of a new ideology, or, if we wish to avoid that rather unpleasant word, a new system of ideas appropriate to man's new situation?

What are the characteristics of this new situation which would seem especially relevant to the task of adaptively transforming the organization of our thought? First of all, the world of man is beginning to emerge as unavoidably destined to be one: in many particular aspects it has already acquired a *de facto* unity. Yet in spite of this, it is also abundantly split, especially in its thinking.

There are two main kinds of splits in thought. There is the split between the thought of West and East (or non-West), and there are the splits within the thought both of the West and of the non-West.

The dominant idea-system of the non-West, the system of Marxism and dialectical materialism, began by taking over the emerging idea of process and the historical outlook from Hegel and Darwin. It then took the idea of scientific method from the Western world, the materialist outlook from physical science and technology, and the economic and class outlook (but not the individualist outlook) from the social structure of the nineteenth-century West. In so doing, Marxism accomplished a curious feat: it took over the basic dualism of Western European thought, but then proceeded to transform it into a phony monism, a sham unitary system, by denying validity to one of its two components, namely the mental aspect.

The Marxists, perhaps unconsciously, took over the idea of their power structure from the dogmatic authoritarianism of medieval Christendom, the idea of universalism from the past of Russia, and the idea of universalism from the Enlightenment; and these three ideas in combination inevitably produced the idea of a monolithic state, exclusive but expansionist, based on a dogmatic cultural and political imperialism.

However, it is really only the façade of the Marxist system that is monolithic, and behind it there are many splits. The chief split is the result of the tension between the individual, whose significance *qua* individual is denied or repudiated, and the State as organized domination and as an object of subservience. There is the split between the overt materialism of the system and its repressed mental and spiritual aspects. Finally, there is the split in intellectual and cultural life between the scientific and the dogmatic methods of organizing and expressing thought; this was most strikingly exemplified by the Lysenko controversy, but is apparent also in many other fields of science, learning, and art.

But we in the West are more immediately concerned with the splits of our own system. It would be possible to list a large number of such splits operating within our present thought: the split between nature and man, between subject and object, between religion and science, between good and evil, between free will and necessity, and dozens more. However, these are all in a sense only symptoms or products of our one basic split, the fundamental dualism of Western thought, which has resulted in a radical dissociation of Western culture and personality. This has been in operation ever since the time of Plato and Paul, though it has been manifested in all sorts of different ways in different periods: the split persists, but its manifestations change according to circumstances.

What are the chief current manifestations of this basic split? I would suggest, first of all, our over-specialization as against the development of an all-round approach, too much reliance on analysis into separate elements, too little on unitary comprehension: in general terms, too much differentiation and not enough integration. A special case of this is the over-emphasis on quantity, as against quality and the significance of qualitative values. This over-emphasis, though most marked in scientific thought, has also been characteristic of economics, and its value-debasing influence has spread over many aspects of everyday life. To-day, we are just beginning to realize that far from the principle of quantity being fundamental, it is not even inherent in the nature of the universe. It is we ourselves who have put quantity and number and mathematics into the universe. We have done so by employing the technique of measurement for our own purposes: measurement and mathematical formulation are essential for certain kinds of comprehension, and for the precision control which is needed for efficient technology. Sir James Jeans' pronouncement that God must be a mathematician was just another example of man's age-old practice of creating God in his own image.

Then there has been the collapse of the traditional confidence-giving beliefs, a collapse largely brought about through the rise of science; while in the meantime science, by clinging to the pretence that it was ethically and morally neutral, has debarred itself from providing confidence or from assisting in the building up of new systems of belief in place of the old.

Meanwhile a further depth of insecurity and fear—man's fear of his own self—has resulted from the revelation of sadism and bestiality which came to the surface in the last war. As a consequence an old problem has been aggravated —the projection of our own fears and repressed aggressivity on to enemies, who can then serve as convenient scapegoats for our own guilt. We are constantly searching for enemies, or even creating them, in order to justify ourselves: and that inevitably enlarges minor differences into major ones, and makes any actual splits appear as apparently unbridgeable chasms and irreconcilable conflicts. One of the reasons why the split between East and West is so grave is that we have ourselves magnified both its size and its gravity, largely by thinking about our admittedly serious differences in terms of black-and-white opposition. Many Westerners have ceased to think of Russians as human beings: they have become, in some non-rational absolute sense, just "enemies".

Finally, there is the inhibition, the negativist pessimism, the energy-consuming conflict, and the essential destructiveness of all split thought, in place of the rational faith, the

positive facilitation, and the energy-releasing constructive-
ness which could be ours if we could but unify our thinking—conflict as against unitary purpose, frustration as
against fruition.

This brings me back to the emergent idea-system, the new
organization of thought, at whose birth we are assisting. It
takes account, first and foremost, of the fact that nature is
one universal process of evolution, self-developing and self-
transforming, and that it includes us. Man does not stand
over against nature; he is part of it. We men are that part of
the process which has become self-conscious, and it is our
duty and our destiny to facilitate the process by leading it on
to new levels.

Our chief motive, therefore, will derive from the exploration and understanding of human nature and the possibilities
of development and fulfilment inherent in it, a study which
will of course include the limitations, distortions, and frustrations to be avoided.

Such a philosophy might perhaps best be called Transhumanism. It is based on the idea of humanity attempting to
overcome its limitations and to arrive at fuller fruition; it
is the realization that both individual and social development
are processes of self-transformation.

The accumulation and organization of knowledge provide
both the necessary basis and the main mechanism for
human transformation. In the light of that fact, truth can
be defined as the organization of our knowledge in greater
concordance with reality. The truth of the transhumanist approach and its central conception is larger and more universal than any previous truth, and is bound in the long run to
supersede lesser, more partial, or more distorted truths, such
as Marxism, or Christian theology, or liberal individualism,
or at any rate to assimilate those of their elements which
are relevant to itself.

In the light of such an overriding idea, the individual is
seen as a part of the social process, and a very important
part of it, just as man is seen as a very important part of the
cosmic process. He need no longer feel insulted by the fact
of death or by his own insignificance. Once he can grasp that
he is a part, and an operative part, of an enduring process,
he need not continue to compensate for his isolation by
mere personal ambition or by frantic striving for superior
status or superior achievement. Once he grasps that his main
job is the optimum realization of the possibilities of his own

development, and that this, if well and truly accomplished, will at the same time inevitably facilitate or contribute to the realization of the possibilities of society, and of mankind, and of the cosmic process as a whole, he can acquire a new sense of oneness with the rest of existence.

Various elements in other previous systems could and should be taken over by the new system of thought, and assimilated into its new pattern. There is the equal worth or intrinsic value of all human beings, taken over from Christianity and Western democracy; the importance of the individual, taken over from the post-Renaissance era, the scientific method of objective testing and the principle of limited certitude, from the three centuries of natural science; the importance of quantitative thinking, from technology and precision control; the importance of quality, from the arts and from philosophy; the application of the evolutionary or historical idea to society, from Hegel and Marx; the value of variety, both for individuals and for cultures, from social anthropology; the idea of what we may call external adventure—activism, exploration, control of nature—from the Renaissance and natural science, from technology and sport, and from Marxism; but also the correlative of this, on the other side of the basic split, the idea of internal adventure—contemplation, self-discipline, and control of oneself—from the poets, artists, philosophers, and mystics of all continents.

Then we very much need to take over the ideas of wholeness and harmony, largely from Oriental thought; and, of course, the idea of order, law, and the necessary hierarchy of authority from various sources in past history.

We may have to combine and adjust these elements in various ways. For instance, one may combine the scientific approach with the idea of hierarchy of authority, in the affirmation that the final authority in the society of the future will be that of knowledge: we cannot help but obey the truth once we have successfully made the effort of clearly identifying and recognizing it.

And so our new idea-system gradually begins to take shape. Its central ordering concept is the idea that our human destiny is to have the unique privilege and responsibility of leadership in the process of evolution: there is one reality, and man is its prophet and pioneer.

The long-term component of this is the discovery that the process is universal, the process of the universe as a whole; that it is a creative, open process with indefinite possibilities of fulfilment still unrealized before it, one to be fully grasped and comprehended only in the active process of realizing it. This automatically heals the basic split between man and nature. And the split between the individual and society is healed by the discovery that in self-fulfilment, through the development of his personality, the individual is making his particular contribution to the cosmic process.

What we may call the medium-term component, applicable to all human activities, whether of individuals or groups, is the idea of participation in the enterprise of human evolution, contributing to the creative self-transformation of man. The chief dynamic or central motive here is the exploration of human possibilities and opportunities.

The short-term component, that which is immediately applicable to the present situation, is the idea that the world of man *can* be unified, but only on the basis of widespread understanding of the meaning of unification and the need for it. In other words, the human species, as an operative agency, must become conscious of itself as a single process which will only operate efficiently and freely if unified. And this will only happen if the mass of people everywhere are free to think about the problem; only when they are liberated from the compulsions of ill-health, material misery, and ignorance, will they be able to turn their attention away from themselves and their particular frustrations and direct it on to their relations to the world at large.

The chief dynamic here is, on the one hand, the already widespread belief that science can provide at least a minimum adequacy of food, health, and material well-being, with the resultant demand for this on the part of the under-privileged millions; and, on the other, the dawning belief that only knowledge can set man truly free, with the resulting demand for more knowledge, more science, and better education.

All this has direct implications for morality. Thus one immediate moral duty is to try to identify and understand the transformation of human development which the present situation calls for, and to devise appropriate methods for thinking about it.

I must now speak about some of the implications and applications of any such unitary approach to the problem of human destiny. The first is that we must learn to adopt a unitary and evolutionary mode of thinking, in terms of total pattern and continuing process.

This means using intuition and imagination—unitary comprehension of truth and total significance, imagination of new possibilities and of the consequences of new facts and ideas—as well as the analytic processes of reason. Of course, they must be employed in conjunction with analytic reason and with the laborious process of testing against reality. We must learn to regard intellectual analysis and scientific objectivity, not as the sole or main, or even as a separate method of thinking, but as a means for improving intuitive comprehension and appreciation and their applications.

This is not easy. It is a new technique, a new type of skill which we have to learn, like mathematical skill, or skiing, or playing the piano. It demands time and effort and will inevitably meet with resistance, not only from the vested interests of other modes of thinking but from our natural laziness and our existing mental habits and established organizations of thought. But like other skills, it is a pattern of activity which, once acquired, can be applied in a great variety of detailed situations, and a capacity whose free exercise provides new sources of satisfaction.

Throughout life we are confronted by the need for organizing our experience and our thought. This is illustrated by the way in which we organize our perceptions and our concepts. The need here is to organize the primordial chaos of sense-data with which our infant minds are confronted into a first degree of order. When we say that we perceive an object, we imply that we have intuitively recognized a particular example of some general configuration of sense-data, which we have unconsciously learned in our past lives to associate in a single general pattern. From one point of view, a perceived object is thus a pattern of assumptions, as can be demonstrated by experiments on illusions.

But the assumptions are also predictions, in that they have all sorts of potential significance for our future. For instance, we unconsciously predict of a heavy solid object that it will need effort to handle and can hurt us mechanically; of fire that it may burn us; of food that it will taste good.

Concepts are organizations of thought involving generality. Into them too we often put assumptions: for instance, the assumption that the immediate separability and temporary persistence of what we call objects or things are absolute, permanent, and essential to them; and, by extension, that abstract concepts like goodness or truth are also permanent and absolute essence or qualities. Historically, man appears to have generalized his notions of separateness and persistence before he felt the need to generalize those of wholeness or of togetherness in patterned relation, or those of process or orderly change in development.

The need for this new mode of organizing our experience is only now becoming fully apparent. We have at last discovered that the reality with which we have to deal is a hierarchy of patterned processes. We must now learn how to recognize unit processes as we earlier learned to recognize unit objects, to comprehend their characters as we learned to comprehend the properties of objects; in so doing, we shall learn to comprehend the patterns of development which are inherently possible for them, and to make correct assumptions or predictions about their effects.

The principle of causality and the formulation of regularities in the shape of scientific laws represent, I suppose, the highest achievements of the analytic and static method. Today we need, not to abolish them, but to transcend them. This we can do through proper formulation of the principles of relational adjustment and of order in terms of intrinsic modes and forms of development.

Now for some of the implications of any such formulations. I will begin with one relevant to psychiatry. In the recent past there has been a tendency to minimize the importance of reason by interpreting it mainly as rationalization, and to consider the organization of thought as a secondary product of our instinctual and emotional life. Thus any split thinking we may display has tended to be regarded as a resultant, a symptom of basic personality dissociation or primordial conflict, in conjunction with social tensions and cultural splits. This, however, is turning out to be incorrect: indeed, the tendency itself results from our thought being unintegrated.

We in the West grow up in a system of thought which forces its own dissociation on to the unitary reality of things. The very organization of our language, and all our habitual ways of thinking, artificially dissociate real and ideal, object and subject, quantity and quality, material and spiritual, right and wrong, good and evil, "we" of the in-group and "they" of the out-group, individual and society, intuitional appreciation and intellectual analysis. How can we expect people to grow up whole in a world which is presented to them already split by the organization of thought, and when the main instrument we give them in education is one for carving reality into separate slices? It is true that art is a

method for putting some of the slices together again, sometimes even for presenting situations as wholes without preliminary carving up; but it is also true that the entire trend
of the modern West has been to relegate art to an inferior
position vis-à-vis analytic science.

Of course I do not intend to imply that we should go to
the opposite extreme and say that either split personality or
social tension is only the symptom or resultant of split
thought. That would be to perpetuate the same basic error,
after merely turning it upside down. No, we must learn to
think in unitary terms. Then we shall see thought as an
element in the totality of human life and social transformation, inevitably related to and reacting with other elements
in the process—an element whose organization is in part
determined by the rest, but which also helps to determine the
whole. For unitary thinking, nothing is merely cause or merely
effect, nothing solely symptom or solely determinant; everything is related together in mutual interaction to produce a
characteristic pattern of development.

The pattern-process type of thinking inevitably substitutes
the idea of wholeness for anything in the nature of a final
goal or static absolute, and that of harmony for ideal perfection. It is perhaps not irrelevant to recall that etymologi-
cally the very word "health" means "wholeness".

In laying stress on conscious thinking, I do not wish to
minimize the importance of the unconscious. Indeed, the
unitary and evolutionary approach cannot draw so sharp a
distinction between the conscious and the unconscious as is
done either by theology, by idealist philosophy, or by most
psycho-analytic formulations. For unitary thought, conscious
thinking represents merely the most highly developed and
most fully integrated process of organizing and dealing with
experience. Sometimes the process of the brain raises itself
above the threshold of consciousness, sometimes it sinks below
it; but so long as the entire brain is functioning, the character
of the process remains the same. It is only through dissociation or active repression that any sharp division is introduced
between the conscious and the unconscious.

Once we learn to see reality as a pattern of unitary processes, freedom acquires a new meaning—the felt necessity
of unfrustrated development, the active creativity of self-
realization. Similarly with morality. What we have been used
to call "morality" is essentially superficial; it deals with
symptoms of maladjustment or dissociation. Morality now

becomes more or less synonymous with right direction, with behaviour which facilitates the fullest and speediest realization of characteristic development.

Our new unitary approach transforms the Marxists' claim that "history is on our side". Marxism does its best to remove thought and mind from any active share in determining events; our new approach, by putting them back into the historical process as operative agents, enables us to reformulate the phrase thus: "We are participants in the adventure of history and can, if we think rightly, facilitate its right development".

It gives the individual a different position in relation to society. Against this new background he can satisfy his longing to be in relation with something bigger than himself, in many ways. Since the development of human personalities is one of the most important ways in which the cosmic process fulfils itself, he can feel united with it, not selfishly withdrawn from it, in virtue of developing his own personality or in realizing particular aspects of it fully, for instance in art or science or athletics. He can also obtain satisfaction by consciously acting as a cog in the great dynamic machine, by contributing his energy or his skill to its service. If he is fortunate, he can do so by helping to lead the process on through an effort of creative thought or scientific discovery; or by bearing witness, as it is fashionable to say in literary circles now, through literature or art to the significance, the beauty, the interest, or the value of some aspect of the process.

That remarkable man, Abdul Baha, wrote that "the greatest prison is the prison of self". That is true—but it is only half the truth. It is true that the self can become the individual's greatest prison. But for those who have found themselves, discovering their unity with their own deeper natures, with others, and with the rest of the universe, the self can be the root of unlimited freedom, the jumping-off place for infinity. As Whitman said after he had found himself,

> . . . I, turning, call to thee, O soul, thou actual Me,
> And lo! thou gently masterest the orbs,
>
> . . . . . .
>
> Greater than stars or suns,
> Bounding, O soul, thou journeyest forth . . .

I would like to return a moment to the problem of adapting

the organization of our thought and its conscious formulations to reality and our knowledge of reality. An obvious
example is the way in which man has formulated persistent
regularities in nature. The old way, current right through
the Middle Ages, was to *ascribe* such regularities to inherent principles or qualities; to-day we *describe* the regularities that we discover, but describe them in the concentrated
form of scientific laws and theories. Thus the old principle
of there being four elements with different qualities has
been superseded by the particulate theory of matter and the
laws of atomic structure and combination: the old idea of
opposed qualities of lightness and heaviness inherent in matter
has been superseded by the law of gravitation.

The very terms we use may express the type of organization
of our thought. For instance, the description of human
nature in the old terms of the different humours has now
long been superseded by description in terms of genetics,
endocrinology, neurology, psychosomatic types, and so on.
The advance of science has often depended on the supersession of terminology involving a dualistic approach by one
based on a unitary approach. Thus, for instance, Newton
could not formulate the laws of gravitation before the dualism
of lightness versus heaviness had been superseded by the
unitary idea of greater or less degrees of weight or mass.

The example of temperature shows how terminology is
not a mere matter of academic semantics but a method of
organizing and handling our experience. In the old days, heat
and cold were thought of as due to antagonistic principles or
qualities of hotness and coldness, inherent in matter. Since the
seventeenth century, that idea has been superseded by the
single concept of temperature, degrees of one thing instead of
a balance between two opposing things. We can still usefully
employ the terms "hot" and "cold", but merely to denote
certain aspects of our subjective experience; the terms now
only have significance against the background of the single
scale of temperature.

In a somewhat similar way, motion and rest have been
subsumed under the single head of relativity, though the
dualistic terminology is still useful within that framework.
The old opposed ideas of complete material occupancy of
space or its complete emptiness have been co-ordinated in the
gas laws under the single idea of degrees of pressure, and in
the material universe at large under that of degree of concentration of matter. It is true that we can still use the word

"vacuum," but only in a rather derivative sense, of extremely low concentration of matter in space.

One of the intellectual urgencies of to-day is to reorganize thought, wherever it is still dualistic, under the head of new unitary concepts. In many fields this will involve inventing new terminology. For instance, how are we going to subsume the apparently opposed qualities of variety and unity? Perhaps under the head of "pattern" or "degree of organization". The duality of cause and effect perhaps can be subsumed under the one idea of the most probable tendencies of a process. The ancient duality of good and evil can perhaps be unified in relation to the degree of undistorted self-development, and the opposed ideas of "friend" and "enemy" under the one head of degree of participation in a common effort.

Sometimes the very principle on which a concept organizes experience and thought turns out to be incorrect, in the sense of not being adapted to the nature of reality. If so, the concept is assuredly destined to disappear, just as some animal types were doomed to extinction through not being adapted to the reality of the evolutionary situation. This has actually occurred with our previous examples of the four elements and the humours, and, in civilized countries, also with the concept of sympathetic magic.

I would like now to consider certain aspects of religion, notably the concept of God. This affords one of the best examples of the influence of the formulation or mode of organization of knowledge on everyday life and practice. It also illustrates how a concept with a high degree of organization, which at first sight appears to be solely a unifying one, may turn out to be fundamentally dualistic.

The word "God" formulates in one single term and concept various features of man's experience, such as sacredness, transcendent significance, permanence, ultimacy, personal authority (including its functions such as responsibility and loving care as well as justice and compulsion), and power.

So long as all this was formulated in the single concept of a divine ruler, man's idea of his destiny received a certain slant, and rituals of propitiation were inevitable. Such a formulation introduces a split into the world, between man and God, between natural and supernatural. Indeed, the concept of God was brought into existence by virtue of split thinking.

Here I cannot forbear recounting an incident about my grandfather, T. H. Huxley, at the inauguration of Johns

Hopkins University. His invitation to deliver the inaugural address raised a storm, partly because he was a controversial figure and partly because the ceremonies were conducted without the customary opening prayer. President Isaiah Bowman of Johns Hopkins, before his lamented death, showed me a letter from a Congregationalist minister in New York to a colleague of his in Baltimore apropos of the situation. His words are firmly engraved on my memory: " 'Twas an ill thing to have invited Professor Huxley; 'twere better to have invited God; 'twould have been impossible to have invited both." To-day, I am coming to believe that it is impossible to invite the aid of the concept of unitary thought without dropping our invitation to God.

The particular system of thought, feeling, and action known as religion has always involved our knowledge, beliefs, and assumptions about human destiny, and has always been concerned with our relations with some power apprehended as existing outside or beyond our life, irrespective of our individual desires—something not ourselves, given in the nature of reality. Further, it always involves the sense of psychological or spiritual significance and effectiveness in life, and in particular what Otto has called the sense of the sacred.

It seems to have begun by combining these two apprehensions—the apprehension of power with the apprehension of sacredness—and so becoming concerned with what may be called "sacred power". Historically, it has consisted of the beliefs, actions, rituals, and experiences which express and embody the significance and effectiveness of that power.

During history, religion has undergone protean transformations. This is inevitable, since its form and organization, the modes in which it exercises its dynamic force, are conditioned by the picture which men are able to formulate of the sacred power underlying religion, and this in its turn is conditioned by the knowledge available and the comprehension reached at any stage.

The main types of formulation so far made appear to be as follows.

First of all, the magic stage. In this sacred power is assumed to be widespread in nature, but especially concentrated in certain striking objects and events, and in certain rituals. Divinity, or "godness", if we may coin a word, is thus thought of as diffused, and is not yet distinguished from mere sacredness.

The next stage is the animistic. In this, sacred power is assumed to emanate from beings similar to human personalities; but these are regarded as being somehow still *in* the sacred or magic objects or events. Men projected certain of their own capacities, of will and purpose, emotion and knowledge, into the elements of nature which were felt to be sacred. The strangeness or other psychological effectiveness which led to the ascription of sacred power to objects, events, or rituals is now more definitely held to be divine, and somehow organized into person-like forms, though ideas on this point are usually vague and often contradictory, as one can see by studying early forms of religion in the neolithic dawn of civilization in the Middle East. Here "godness", the quality of being divine, is beginning to be concentrated into a large number of minor divinities, none of which, however, have much resemblance to the gods of more highly developed religions. Furthermore, "godness" may be projected into men as well as into divinities, giving rise to heroes and demigods and divine human personages such as the Egyptian Pharaohs and, later, the Roman Emperors, not to mention the bizarre contemporary phenomenon of "God" in the person of Father Divine. Essentially the same process, of endowing human beings with superhuman attributes, has been applied to modern dictators, though here the quality of sacredness is not usually used explicitly. But the practical, though not the semantic result, is the same—a divine human personage.[2]

Next came the theological stage, in which the diffuse principle of divinity is not merely condensed into gods of more definitely personal nature, but is to an increasing extent placed *behind* instead of *in* phenomena. There are two distinct substages of this stage, the polytheistic and the monotheistic, though again all transitions between them are to be found. This seems to have been the mode of development in the West, though various religions in the East, notably pure Buddhism, have pursued a rather different course.

Once personality is ascribed to divinity, the gods must be treated as one would treat absolute human rulers, and worship, propitiation, and sacrifice inevitably become prominent features of religion. They can and sometimes do appear in the earlier preanimistic stages, but in much less developed forms.

Each of these main stages clearly embodies a different

[2] Since this was written, Stalin has been brusquely "de-deified" by his successors.

hypothesis or set of assumptions. The first makes the naïve assumption that a psychological quality resides in its object. The second takes the elementary first step in pseudo-logical thinking (one taken by most children at an early stage), namely, the assumption that objects or events which affect us, or operate so as to produce effective results in our lives, can do so because they are animated by something akin to human personality, endowed with will, emotion, and knowledge. In so doing, it utilizes the psychological mechanism of projection.

The third stage takes the second stage farther, in two steps. In the first, man is forced to come to terms with his increasing empirical knowledge about material phenomena; he realizes that material objects, however sacred, cannot well be actually animated by personality, and therefore places divine personalities behind the objects. The second step, from polytheism to monotheism, seems to be taken partly under the pressure of an inner psychological logic, a felt need for unity, partly as a result of realizing the objective fact of the interrelation of all phenomena.

To-day, a fourth stage is in process of being reached. The critical intellect is realizing that these different ways of envisaging sacred power are all merely hypotheses or assumptions, and almost wholly subjective; that the earlier ones—of mana, magic, animism, and multiple divinity—have failed to be verified and indeed have been disproved; and that the third, of a single God, is in danger of suffering the same fate. The theistic assumption cannot make the positive advance towards scientific respectability, since it is objectively unverifiable (except by way of so-called miraculous occurrences which the scientific mind of to-day refuses to accept as evidence); and negatively it is in danger of being rendered untenable by virtue of advances in knowledge. In this new emergent stage, human minds, critical in the light of new knowledge, are no longer able to accept a God as a working hypothesis to explain phenomena, still less to accept Christian or any other theology as a scientific theory of human destiny. Laplace told Napoleon that God was no longer a necessary hypothesis in celestial mechanics: to-day God is becoming an erroneous hypothesis in all aspects of reality, including man's spiritual life.

The first result of this change in attitude and organization of thought has tended to be negative. Sometimes the baby is thrown out with the bath; the rejection of the idea of a personal God comes to involve the more or less complete rejection of what are generally termed spiritual values and realities, as in orthodox Marxism, or at least the rejection of their efficacy or relevance to practical affairs, as in *laisser-faire* economics and hard-shell rationalism. Often it has led to the radical separation, both in thought and practice, of the material and practical from the sacred and spiritual, of business and politics from religion and morality. This is the phase through which many people are now passing in the Western world, and which the representatives of established religious systems characterize as "irreligion" or "loss of faith".

However, with the development of a fully naturalistic outlook the transformation of thought is capable of passing from a negative to a positive phase. Men can cast off the blinkers of dualism. They find that, after all, spiritual experiences, including the sense of the sacred, are an important part of reality. They realize that it was merely the assumptions about the relations of spiritual experience with the rest of reality which they were unable to accept. They also realize that, once the formulation of gods, as personal beings behind phenomena, had been made, and dissociated thinking had built its artificial fence between God and nature, the transition to monotheism was not merely logically but empirically indicated, as a step towards expressing the real unity and continuity of the cosmos, but was an incomplete step, since the concept of God itself involves dualism. Regarded in this light, the fall of man is not a fall from good to evil, but a falling apart of the universe into good and evil, consequent upon man having split it into Nature and God.

Even when under the influence of a prevailing dualism, men have been unwilling to put all the elements of divinity on the other side of the fence they have erected between nature and the supernatural. Priest-kings endowed with the attributes of god, rulers deified during their lifetime, from the Roman Emperors to Joseph Stalin, manage to keep some of the elements of divinity on the natural side of the fence: the doctrine of the incarnation is a brilliant device to put back some of God into man: all theories of divine immanence and of pantheism attempt to take down the fence itself; and the great mystics have learnt by experience that divinity is to be found within us.

One way in which religion can properly be described is as man's conception of his destiny. To-day, this can be formulated in a unitary way, as a spear-heading and condensation of evolution, by realizing new possibilities for life. Such a unitary formulation does not take the sacred power from where it belongs—namely, in particular relations between particular human beings and particular objects and events—and erroneously project it into a single supernatural being. It can recognize the plurality and multiple variety of the world and of life, and yet superimpose unity upon it by way of a unitary formulation.

Man inevitably discovers that existence involves mystery. Perhaps the latest revelation of inherent mystery is the discovery by science of the unexpected unity of all nature. All the realities which were taken out of nature and put together in the supernatural concept of God can now be put back into the natural process. And there, if their relation to the whole process is properly grasped, they can exert at least as much and perhaps more force than they did under the old dispensation.

I must now pass to some of the implications of such a view for science. It seems to me we are in danger of introducing a new split into thought by thinking of science as in any sense an unchanging entity, separate from the rest of reality, and possessing a different kind of validity and certainty from that of other modes of organizing experience.

We speak of scientific certainty; on the other hand, the growth of science has undoubtedly led at the present time to the growth of uncertainty. This is due partly to the rapidity of new discovery, and to its exploitation by sensationalism. The mere fact of realizing how many surprising, disconcerting discoveries science has made in the last fifty years, and yet how much we still do not know, is also unsettling. Finally there is the uncertainty caused by the conflict between scientific knowledge and traditional beliefs, and also by the contradiction between scientific method and the methods of thinking which appear natural to the bulk of the community. Under this last head I include not only the naïve attitudes of the relatively uneducated masses but also the thinking of those educated in the humanist or religious tradition. This last conflict will continue so long as people fail to understand that science is a limited activity, though with an unlimited field, immensely successful within that field and eventually influencing other fields, but not directly applicable to aesthetic creation or appreciation, intuitive comprehension, or spiritual experience.

The unsettling effect of science can be overcome if we stress its other effect, in establishing an increasing body of increasingly accurate knowledge. That is something which is often forgotten by the critics of science. It is the outcome of the principle of limited but increasing certitude. This is the underlying strategical principle on which the scientific method operates. Tactically, science proceeds by means of working hypotheses, which are later tested out by checking against factual observation. The campaign for certitude then proceeds to organize prediction by formulating observed regularities in the form of scientific laws, and to organize comprehension by formulating our ideas in the form of scientific theories.

Scientific laws, let us remind ourselves, are never more than an approximation to the truth, though the approximation may be an extremely close one; and scientific theories never have more than a limited comprehensiveness. But the scientific method is by far the best so far discovered for acquiring and organizing natural knowledge.

Its effectiveness is at once shown by reminding ourselves of some of the ideological and moral effects of the advance of scientific knowledge. As examples we may take the realization that earthquakes, droughts, and other physical catastrophes are natural phenomena, and not due to divine intervention or supernatural agency; or the realization that disease and death are due to infective agents, not to divine punishment or witchcraft. We have only to read Boccaccio's *Decameron* to realize what horror and fear were aroused in civilized Europe only a few centuries ago by this uncomprehended mystery of epidemic disease. We have only to take a plane to Africa to realize that the tribal African to-day still firmly believes that no death is ever natural, but must always be due to witchcraft.

There is the realization that all objects, organic or inorganic, consist of the same matter and operate by the same energy, so that neither life nor man is set apart from the rest of the world in these two basic respects; the fact that the mind is not an incalculable extranatural entity, but develops and operates according to ascertainable laws or rules, and that its workings can most fruitfully be regarded as one aspect of the unitary organism; the fact that man has not been created helpless or as a slave of some external authority, but is the most creative part of the total creative process.

It is thus urgent that we should take this basic scientific principle of limited but increasing certitude, constantly checked against the facts of nature, and adapt and transpose it for use in other fields—limited but increasing rightness in the field of morality, in the place of absolute rightness as against absolute wrongness; limited but increasing significance in the field of art, in the place of right or good art as against wrong or bad art; limited but increasing comprehension in the field of religion, in place of the false absolutes of authoritarian dogma, in which absolute "truth" is set against absolute "error"; limited but increasing faith and confidence, checked and validated by experience, in place of the false certitudes of purely subjective feeling.

Finally, let us remember that science is not an unchanging entity: it evolves and changes its character like everything else. Indeed it is becoming clear that science itself needs considerable overhauling and transformation. As indicated earlier, it needs to devise methods for dealing with pattern, process, and quality, as well as with isolated elements, static or reversible events, and quantity. And in so doing it is bound to abandon its isolationism, its pretence of sovereign separateness and its pretence of being morally neutral, for it will find itself operating as part of the total human process, in common harness with emotion, value, and purpose.

Thus, one might seek to apply the unitary outlook to political science. The main point is that, in the light of our present knowledge, the only way to envisage the state or the community is as an organization to facilitate and promote the development of its members and the fullest realization of their individual potentialities. This, as is immediately evident, knocks the bottom out of Fascism and Stalinist Communism and any other kind of totalitarianism or State-worship. Furthermore, it puts political nationalism into its proper place and perspective as a temporary expedient, a means which may sometimes have to be employed to realize certain ends.

Then there is the gathering belief, based on the awareness of what science has already done and the resultant myth of scientific omnipotence, that science could provide minimum standards of food, health, and material comfort for everybody; and the gathering demand, by the great underprivileged majority, for the raising of the standards of their life.

These facts have direct implications for the great powers, and particularly for the United States as the greatest power in the present world: but the implications must be drawn in the light of a unitary approach. The United States can assume a decisive leadership in the present crisis only if it can see itself in relation to the process of transformation as a whole. It could provide essential leadership in facilitating the transformation of the world to higher minimum standards of material life for the under-privileged and more freedom for the exploited and backward: it will inevitably do so if it can learn to think of them and itself as joint participants in man's global adventure. The great powers must learn to see themselves in the role of an active partner in this joint enterprise. Their leadership will consist partly in introducing to the backward, upsurging masses the idea that material standards are only the basis for a fuller development, the necessary foundation on which further possibilities of knowledge and enjoyment may be realized; for to concentrate on material standards alone would inevitably degenerate into a scramble for material goods, unless it is transcended by the more inclusive motive of realizing total human possibilities.

It is not by exploiting economic concessions or by establishing bases or by purely military victories that a nation will win. Indeed, "winning" is not the right word: world affairs are not a game of football, and mere victory, whatever General MacArthur may say, is *not* the ultimate aim of war. What the United States and other great powers should aim at is to *succeed*—in providing leadership and in facilitating right development for the world at large; and this it can do if it successfully provides good-will and expert assistance, material and mental aid, to the world's development.

I will conclude with the idea with which I began, the idea of human destiny. We can no longer envisage human destiny in such terms as the will of God set over against the sinful will of man, or as the plan of a divine creator frustrated by the imperfections and wilfulness of his creation. Human destiny is to participate in the creative process of development, whereby the universe as a whole can realize more of its potentialities in richer and greater fulfilments.

For man to fulfil his destiny truly and effectively, the first step must be one of discovery. He must learn to recognize and identify the systems of transformation operating in reality, the nature of the self-creative process as a dynamic organization, its form, and the modes of the transformation of that form to new and richer forms; and in particular the particular transformation now under way.

Once the nature and character of a process have been truly and effectively grasped, prediction, in the sense of justifiable assumptions on which to base purposive action, at once becomes possible, for the laws governing the development of such a system are implicit in its nature and form. In truly unitary thought, effectively adjusted to deal with the unitary processes of nature, to recognize is to be able to comprehend, and to comprehend is to be able to act. Any such new formulation of thought will need time and effort to achieve: but in it, once achieved, thought will become involved with action, and science acquire a morality in helping man to recognize his destiny.

EVOLUTIONARY HUMANISM [1]

AMONG the many things for which T. H. Huxley is remembered is the fact that he coined the word *agnostic* as a label for himself. I would guess that to the majority of people to-day that word connotes a rather arid rationalism, something essentially negative and even destructive. Yet in point of fact it was only the philosophical obverse of his belief in science, and did not prevent him from cherishing a strong and positive faith.

In one of his essays he equates the principle underlying agnosticism with the ancient prescription "Try all things: hold fast by that which is good", and calls it "the fundamental axiom of modern science". In his remarkable letter to Charles Kingsley he proclaims the very positive thesis that "the most sacred act of a man's life is to say and to feel 'I believe such and such to be true'". He was, in fact, deeply preoccupied with the central problems of human destiny, and in his Romanes Lecture on *Evolution and Ethics* summed up that life-long preoccupation in a justly celebrated but now out-moded exhortation: "Let us understand, once and

[1] The material of this essay was compiled in preparation for the Huxley Memorial Lecture at Birmingham University in 1953, and formed the basis for the third of the series of Dyason Lectures delivered in Australia later in the same year.

for all, that the ethical progress of society consists not in imitating the cosmic process, still less in running away from it, but in combating it."

The problems of human destiny concern us to-day as acutely as they concerned T. H. Huxley. Indeed, I could have defined my subject as the relation between science and man's beliefs concerning his place in the cosmic process.

The problems are as basic as ever: but we look at them from a somewhat different position. The main difference is that whereas T. H. Huxley never quite rid himself of the dualistic premiss of his age, we are perforce monists, in the sense of believers in the oneness of things, the unitary nature of reality; we see ourselves, together with our science and our beliefs, as an integral part of the cosmic process, instead of somehow outside it. And from this new angle of approach we obtain a new view of the cosmic landscape, a new picture of our place in it.

Man is always concerned about his destiny—that is to say, his position and role in the universe, and how he is to maintain that position and fulfil that role. All societies of men develop some sort of organs for coping with this problem—organs for orientating their ideas and emotions and for constructing attitudes of mind and patterns of belief and behaviour in relation to their conception of their destiny. All these social organs concerned with destiny can, I think, properly be included under the head of religions. Even if some of them are exceedingly primitive and consist of little but magic rituals, while others are highly developed and claim to be entirely rational, they are all, from Haitian voodoo to Roman Catholicism, from neolithic fertility religions to Stalinist Communism, concerned with this same general function. In the same sort of way, the tube-feet of a starfish, the legs of a horse, the pseudopods of an amoeba, and the wings of a bird, though profoundly different from each other, are all animal organs concerned with the same general function of locomotion.

Homo sapiens—man, for short—is a unique organism, whose maintenance and transformations depend primarily on psycho-social mechanisms, in which mental activities play a dominant role; while those of all other organisms depend primarily on the biological mechanisms of heredity, mutation, and natural selection.

Although the terms *mind* and *mental* have been bedevilled

by differences in common usage, I shall employ them, *faute
de mieux*, in the widest possible sense, to describe all activities involving awareness, from cognitive to emotional awareness, from purely intellectual to spiritual and aesthetic, from
intensely conscious activities to those that are subconscious
or even, in Freudian terminology, unconscious. It would be
convenient to have some new term, uncontaminated by
earlier modes of thought, to characterize all psycho-social
mechanisms in which communicable mental activities play
a predominant role. If so, I suggest the term *noetic;* and I
shall sometimes employ it with this connotation.

Religions are thus noetic organs of evolving man. Their
special function concerns his position and role in the universe, his relations to the rest of the cosmos, and in particular
his attitude to the powers or forces operating in it, including
those of his own nature: or in the fewest possible words, with
his attitude towards his destiny. Furthermore, this attitude
always involves the sense of sacred power in some form or
other—a feeling of reverence, or mystery, or wonder, or
transcendent power or beauty. To perform this function, a
religion requires some interpretative beliefs, notably about
the spiritual powers in the universe; some picture of the
cosmos in which man's destiny is cast; some mobilization of
the emotional and spiritual forces at work within man himself; some form of ritual, in the widest sense of the term, to
express and maintain this religious attitude; and some relation to the moral and practical problems of existence, both
individual and social.

The beliefs may be mere assumptions lacking precise
definition, as in those underlying the magic rituals of many
primitive peoples; or they may be elaborate systems involving precise intellectual formulation, like the creeds of Christian theology; or they may be *post-hoc* rationalizations, quite
subsidiary to the ritual elements of the religion, as in Chinese ancestor-worship.[2] The inner psychological forces may
be given violent expression as part of a sacred ritual, as in
orgiastic cults like that of Dionysos or in some aspects of
Haitian voodoo; they may be sternly disciplined, or even
repudiated, as in some Protestant sects or in the various
forms of asceticism; or they may be cultivated and developed
so as to provide new fulfilments, as in the various systems

[2] See A. R. Radcliffe-Brown, *Structure and Function in Primitive Society,* Cohen and West, London, 1952, pp. 153f.

of mysticism. The ritual may be magical, or dramatic, or symbolic; it may consist in formalistic observances, in prayers, in orgiastic releases, in mass celebrations, like those of the Holy Year or the rallies and parades of Nazism and Communism, in pilgrimages, or in sacrifices and rites of propitiation. And the relation to practical existence may be one of escape, as in asceticism or pure Buddhism; or of full participation, as in classical Greece or the city-states of ancient Mesopotamia; or of rendering unto Caesar the things that are Caesar's, as in usual Christian practice.

The form of the beliefs about the spiritual forces at work in the universe colours and affects the rest of the religious system. The three chief hypotheses on which past religious belief-systems have in fact been erected are the magic hypothesis, the animist or spirit hypothesis, and the daimonic or god hypothesis.[3]

Both the magic hypothesis and the god hypothesis appear to be based on the well-known psychological tendency to projection. Putting the matter rather crudely, man has experiences of sacred power. On the magic hypothesis, he projects the sacred power *into* phenomena, into some external object or event, including rituals and forms of words. On the god hypothesis, he projects the sacred power *behind* phenomena, and clothes it in the garb of a personality.

The magic hypothesis leads man to ascribe practical efficacy and importance to dramatic rituals like rain-making ceremonies, to witchcraft with its spells and curses, and to omens and auguries. The god hypothesis, with its central idea of personal spiritual powers behind phenomena, leads naturally and almost universally to the idea that misfortunes like earthquakes and pestilences are divine punishments for sin,[4] to the belief that gods need propitiation by sacrifices and offerings and glorification by worship, and that they can be influenced by petitionary prayers. The combination of magic and god hypotheses may produce singular results, such as the development of prayer-wheels worked by wind- or water-power in Tibet.

[3] *Daimonic* is a useful term to cover all classes of superhuman spiritual beings, whether good or evil or ethically neutral, including both gods and devils of various kinds and various degrees of importance, angels, local spirits, tutelary deities, etc. See R. Turner, *The Great Cultural Traditions*, McGraw-Hill, London and New York, 1941, I, p. 92, on "The Concept of the Daimonic Universe".

[4] See T. D. Kendrick, *The Lisbon Earthquake*, Methuen, London, 1956.

The bases of the spirit hypothesis appear to be more complex; but its effects on practice are equally obvious. When sacred power is supposed to reside in the spirits of the dead, we may find special rituals of burial designed to keep the dead from plaguing the living, or the cult may develop into an elaborate system of ancestor-worship. And of course when religious beliefs are largely concerned with survival in a supernatural world, the practical effects may be enormous. We need only think of the pyramids, and the economic importance of the mortuary priesthood of ancient Egypt; or of the role of Indulgences in helping to bring about the Reformation.

Many religions utilize all these belief-hypotheses. Thus in Roman Catholicism, while the god hypothesis is central and basic, the spirit hypothesis plays a not inconsiderable part, for instance in assigning an important role to the spirits of dead saints; and certainly for most Protestants as well as for rationalists, Catholic beliefs about the efficacy of relics and pilgrimages and various ritual observances involve the magic hypothesis. Furthermore, the three hypotheses often combine to exert a joint effect on religious attitude and practice.

The belief in spirits, and still more markedly the belief in gods, involves another basic hypothesis—the hypothesis of dualism. In general, theistic religions are based on the assumption of a dualism between the material and the non-material or spiritual.[5] For brevity's sake I shall use the term supernaturalism to include the combination of the god hypothesis and the spirit hypothesis which characterizes most higher religious systems.

An almost universal and perhaps inevitable consequence of the god hypothesis in its developed forms is the assumption of absolute truth. A monotheistic religion almost invariably claims to be in possession of the absolute truth about human destiny: the fact that rival religions make similar claims is disposed of by affirming that they are "false", while only one's own religion is "true".

Furthermore, theistic religions usually adopt the hypothesis of revelation: they assert that the truth has been revealed in a set of god-given commandments, or a holy

[5] For the historical development of dualism between matter and spirit, see V. G. Childe, *Society and Knowledge*, Allen and Unwin, London, 1956.

book, or divinely inspired ordinances. The beliefs of theistic religions thus tend inevitably to be authoritarian, and also to be rigid and resistant to change. When religious change does occur, as is sometimes inevitable in our changing human world, it often involves merely the substitution of one authoritarianism for another, as when the Protestant reformers set up the authority of the Bible in place of that of the Church or the Pope.

Hypotheses are valuable and necessary instruments of the human mind for its dual task of adding to and organizing its knowledge. But they become dangerous when they are erected into absolute affirmations or dogmas, and pernicious when they claim immunity from constant testing against fact.

The magic hypothesis in its straightforward form can no longer be seriously entertained, even though elements of it continue to colour theistic religious practice, and though it survives in many forms among the illiterate, and has given birth to new versions of old superstitions (such as astrology and numerology) among the half-educated.

The supernatural hypothesis, taken as involving both the god hypothesis and the spirit hypothesis and the various consequences drawn from them, appears to have reached the limits of its usefulness as an interpretation of the universe and of human destiny, and as a satisfactory basis for religion. It is no longer adequate to deal with the phenomena, as revealed by the advance of knowledge and discovery. This is the crux of the so-called conflict between science and religion, which should more properly be described as a conflict between the progress of established knowledge and a particular type of religious hypothesis.

It would be interesting to discuss the history of this conflict, and to show how, for instance, the advance of knowledge, both in the natural and the human sciences, has led to modifications in the god hypothesis—how the Newtonian and the Darwinian revolutions combined to push the Deity ever farther into the background, until his only role in cosmic affairs appeared as that of initial creator of a self-running machine; how, with our increasing knowledge of the orderly working of nature, the idea of miraculous intervention has grown progressively less and less tenable, until it has now become repugnant and indeed intellectually immoral to a growing body of those trained in the scientific tradition; how theistically minded astronomers and philosophers have been reduced to presenting god in the unsatisfying role of a cosmic mathematician, or the nebulous guise of an absolute principle. But I have no space for such as excursus and can merely state the plain fact that the advance of knowledge is making supernaturalism in general, and the god hypothesis in particular, untenable for an increasing number of educated people.

The vital question is this: Can we find any other basic hypothesis about the spiritual forces at work in the cosmos on which to build our beliefs? Such a hypothesis must square with the facts of established knowledge, and must be religious in the broad sense, in being relevant to the problem of human destiny and to man's experiences of sacredness.

Marxist Communism has adopted the hypothesis of materialism, which denies any real importance or indeed validity to spiritual forces. For Marxism, mental or psychological activities in general are essentially epiphenomena, always the resultant and never the cause of "objective" material events. I am, of course, aware that, through a complicated process of fine-spun dialectic, Marxist philosophers manage to rescue a good many psychological phenomena from this wholesale jettisoning and keep them safely aboard the Communist ship; and that in practice a great deal of attention is paid to activities like art and philosophy and science, which to most of us would appear to involve a major mental or noetic component. But the underlying hypothesis is explicitly materialist; and this fact has all kinds of important consequences, not least among which will be its ultimate consequences for the religious efficacy of Communism, as a system of beliefs and attitudes concerning human destiny.

Again it would be interesting to pursue the subject; but again I have no space. I would only say that the materialist hypothesis, in denying the intrinsic validity of mental and spiritual factors and their importance in the cosmos, is to me as erroneous as, though more sophisticated than, the naïve notions of the magic hypothesis, which projects spiritual force into material events. It is still, perhaps unconsciously, dualist, and, through failing to take account of a large body of fact, is as untenable as the supernaturalist hypothesis. But it has provided the basis for the first important nontheistic religion of modern times, and its existence makes the task of finding an adequate alternative even more urgent.

I submit that the discoveries of physiology, general biology, and psychology not only make possible, but necessitate, a naturalistic hypothesis, in which there is no room for the supernatural, and the spiritual forces at work in the cosmos are seen as a part of nature just as much as the material forces. What is more, these spiritual forces are one particular product of mental activity in the broad sense, and mental activities in general are seen to have increased in intensity and importance during the course of cosmic time. Our basic hypothesis is thus not merely naturalistic as opposed to supernaturalist, but monistic or unitary as opposed to dualistic, and evolutionary as opposed to static.

Another postulate of modern thought is that truth is not revealed once and for all, but has to be progressively discovered. This is itself a scientific discovery, and one of the first magnitude. It is also an inevitable consequence of our basic hypothesis of evolutionary naturalism; and the fact that modern science has resulted in the progressive discovery of more truth is a confirmation of that hypothesis.

It may well be that future discoveries, in parapsychology for instance, will alter our views on the nature of the relation between material and mental or spiritual events and activities; but meanwhile the monistic evolutionary hypothesis best meets the known facts, and its implications need to be followed out and tested in detail, in full confidence that they will be fruitful.

In the light of such a view, religions, like sciences or philosophies, are creations of man, and gods are products of the human mind just as much as scientific "laws of nature". The comparison is illuminating. Both gods and scientific generalizations must be derived from experience and must have some basis in reality. The question is how much of a basis: how far do they correspond with reality, how accurately do they embody experience? The laws of nature did not exist as such before men began scientific investigation: what existed was the welter of natural events, and the laws of nature are constructions of human thought which attempt to give comprehensible general formulations of how those events operate. Similarly gods did not exist as such before men built up theistic religious systems: what existed was the clash of natural forces, physical and spiritual, including those of the human mind, and the gods are attempts to give a comprehensible formulation of these forces of destiny. The difference—but an important one—is that, in the history of religion, gods correspond to men's pre-scientific constructions in the investigation of natural phenomena—products of imaginative speculation like the four "Elements", or the principle of the Humours, or the idea of spontaneous generation.

With evolutionary naturalism as our basic hypothesis, we can begin exploring the new religious situation of our twentieth century, without spending more time in the unprofitable task of pointing out the theoretical or practical inadequacies of earlier religious systems.

Twentieth-century man, it is clear, needs a new organ for dealing with destiny, a new system of religious beliefs and attitudes adapted to the new situation in which his societies now have to exist, including the new knowledge which they have discovered and amassed. The radically new feature of the present situation may perhaps be stated thus: Earlier religions and belief-systems were largely adaptations to cope with man's ignorance and fears, with the result that they came to concern themselves primarily with stability of attitude. But the need to-day is for a belief-system adapted to cope with his knowledge and his creative possibilities; and this implies the capacity to meet and to inspire change. In other words, the primary function of earlier systems was of necessity to maintain social and spiritual morale in face of the unknown: and this they accomplished with a considerable measure of success. But the primary function of any system to-day must be to utilize all available knowledge in giving guidance and encouragement for the continuing adventure of human development.

I am here treating of religious systems as social organs whose function it is to adjust man to his destiny. No previous systems could perform this function with full adequacy, for the simple reason that no previous age had sufficient knowledge to construct an adequate picture of the drama of destiny or of its protagonist, man. The present epoch is the first in which such a picture could begin to take shape. This is due to the fact that scientific investigation has now for the first time begun to cover the entire range of phenomena involved in human destiny. Beginning with the physical phenomena and proceeding to the biological, it has now invaded the social, psychological, and historical fields, and is at last being forced to deal with the phenomena of values. Immense tracts of ignorance are still to be explored and await annexation to the growing empire of knowledge; but we can already affirm that the cosmos is unitary, that it is a process of transformation in time, and that values and other products of mental and spiritual activity play an important operative role in that sector of the process with which we are involved.

More specifically, the present is the first period in the long history of the earth in which the evolutionary process, through the instrumentality of man, has taken the first step towards self-consciousness. In becoming aware of his own destiny, man has become aware of that of the entire evolutionary process on this planet: the two are interlocked. This is at once an inspiring and a sobering conception.

The present age also differs from all earlier ages in the increased importance of science and its universal extension. There should no longer be any talk of conflict between science and religion. Between scientific knowledge and certain religious systems, yes: but between science as an increasing knowledge of nature and religion as a social organ concerned with destiny, no. On the contrary, religion must now ally itself wholeheartedly with science. Science in the broad sense is indispensable as the chief instrument for increasing our store of organized knowledge and understanding. Through evolutionary biology it has already indicated the nature of human destiny. Scientific study is needed to give religion a fuller understanding of destiny, and to help in devising better methods for its detailed realization. Meanwhile, science must not allow any ancient prejudices against certain aspects of previously established religions to hold it back from giving its aid when called upon.

Industry and agriculture, after a good deal of resistance on the part of so-called practical men, have already discovered the indispensability of science, both pure and applied. It now remains for religion, together with other social activities, to make the same discovery. For without the fullest aid from science we will assuredly not be able to bring into being a religion adequate to our needs, any more than we could have brought into being an aeroplane capable of flying or antibiotics capable of killing disease-germs.

Once it is realized that religions are the product of man's creative mind, working on the data provided by personal and collective experience, the need for enlisting science in the religious task becomes apparent. In any event, the march of knowledge and events has made it imperative to reach a new formulation of human destiny and a new attitude towards it. This is a task for the human species as a whole, to which all can bring their contribution. The co-operation of the re-

ligiously minded and the scientifically trained is essential for
its adequate performance.

The contribution which science can make is two-fold. It
can contribute an enormous body of hard-won, tested, organized knowledge; and also a spirit of disinterested devotion
to truth, and a willingness to apply this spirit to any problem,
irrespective of prejudices or possible consequences. An immense co-operative effort of creative discussion is needed. In
what follows I submit the thesis which I am calling evolutionary humanism to that discussion, fully conscious that,
though based on the accumulated results of unnumbered
others, it is only the personal contribution of one biologist.

In the first place, evolutionary biology has given us a new
view, impossible of attainment in any earlier age, of our
human destiny. Our destiny is to be the agent of the evolutionary process on this planet, the instrument for realizing
new possibilities for its future.

The picture of the universe provided by modern science is
of a single process of self-transformation, during which
new possibilities can be realized. There has been a creation
of new actualities during cosmic time: it has been progressive, and it has been a self-creation.

The entire cosmos, in all its appalling vastness, consists of
the same world-stuff. Following William James, I use this
awkward term deliberately in place of *matter*, because "matter" is commonly opposed to "mind", whereas it is now apparent that the world-stuff is not restricted to material properties.[6] When organized in certain ways—as, for instance, in the
form of human bodies and brains—it is capable of mental as
well as material activities. Furthermore, the study of animals
shows that there is no sharp line to be drawn between human and animal behaviour, except in the essential human
capacity for the cumulative transmission of experience, knowledge, concepts and ideas; and it is now clear that minds, in
the sense of all activities with an obvious mental component,
have evolved just as much as have material bodies; during
evolutionary time, mental activities of every kind, from awareness and knowledge to emotion, memory and will, have
become increasingly intense and efficient, and mental organization has reached ever higher levels. Through sense-organs

6 Physics has also revealed the inseparability and interchangeability
of matter and energy. For simplicity's sake, I am using *matter* as
equivalent to matter-and-energy, and *material* for material-and-energetic
or physically measurable properties.

and brains, the mind-like potentialities of the world-stuff have been progressively intensified and actualized, in the same sort of way as its electrical properties have been intensified in the electric organs of the torpedo-fish or through human agency, in constructions like dynamos.

Since natural selection is the sole or main method of biological evolution, and since it can only operate to produce results of biological utility, it is clear that the mental properties of organisms cannot be mere useless by-products, but must be of value to their possessors. Furthermore, they can and do play an operative role in the evolutionary process: thus the awareness of colour and pattern found in some higher animals has led to the further evolution of colour-patterns of various sorts, and has assisted in the birth of that evolutionary novelty we call beauty. If the self-creation of novelty is the basic wonder of the universe, this eliciting of mind from the potentialities of the world-stuff, and its intensification and increasing importance during evolution, is the basic wonder of life.

During evolution, the onward-flowing stream of life breaks up into a vast number of branches or trends, each resulting in improvement of one sort or another. The great majority of these become so specialized that life in them finds itself in a blind alley, incapable of further improvement or of transformation for another way of existence. After this, they either remain essentially unchanged for tens or even hundreds of millions of years, or else wholly die out, becoming extinguished in the sands of time. We need only recall the extinction of the dinosaurs and other strange reptiles of the Mesozoic, or the lack of any essential change shown by such successful groups as the birds for over fifteen million years, or the ants for over fifty.

But through this radiating fan of restricted improvements and blind-alley specializations there runs a trend towards major advance; and this current of biological advance has continued through the two thousand million years of life's existence. It is marked by increase of over-all biological efficiency and by improvement in general plan of working. During its course, there has been an enormous rise in level of complex but harmonious organization—think of a bird or a mammal as against a flatworm or a jellyfish; in flexibility and the capacity for self-regulation; in physiological efficiency, as shown in muscular contraction or rate of nervous conduction, or manifested in sheer strength or speed; in the range of awareness, as seen in the evolution of sense-organs—think of an eagle's eyes or an antelope's ears as against the blindness and deafness of a polyp or an amoeba; and in the intensity and complexity of mental processes such as knowing and perceiving, feeling and willing, learning and remembering—think of dogs or elephants as against sea-anemones or snails.

In the actual course of the evolutionary process, general biological advance has been achieved in a series of steps, through the emergence of a series of dominant types. Each new dominant type possesses some improvement at the expense of the previously dominant group from among whose less specialized members it has evolved. This progressive replacement of dominant types and groups is most clearly shown in the later history of vertebrates. The reptiles replaced the moist-skinned amphibians as dominant type of land animal, and were in turn replaced by the warm-blooded mammals and birds. It is thus perfectly proper to use terms like *higher* and *lower* to describe different types of organism, and *progress* for certain types of trend. A higher organism is one which has realized more of the inherent possibilities of living substance, and biological progress denotes those trends which do not restrict the further realization of those possibilities.

The next fact of importance is that during evolutionary time the avenues of possible progress have become progressively restricted, until to-day only one remains open. Well before the end of the Cenozoic Era, the limits of physiological efficiency seem to have been reached by life. The largest size possible to efficient land animals was attained by the dinosaurs over sixty million years ago: the temperature-regulating mechanism of higher mammals reached the profitable limit of accuracy perhaps halfway through the Cenozoic, and their locomotor efficiency during the Pliocene: it appears to be physically impossible to evolve an acuity of vision or a speed of flight greater than that of a falcon.

The only avenue of major advance left open was through the improvement of brain and mind. This was the line taken by our own ancestors, and it was this advance which enabled man to become the latest dominant type in evolution. His rise to dominance is very recent—an affair of less than a million years—but its later course has been spectacularly rapid, in the extremely short period since the waning of the last phase of glaciation; and it has been accompanied by marked decline and widespread extinction of the previously dominant mammals, as well as by a radical transformation of his environment by man. Furthermore, it is clear that man is only at the beginning of his period of evolutionary dominance, and that vast and still undreamt-of possibilities of further advance still lie before him.

Biology, I repeat, has thus revealed man's place in nature. He is the highest form of life produced by the evolutionary process on this planet, the latest dominant type, and the only organism capable of further major advance or progress. His destiny is to realize new possibilities for the whole terrestrial sector of the cosmic process, to be the instrument of further evolutionary progress on this planet.

The past history of biological evolution gives us a certain further guidance. We can justifiably extrapolate some of the main trends of progress into the future, and conclude that man should aim at a continued increase of those qualities which have spelt progress in the biological past—efficiency and control of environment, self-regulation and independence of outer changes, individuality and level of physiological organization, wholeness or harmony of working, extent of awareness and knowledge, storage of experience, degree of mental organization. In particular, man is likely to fulfill his destiny more successfully if he exploits to the full those improvements which have given him his position as latest dominant type, notably his properties of reason, imagination, and conceptual thought, and his unique capacities of accumulating, organizing, and applying experience through a transmissible culture and set of ideas. These include the capacity to construct religions in the broad sense—systems of attitude, in which knowledge can be combined with ideals and imaginatively fused with our deep spiritual emotions to form a stable framework of sentiments and beliefs, which in turn will influence behavior and help to determine moral and practical action.

From this point of view, the religion indicated by our new view of our position in the cosmos must be one centred on the idea of fulfilment. Man's most sacred duty, and at the same time his most glorious opportunity, is to promote the maximum fulfilment of the evolutionary process on this earth; and this includes the fullest realization of his own inherent possibilities.

Let us follow up some of the implications of this general conclusion. Evolutionary biology makes it clear that the developed human individual is, in a strictly scientific sense, the highest product of the cosmic process of which we have any knowledge; accordingly, we can formulate the ultimate aim of the human species as the realization of more possibilities by more, and more fully developed, individuals. On the other hand, human individuals cannot realize their possibilities except as members of social groups, and through means which only organized societies can provide. Furthermore, organization on the human level cannot be reproduced, still less improved, except through the social agency of cultural transmission. Thus the paramountcy of the individual is not absolute: it is limited by the need of maintaining and improving social organization.

Man inhabits a world of ideas which he has created, and of social institutions and achievements which those ideas have generated. In this psychosocial world he lives and moves and has his being. It is in a certain sense an artificial environment which he makes for himself, but can better be regarded as an essential part of the radically new type of evolving organization represented by the human species. There is inevitably some conflict between the interests of individuals and those of society. But the conflict is in large measure transcended in this conception of man as an evolving psychosocial organism. This dictates certain conclusions. In the longest-term point of view, our aim must be to develop a type of society and culture capable of ever-fresh evolution, one which continually opens the way to new and fuller realizations; in the medium-term point of view, we must secure the reproduction and improvement of psycho-social organization, the maintenance of the frameworks of society and culture and their transmission and adjustment in time; and in the immediate point of view we must aim at maximum individual fulfilment.

What needs stressing, however, is that, from the angle of evolutionary humanism, the flowering of the individual is seen as having intrinsic value, as being an end in itself. In the satisfying exercise of our faculties, in the pure enjoyment of our experience, the cosmic process of evolution is bringing some of its possibilities to fruition. In individual acts of comprehension or love, in the enjoyment of beauty, in the inner experiences of peace and assurance, in the satisfactions of creative achievement, however humble, we are helping to realize human destiny. Above all, the individual should aim at fulness and wholeness of development. Every human being is confronted with the task of growing up, of building a personality out of the raw materials of his infant self. A rich and full personality, in moral and spiritual harmony with itself and with its destiny, one whose talents are not buried in a napkin, and whose wholeness transcends its conflicts, is the highest creation of which we have knowledge, and in its attainment the individual possibilities of the evolutionary process are brought to supreme fruition.

But if the individual has duties towards his own potentialities, he owes them also to those of others, singly and collectively. He has the duty to aid other individuals towards fuller development, and to contribute his mite to the maintenance and improvement of the continuing social process, and so to the march of evolution as a whole.

However, to realize the practical importance of such general conclusions, we need to amplify and illuminate them by following out their implications. To do this satisfactorily in any detail is beyond the possibilities of a single article, or indeed of a single individual. But I must at least make some attempts at annotation, in the hope that they will serve as a stimulus to further exploration by others.

The basic postulate of evolutionary humanism is that mental and spiritual forces—using the term *force* in a loose and general sense—do have operative effect, and are indeed of decisive importance in the highly practical business of working out human destiny; and that they are not supernatural, not outside man but within him. Regarded as an evolutionary agency, the human species is a psycho-social mechanism which must operate by utilizing those forces. We have to understand the nature of those forces; where, within the psycho-social mechanism, they reside; and where their points of application are.

In the first place, there is evil in man as well as good. This obvious ethical fact has found theological expression in elaborate doctrines like that of original sin, and has been projected into hypotheses of supernatural powers of good and evil, like God and the Devil, Ormuzd and Ahriman. But the crude distinction in terms of ethical absolutes like "good" and "evil" requires reformulation in the light of psychology and history. We then see that the important distinction to make is between positive and negative, between constructive and destructive or restrictive. On the negative side we have such forces as hate, envy, despair, fear, destructive rage and aggressiveness, restrictive selfishness in all its forms, from

greed to lust for power, and negations of effectiveness such
as internal disharmony, frustration and unresolved conflict;
on the positive side we have comprehension, love in the
broadest sense, including love of beauty and desire for
truth, the urge to creation and fuller expression, the desire to
participate and to feel useful in contributing to some larger
enterprise or purpose, pure enjoyment and the cultivation
of intrinsic talents and capacities, and that constructive disposition of forces that we may call inner harmony.

These forces operate not only through individual minds,
but through the social framework. A society may be so
organized that it generates large amounts of hate or envy or
despair; or creates vast tracts of ugliness; or imposes subnormal health or inadequate mental development on large
sections of its population. Or its organization may serve to
encourage and facilitate constructive enthusiasm, to create
beauty, and to promote full and healthy individual development. This is so obvious that we are sometimes in danger of
disregarding it. The fact remains that social organization
does canalize and concentrate the psychological forces of
human nature in different ways, so that society can act
either as an organ of frustration or an organ of fulfilment.
Once we have grasped that fact, it is up to us to make the
attempt to improve the design of society.

Evolutionary humanism has the further implication that
man is at one and the same time the only agent for realizing
life's further progress, and also the main obstacle in the path
of its realization. The hostile outer world was his first obvious adversary; but the only opponent ultimately worthy of
his steel is himself. Man has learnt in large measure to
understand, control and utilize the forces of external nature:
he must now learn to understand, control and utilize the
forces of his own nature. This applies as much to the blind
urge to reproduction as to personal greed or desire for
power, as much to arrogance and fanaticism, whether na-
tionalist or religious, as to sadism or self-indulgence.

Let me pursue one example in a little more detail. Most
individual human beings feel themselves saddled with some
burden of guilt or uncleanness or unrighteousness, and desire a positive assurance of righteousness or cleansing or
worth. The exact nature of the sentiment varies from culture
to culture, and also as between different individuals, but it
always involves feelings of rightness and wrongness. The
simplest and most primitive method of coping with this dual

problem is to increase one's assurance of rightness by projecting one's own guilt or wrongness outwards on to events or, if possible, on to a human or humanly personified enemy. The process may be wholly unconscious, or merely rationalized; but this does not render it any less wrong or any less dangerous. It prevents the proper development of the individual personality by standing in the way of its wholeness and harmony of organization; and it obstructs the development both of society and of the species as a whole by magnifying or even creating conflicts and by converting potential partners into actual enemies. The text-books of psychology illustrate in detail the workings of this subconscious tendency to justification by projection. It is clearly an opponent of progress, standing in the way both of individual and evolutionary fulfilment, and if man is to advance, it needs to be understood, faced, and overcome.

The business of individual development thus poses a triple problem. The individual has to come to terms with the battery of powerful and often conflicting impulses with which he has been equipped willy-nilly by heredity; with the forces of his immediate social environment—family, class, and nation; and with what I may call transcendent forces—all those which transcend that immediate environment, such as the impact of the enduring framework of nature, the concept of the human race as a whole and its welfare, the driving force of man's own ideals and aspirations.

Freud has shown how the infantile and often unconscious struggle between love and hate colours all early development, and can become transformed into a frustrating conflict between the sympathetic impulses making for interdependent co-operation and the aggressive and power-greedy impulses making for hostility and violence. And we all experience consciously the shock of the powerful emergence of the sex-impulse in adolescence, and the difficulty of harnessing it satisfactorily to our vital chariot.

The immediate social forces will influence the way in which the individual's impulses are adjusted: for instance, social approval and disapproval largely determine the form in which conscience develops. As modern anthropological research has served to emphasize, the personality-moulding forces of the social environment vary from society to society, so that the types of individual psychological organization found in South Africa, for instance, will differ from those in Bali or in Soviet Russia.

The transcendent forces have tended to be neglected by social scientists, perhaps partly in reaction against their over-emphasis by religious thinking, and partly because the very phrase *social science* tends to focus scientific attention on actual immediate social organizations. But they are of great importance. When Wordsworth wrote of

> High instincts before which our mortal nature
> Doth tremble like a guilty thing surprised

he may not have provided a scientific formulation, but he gave convincing expression to a potent element in life. In any case, man's capacity for generalization and abstract thought inevitably generates what we call ideals, and ideals inevitably affect behaviour and personal development. Furthermore, the basic human sense of dependence and need for maximum assurance makes it inevitable that man will seek for the enduring elements in or behind the disconcerting flux of experience, and will attempt to express them in psychologically effective form. Here, as elsewhere, the problem is to ensure that the resultant formulations shall be not only effective but true, in the sense of corresponding with reality to the greatest possible extent. From our evolutionary humanist point of view, they need to be related to the optimum future development of humanity.

Individual mental and spiritual development thus always and inevitably involves the adjustment or reconciliation of conflicts of various sorts—between different impulses, between the practical or immediate and the transcendent or enduring. This last conflict can to-day be more precisely formulated as the conflict between the demands of the existing society into which the individual happens to be born, and those of the evolving human species as a whole.

It is easy to say that evolutionary humanism establishes the duty of the individual as the optimum realization of his possibilities: but this is too general. The fact that he must reconcile his individual demands with the needs of society and the claims of further evolutionary progress defines the problem rather more closely, but still leaves it vague in many important details. In the first place, it is clear that there are different degrees of fruition, different levels to be attained by the developing personality. In religious phraseology (which can readily be translated into the more cumbersome terms of scientific psychology), the organization of the soul can reach different grades of perfection. It is always possible to know and understand more, to feel and to sympathize more comprehensively, to achieve a fuller internal harmony. The right kind of individual development is thus one which leaves the way permanently open for fresh possibilities of growth (just as evolutionary progress was only achieved through trends of improvement which did not bar the way to further improvement).[7] The developing self has the possibility of transcending itself in further development; but in practice, different selves stop at different levels. There is thus in some sense a hierarchy of development among personalities, more or less corresponding to the hierarchy of higher and lower among non-human organisms.

In the second place three main contrasted ideals of personal development are possible. One is specialization: the fullest exploitation of some particular capacity, as seen in many successful professional men. The second we may call all-roundness by summation: the cultivation of every kind of fulfilment separately. This was, broadly, the ideal of the ancient Athenians and of our own Elizabethans. The third is difficult to characterize in a word: we may perhaps call it comprehensive wholeness: the cultivation of inner harmony and peace, the development of a unitary and comprehensive pattern of intellectual and spiritual organization. This has been the aim of the saints, the sages, and the mystics.

The first is in some degree necessary for personal success in life: but pushed to extremes it is as dangerous as biological specialization, and stands in the way of the higher levels of personal development. The second does justice to the variety of apparently conflicting fulfilments possible to man. The Greeks gave it a religious sanction by divinizing various separate human activities or modes of fulfilment. The co-existence of Aphrodite and Artemis, of Ares and Athena in the Greek Pantheon implies that, to the same individual at different times, both physical love and chastity can be sacred, that a man can find high fulfilment both in war and in peaceful learning. The organization of personality round a number of separate and apparently disparate modes of fulfilment corresponds roughly on the human plane to the organization of behaviour round a number of separate and mutually exclusive instincts in an insect, or impulses and drives in a bird or a mammal. It is an important method of utilizing ap-

[7] See Charles Morris, *The Open Self*, Prentice-Hall, New York.

parently conflicting or contradictory capacities to achieve a high sum-total of fulfilment. But it does so by the avoidance of conflicts, not by their reconciliation. It thus, if pushed to its logical extreme, stands in the way of achieving the third ideal—wholeness, the unity and continuity of the highest types of personality—just as the mammals' separate emotional drives and their series of isolated experiences had to be brought together in consciousness before the continuity of man's mental life could be realized.

Some kind of wholeness, some degree of unification, is thus indispensable for the higher levels of human fulfilment. But here again restriction or over-specialization can have unfortunate results. The dangerous over-specialization here is emphasis on unity and harmony to the neglect of comprehensiveness, richness and variety. A holy life may be strongly unified, but may be sadly restricted in scope. Its pattern may be a whole in the sense of having a well-marked unity; but it may fall far short of possible wholeness in failing to utilize many of the potentialities of human development. Wholeness, however, if properly understood, remains the key to the higher reaches of personal development and fulfilment. The personality is a spiritual and mental construction, a work of art like other human constructions. Wholeness is to this construction what design is to a building, conferring a new beauty and significance on what would otherwise be a mere assemblage of separate parts. This applies whether the building be a cottage or a cathedral, whether the personality be that of a simple labourer or a great archbishop.

It is all too obvious that, in the great majority of human beings, the great majority of their possibilities, whether physical or spiritual, intellectual or aesthetic, remains unrealized; while our rather meagre knowledge of mysticism and yoga makes it clear that some regions of human potentiality remain virtually unexplored, or at least unavailable to mankind as a whole. I would venture to prophesy that one of the next important steps in human progress will be the development of a science of human possibilities—their nature, their limits, and the communicable techniques for their fuller realization.

Evolutionary humanism, with its naturalism and its twin concepts of present fulfilment for the individual and of long-term progressive realization of possibilities for man and the planet he inhabits, imposes the need for a transvaluation of values. For one thing, it helps to restore our unity with nature. It brings back the objects of our adoration and the goals of our spiritual longings out of supernatural remoteness and sites them nearer home, in the immediacy of experience. As an example, let us consider the beauty and richness of nature. Rare Christian mystics like Traherne have found in it a religious fulfilment, and great poets like Wordsworth, in spite of the theological preconceptions of their time, have succeeded in expressing its transcendent value. The gospel of evolutionary humanism generalizes that value. The enjoyment of the beauty and strange variety of the natural world—an experience engendered jointly by nature and the capacities of man's mind—is seen as one of the indispensable modes of human fulfilment, not to be neglected without peril, involving something essentially religious or sacred even though we may not burden it with any such heavy designation.

As a corollary, we have the collective duty of preserving nature—partly for its own sake, but mainly as one of the necessary means for man's fulfilment. To exterminate a living species, be it lion or lammergeier, to desecrate the landscape, to wipe out wild flowers or birds over great tracts of country, is to diminish the wonder, the interest, and the beauty of the universe.

The same, *mutatis mutandis,* is true of the beauty of art and architecture. For evolutionary humanism, one of the ultimate aims of man appears as the creation of more and fuller beauty. Failure to create beauty is a dereliction of duty, and the creation of ugliness and meanness is immoral. Judged by humanist values, the cities and many other parts of the artificial environment that man has created for himself stand in large measure condemned. The conservation and proper exploitation of natural resources are other essentially sacred duties imposed by a humanist ideology—because they provide the indispensable material basis for higher fulfilment.

We perceive the same need for compromise or adjustment between social values as appeared for modes of individual fulfilment. We obviously should not preserve all wild life everywhere, nor leave all nature untamed for the enjoyment of nature-lovers. But neither should we allow economic exploitation to become universally dominant. Though much can rightly be accomplished in the way of reconciling diverse interest in a single pattern, it is often impossible to do so completely. Then we must be content with all-roundness by summation, and allot areas in which separate interests are paramount—wild life in one area, natural beauty in another, exploitation of resources in a third, and so forth.

The most important of all the major trends that we find in evolution concerns the *awareness* of organisms, in the broadest possible sense—the organs of experience, by which they become aware of happenings in the external environment and in themselves, of the world and of their situation in it.

I cannot embark on a detailed discussion of this improvement of biological awareness. It must suffice to remind my readers that there has been a great increase in the range and acuity of sense-organs; that the awareness of pain has been specialized so as to help animals to profit by experience; that the higher animals are aware of a wide range of emotional states, often intense, and closely linked with adaptive instinctive actions; that there has been a trend towards the integration of different elements of awareness into increasingly complex patterns, as illustrated by the evolution of pattern-vision, or later by the combination of sight and touch and muscular sense to provide perceptual awareness of solid and coloured objects in three-dimensional space; that the capacity to organize awareness in transmissible and cumulative form is the distinctive property which has permitted the evolutionary rise of man; and finally, that man's future progress depends very largely on how he continues this trend towards the greater extension and better organization of awareness.

Let me recall that the organizations of awareness that play a part in our mental life are all our own creations—of course in partnership with external fact, but none the less human productions. This is true even of our perceptions, as is illustrated by such work as that of Ames and Cantril and by the study of how blind people learn to see after recovering their power of vision.[8] We do not merely receive direct impressions or representations of some external reality. We have to learn, albeit for the most part quite unconsciously, to organize the chaos of coloured patterns, which is all we receive in sensation, into coherent perceptions, on the basis of repeated experience. Perceptions, in other words, always involve some degree of assumption and interpretation.

An obvious example is the night sky: the "natural" inter-

8 See J. Z. Young, *Doubt and Certainty in Science*, Oxford University Press, London, 1951, and my *Evolution in Action*, Chatto and Windus, London, 1953.

pretation of this was to perceive the sky as a hemisphere studded with equidistant stars; now, with the aid of telescopes and astronomers' brains, we see it as a fathomless depth of space. Even when, as with the night sky, such interpretative assumptions are largely dependent on conscious intellectual processes, they modify the way in which our raw awareness is perceptually organized. This is still more obviously true of the concepts and verbal symbols which are the chief vehicles for communication. Human societies have to create them: individuals have to learn them: each of us has to build up his own organization of significance round verbal symbols like *horse* or *mathematics*. And so it continues up to the most complex levels of organization, to the construction of laws of nature to subsume vast quantities of observations and experiments on the welter of events, of works of art to bring together many diverse ideas and emotional experiences in a single unified whole, of gods to unify the chaos and the conflicts of spiritual and religious experience.

Collective awareness is thus the distinctive and most important organ of the human species. It can be improved both quantitatively, by adding to knowledge and extending the range of experience, and qualitatively, by improving its organization. Scientific hypotheses and laws are better organizations for coping with our experience of physical phenomena than are trial-and-error methods, or traditional precepts, or pseudo-explanations in terms of metaphysical principles. Monotheism provides a better organization for certain important aspects of religious experience than does polydaimonism.

But meanwhile the total volume of knowledge available to man for the business of living and evolving has increased to a prodigious and spectacular extent, and this very increase in extent demands constant modification of the organizations of knowledge, including sometimes the creation of quite new types of organization and the scrapping of old ones. On this last point, the conclusions dictated by evolutionary humanism can be briefly summed up as follows. First, man finds one of his ultimate fulfilments in comprehension. Fuller comprehension is one of the basic duties (and privileges) of the individual. Secondly, accumulated and organized knowledge and experience are necessary instruments or organs for human advance. Thus scientific research in all fields is essential, and its encouragement is one of the most important tasks of a civilized society.

Then it is clear that the common pools of accumulated and organized knowledge on which civilization and human advance depend will perform their psycho-social functions more adequately as they are more fully available to and more fully utilized by all the members of a community, and as they merge more fully into a single universal pool for the whole human species. Education is extending the possibilities of participation in knowledge and ideas, while natural science is already international, and has laid the foundations for a comprehensive global system of knowledge.

Science has also contributed a discovery of the first magnitude—the discovery of the principle of limited but increasing certitude as the best method of extending and organizing knowledge. The principle of limited certitude not only includes scientific method in the restricted sense—the method of dispassionate observation and, where possible, experiment, of framing hypotheses, and of their testing and modification in the light of further observation and experiment. But it comprises more than this: it involves a general attitude to experience. It implies a fundamental humility, in acknowledging at the outset our enormous ignorance, the vast extent of what we do not know. But it also implies a legitimate pride and assurance—pride in the extent of the areas already annexed to the domain of knowledge from the wastes of ignorance, assurance in the tested validity of the accumulated facts and in the efficacy of the scientific method; and assurance also that the scientific method of accumulating and organizing knowledge can be profitably extended to the entire psycho-social field, to the workings of society and of human nature, in such a way that knowledge can become in a full sense the basis of wisdom.

The scientific spirit and the scientific method have proved the most effective agents for the comprehension and control of physical nature. It remains for man to apply them to the comprehension and control of human destiny. For this to happen, science must understand that a religion of some kind is a necessary organ for coping with the problems of destiny; and religion must not only accept and utilize the findings of science, but must be willing to admit the central principle of limited certitude, with its implication of progressive but always incomplete achievement of a better religious construction.

There are a few other points on which I would like to touch. The importance of the population problem for human destiny is now beginning to loom large. The implications of evolutionary humanism here are clear. If the full development of human individuals and the fulfilment of human possibilities are the overriding aims of our evolution, then any over-population which brings malnutrition and misery, or which erodes the world's material resources or its resources of beauty or intellectual satisfaction, is evil. Among the world's major and immediate tasks is the working out of an effective and acceptable population policy. In the ultimate light of humanist values, the deliberate encouragement of over-population for military or political ends, as in pre-war Italy and Japan, the intellectual dishonesty of the Russian Communists in asserting that over-population is an invention of the "Morganist-Weismannist hirelings of American monopolists"[9] designed to justify American imperialist expansion, and the theological dogmatism of the Roman Catholics which denounces birth-control and prevents the scientific discussion of population problems even in international bodies like the World Health Organization—all are seen as immoral and indeed wicked.

Evolutionary humanism has eugenic implications also. These are, for the moment, largely theoretical, but in due time will become immensely practical. Within a century we should have amassed adequate knowledge of what could be done negatively to lighten the burden of inherited deficiency of mind or body which presses so cruelly on so many individual human beings and so heavily on evolving humanity as a whole, and positively to raise the entire level of innate human possibilities and capacities. When this has happened, the working out of an effective and acceptable eugenic policy will be seen as not only an urgent but an inspiring task, and its political or theological obstruction as immoral.

I must say a word about the arts. Art, science, and religion are the three main fields of man's creative activity: all are indispensable for his fulfilment and the greater realization of his possibilities. In its recent manifestations, Western civilization has tended to exalt science and its technological applications at the expense of the arts. But we can grasp how important and indispensable they really are by imagining a

[9] Quoted from the New York *Herald-Tribune's* summary, April 5, 1948, of an article by Professor Glushchenko in *Pravda*.

world without them. Think of a world without music or poetry, without its churches and noble houses, without ballets, plays, novels, and films, without pictures and sculptures: such a world would be intolerable, and life in it unlivable.

The practice of various arts—painting and modelling, music and acting—can play an important role in the development of individual personality in education; this is especially true of children in whom intellectual interests are not naturally strong, but in any case intellectual interests alone will tend to a one-sided distortion of development. And throughout life the arts can provide individual fulfilments unattainable by any other means.

But for my present purpose it is the social relations of the artist and the social functions of the arts that are more relevant, as well as being in more need of clarification. Two extreme positions are possible. Art may be regarded merely as self-expression, and the individual artist may acknowledge no responsibility to the society in which he happens to live, but only to himself and to whatever ideas of art he may happen to hold. Or it may be regarded merely as an instrument of the State, and the artist be required to subordinate his own ideas entirely to the task of expressing the aims and interests of official policy. At the moment, both these extreme positions are actually held—the former by many among the more rebellious artists in Western countries,[10] the latter by the U.S.S.R. with its officially imposed doctrine of Socialist Realism. Neither extreme is really tenable by itself, but the partial truths embodied in them may be reconciled. In the light of evolutionary humanism art appears not as an instrument of the State, but as an organ of the evolving human species: and though the variety of individual genius and the duty of experimenting with new possibilities of vision and expression must be admitted, humanism insists that the artist, like all other men, has some responsibilities to the community of which he is a member, as well as to the gifts with which, by no merit of his own, he may have been endowed.

Viewed in this light, the duty of the artist comprises not only the duty of cultivating his personal talents and expressing his own individuality and ideas, but also the duty of

10 It is curious to note how in some cases, for instance Picasso, extreme individualism in practice may be combined with a theoretical Communism.

understanding something of the universe in which he lives, of the social process of which he is a part, and of his own relations with and possible role in it.

Evolutionary humanism makes it clear that the essential function of the arts is one of bearing witness to the wonder and variety of the world and of human experience. In more precise but more forbidding phraseology, it is to create vehicles for the effective expression and communication of complex emotionally charged experiences, which are of value in the process of human fulfilment. Both science and art are instruments for comprehending the world, and for communicating that comprehension. They employ different methods, and are important in different ways: but the two are complementary, and both are indispensable.

Indeed, in every sphere, evolutionary humanism appears as one which both necessitates and makes possible the reconciliation of extreme positions and the adjustment of conflicting interests. Conflicts may be transcended in the process of becoming. This central concept of a process of becoming, a self-transformation of humanity with a desirable direction and rate, provides a framework of synthesis in which many conflicts can be transcended. Continuity and change; doubt and certainty; the immediate and the enduring; competition and co-operation; the actual and the possible; individualism and collectivism, at all levels from family, local group, class or nation, to humanity and indeed to life as a whole, are among the many antithetic opposites which can be reconciled. In the actual process of individual development, the stress falls on the reconciliation of conflicting impulses in a harmonious personal unity, in that of social development on the adjustment of conflicting interests in a pattern of maximum fruitfulness. Above all, our central concept of greater fulfilment through the realization of possibilities brings ideals and ultimate values into relation with actual imperfections and present efforts, and links them as participants in the common task of better achieving human destiny.

This brings me back to where I started—the idea of religion as an organ of destiny. It is clear, as I said earlier, that twentieth-century man needs a new organ for dealing with destiny, a new system of beliefs and attitudes adapted to the situation in which he and his societies now have to exist and thus an organ for the better orientation of the human species as a whole—in other words, a new religion.

Like all other new religions, and indeed all other new

movements of ideas, it will at the outset be expressed and spread by a small minority: but it will in due time tend to become universal, not only potentially and in theory, but actually and in practice. The properties of man's psycho-social nature make this inevitable. Man cannot avoid the process of convergence which makes for the integration of divergent or hostile groups in a single organic world society and culture.[11] And an integrated world society cannot operate effectively without an integrated common pool of thought and body of ideas. Thought and practice interact; but in the modern world thought is likely to move the faster. And so a universalist system of ideas, if firmly based in reality, can be expected to play an important part in effecting the process of practical and institutional integration.

Science, as a system of discovering, organizing, and applying mutual knowledge, is already unified and universal in principle, though its efficiency as an organ of the human species could still be much increased. It remains for man to unify and universalize his religion. How that religion will take form—what rituals or celebrations it might practise, whether it will equip itself with any sort of professional body or priesthood, what buildings it will erect, what symbols it will adopt—that is something which no one can prophesy. Certainly it is not a field on which the natural scientist should venture. What the scientist can do is to draw attention to the relevant facts revealed by scientific discovery, and to their implications and those of the scientific method. He can aid in the building up of a fuller and more accurate picture of reality in general and of human destiny in particular, secure in the knowledge that in so doing he is contributing to humanity's advance, and helping to make possible the emergence of a more universal and more adequate religion.

Let me return to where I began—the change in our attitude to the cosmic process since my grandfather's time, the reformulation which the march of knowledge in those sixty years has made imperative. To-day, we must say that the ethical progress of society, and indeed human progress in all its aspects, consists not in combating the cosmic process but in wrestling with it (as Jacob wrestled with the angel), and in finding out what we can do to direct it. And this depends on our understanding of it, and on our learning how to

11 See Père Teilhard de Chardin's remarkable book, *Le Phénomène Humain*, Editions du Seuil, Paris, 1955.

discharge our role of leadership in it. If T. H. Huxley were alive to-day, I believe that he would agree with this formulation (though I am sure that he would have phrased it better), and that he would accept the general way of thinking about man's destiny which I have called Evolutionary Humanism.

In exposing my thesis, I have had to range discursively into many fields. In concluding, perhaps I may be permitted to bring them together in a personal focus. I can, at any rate, testify to the fact that the concept of evolutionary humanism has been of value to myself. It has enabled me to resolve many of the dilemmas and conflicts with which any enquiring and aspiring mind is inevitably beset. It has enabled me to see this strange universe into which we are born as a proper object both of awe and wondering love and of intellectual curiosity. More, it has made me realize that both my wonder and my curiosity (like those of any other human being) can be of significance and value in that universe. It has enabled me to relate my experiences of the world's delights and satisfactions, and those of its horrors and its miseries, to the idea of fulfilment, positive or negative. In the concept of increased realization of possibilities, it provides a common measuring rod for all kinds of directional processes, from the development of personal ethics to large-scale evolution, and gives solid ground for maintaining an affirmative attitude and faith, as against that insidious enemy, Goethe's *Geist, der stets verneint,* the spirit of negation and despair. It affirms the positive significance of effort and creative activity and enjoyment. In some ways most important of all, it has brought back intellectual speculation and spiritual aspiration out of the abstract and isolated spheres they once seemed to me to inhabit, to a meaningful place in concrete reality; and so has restored my sense of unity with nature.

From boyhood, I was deeply impressed by Wordsworth's lines in *Tintern Abbey*:

> and I have felt
> A presence that disturbs me with the joy
> Of elevated thoughts; a sense sublime
> Of something far more deeply interfused,
> Whose dwelling is the light of setting suns,
> And the round ocean and the living air,
> And the blue sky, and in the mind of man.

Yet I was unable to see how experiences of this kind, though I could personally testify to their value, could be linked up with the framework of ideas that I was attempting to build up on the basis of my scientific education. In the light of evolutionary humanism, however, the connection became clear, though the intellectual formulation given to it by Wordsworth was inadequate. The reality behind his thought is that man's mind is a partner with nature: it participates with the external world in the process of generating awareness and creating values.

The importance of this idea of participating, of co-operative partnership in a joint enterprise, had been brought home to me in various separate contexts. I had met with it as a keystone of our colonial policy in Africa; as a necessary basis for the work of Unesco; as the concept inspiring the Colombo Plan and the United Nations' programme of technical assistance; as the basis for Bertrand de Jouvenel's illuminating definition of politics as action directed towards inducing men to co-operate in a common enterprise; indeed, evolutionary biology showed me the destiny of man on earth as a partnership between man and nature, with man in the leading position—a joint enterprise involving the participation of the entire human species for its most fruitful execution.

It has been a deep satisfaction that my almost life-long interest in evolution has led me to a better understanding of the relations between human life and the apparently hostile universe in which it exists. Man, both as individual and as species, turns out to be profoundly significant in the cosmic process. When Hamlet pronounced man "the paragon of animals", "the quintessence of dust", he anticipated Darwin and all the implications of Darwin's work for our ideas about man's origin and destiny. But, he also said, "man delights me not, no, nor woman either", thereby voicing some of the disillusion and horror which we all sometimes feel at human frustration, stupidity, and cruelty. That disillusion and horror have been sharpened for us moderns by the events of the last two decades—though, if we had been willing to cast our eyes backward into history, we should have found abundance of stupidities and cruelties to rival and exceed those of our own times. However, in the light of our newer knowledge of psychology and history, the moral of those failures and horrors is not that human nature is unchangeable or incurably evil. Human nature always contains the possibilities of evil, waste, and frustration; but it also contains those of good, of achievement, and of fruition. The lesson of evolution is that we must think in the limited but positive terms of fulfilment —the degree to which we, individually and collectively, manage to realize our inherent possibilities.

Finally, the concept of evolutionary humanism has helped me to see how, in principle at least, science and religion can be reconciled. It has shown me outlets for ideas and sentiments which can legitimately be called religious, but which otherwise would have remained frustrated or untapped. And it has indicated how vital a contribution science can make to religious progress.

My grandfather, in the same famous essay in which he defined agnosticism, stated as self-evident that "every man should be able to give a reason for the faith that is in him". My faith is in human possibilities: I hope that I have here succeeded in making clear some of my reasons for that faith.

INDEX

Other Books of Interest

On Population: Three Essays *by Malthus, Huxley, Osborn*. Important analyses of a looming global crisis: An important 1830 essay by Malthus, an account by Sir Julian Huxley which brings the reader to 1955, and Frederick Osborn's summary of the situation today—"the population explosion" which is plaguing the overcrowded, undernourished areas of the world. (#MD295—50¢)

Science and the Modern World *by Alfred North Whitehead*. A penetrating study of the influence of three centuries of scientific thought on world civilization. (#MD162—50¢)

Human Destiny *by Lecomte du Nouy*. In this best-selling book, a world-famous scientist proves that science and religion may walk hand in hand and presents a reassuring view of man's dignity and true place in the universe. (#MD165—50¢)

Dialogues of Alfred North Whitehead *as recorded by Lucien Price*. One of the towering figures of 20th century philosophy converses about books, people, events, and ideas in this illuminating book by a friend of 20 years standing. (#MD180—50¢)

Bertrand Russell's Best *edited by R. E. Egner*. Witty and profound observations on religion, politics, education, ethics, sex and psychology by the Nobel Prize winner. (#MD237—50¢)

Heredity, Race and Society *(revised) by L. C. Dunn and Th. Dobzhansky*. Group differences, how they arise, the influences of heredity and environment. (#MD74—50¢)

The Meaning of Evolution *(revised, abridged) by George Gaylord Simpson*. Outlines the whole course of life on earth and its ethical implications for mankind. (#MD66—50¢)